SPORT
FACILITIES

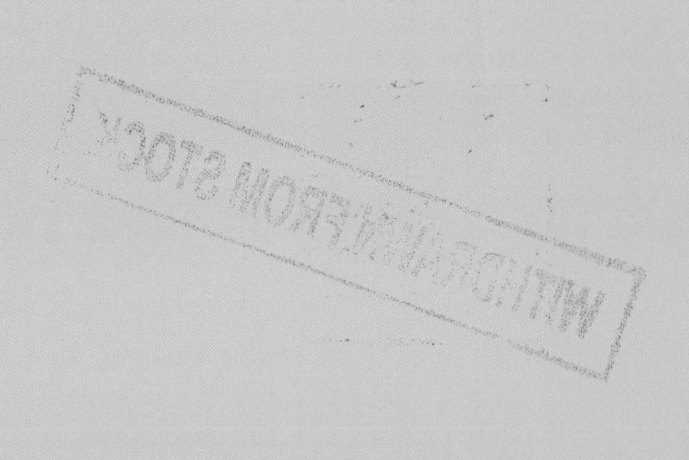

SPORT
FACILITIES

LOFT

Publisher: Paco Asensio

Editor and texts: Aurora Cuito

Art direction: Mireia Casanovas

Layout: Ester Heredia and Emma Termes

English translation: Matthew Connell

Editorial project:

2005 © LOFT Publications
Via Laietana 32, 4° Of. 92
08003 Barcelona, Spain
Tel.: +34 932 688 088
Fax: +34 932 687 073
loft@loftpublications.com
www.loftpublications.com

ISBN: 84-95832-46-1
DL: 27.359-2005

Printed by: Indústries Gráficas Mármol, s.l.

INTRODUCTION

The buildings gathered in this book were all designed to suit the needs of one of the most preponderant activities in modern-day life: sports. As there are few things in life that involve so many millions of people and such massive budgets, it comes as little surprise that the promoters of these activities should commission renowned architects to design unique buildings that will stand out from the crowd—both in terms of their functionality and aesthetics.

Our newfound dedication to our bodies and living a healthy lifestyle has resulted in the opening of a wide variety of centers, all of which strive to offer us the ideal place in which to exercise. Far from the rudimentary gymnasiums of several decades ago, which were sparsely equipped with the odd dumbbell, these new complexes offer a wide variety of services in facilities that have been equipped and designed by prestigious architects.

Additionally, municipal sports centers have also evolved into veritable social centers, in which sports are just one of the multiple group activities that one can engage in. Furthermore, many of these facilities have also taken pioneering steps towards achieving energy savings and overall sustainability—examples of this include the use of

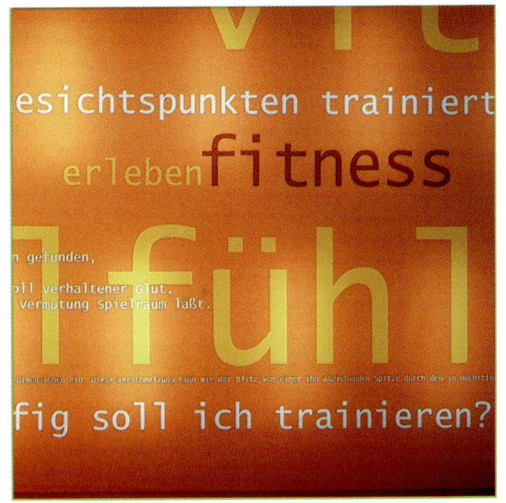

renewable sources of energy, such as solar panels, or increasing these buildings' thermal inertia so as to permit a smaller consumption of electricity. Finally, we should also point out the recent construction of large stadiums for housing the massive spectacles that most modern-day sporting activities have evolved into—the dramatic growth in size of competitions such as the Olympics or the World Cup has entailed the construction of versatile stadiums that are capable of seating numbers of spectators in the tens of thousands. The complexity of these structures, however, does not subtract in any way from their originality or the unique spaces that spring up around them.

SPORT
FACILITIES

GEIBELTBAD SPA

ARCHITECTS: ARNKE UND HÄNTSCH ARCHITEKTEN

PHOTOGRAPHS © WERNER HUTHMACHER

LOCATION: PIRNA, GERMANY
YEAR COMPLETED: 2001

THE ENSEMBLE OF COVERED AND OPEN-AIR POOLS THAT MAKE UP THE GEIBELTBAD SPA EXIST IN HARMONY WITH THEIR SURROUNDINGS, BOTH DUE TO THE WAY THEY ARE ORGANIZED AND FIT INTO THE TOPOGRAPHY, AND THE LOCAL MATERIALS USED IN THEIR CONSTRUCTION.

GEIBELTBAD SPA

This spa is located in Pirna, a village in Saxony on the banks of the River Elbe surrounded by steep mountains. The project consisted in renovating and expanding a series of buildings from the 1930s, and its objective was to highlight the relationship between the indoor spaces and the bucolic landscape surrounding them. Furthermore, as its designers sought to harmonize the complex with its site, they decided to create a large floating roof that would house all the new activities, to design façades that would be almost entirely made of glass, and to puncture the roof with skylights that would flood the entire building in natural light.

To connect the existing outdoor pool with the new indoor pool, a new access courtyard was designed for the complex that also opens onto the restaurant and to the dressing rooms. The organization of the project was also affected by a change in level that coalesced the spaces in a compact body that optimizes the relationship between surface and volume: this is essential in order to make an environmentally-friendly use of energy.

In contrast with the transparency and brightness of the façade in the pool area, a more introverted setting was designed for the area of the saunas— this was achieved through enclosures crafted in locally-found sandstone and granite floors.

Besides practical questions and motives of durability, the selection of the materials and the palette of colors was influenced by the colors of the local soil— different types of stone and granites were used, in addition to strategically located plantings to dilute the boundary between indoor and exterior vegetation.

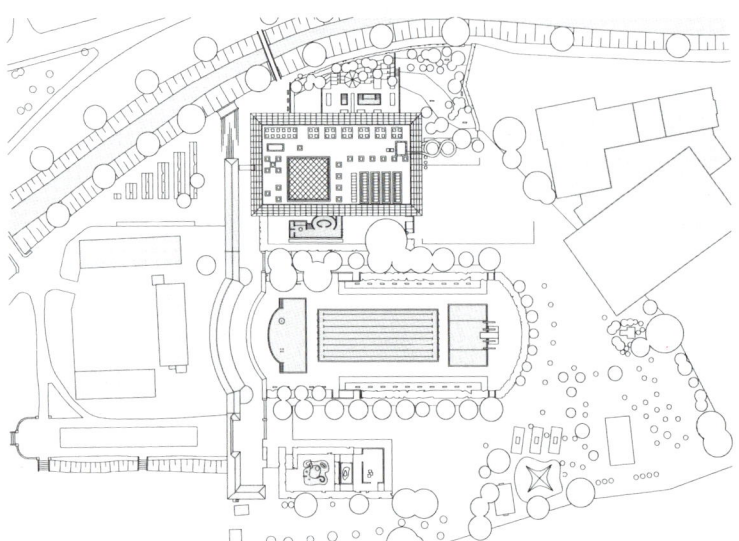

Site plan

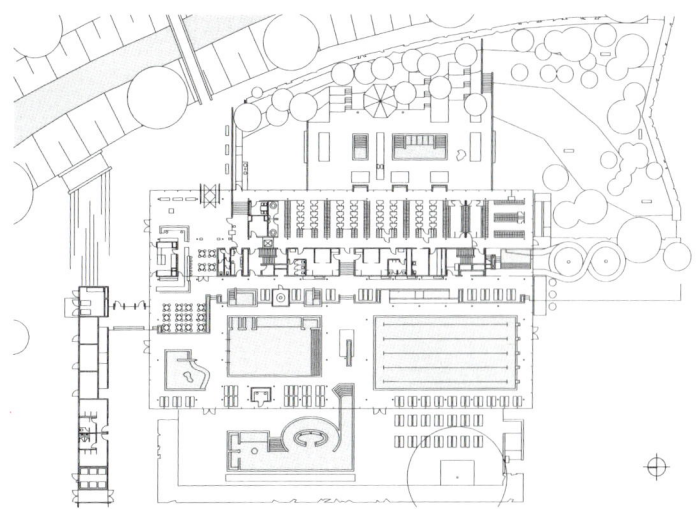

Ground floor

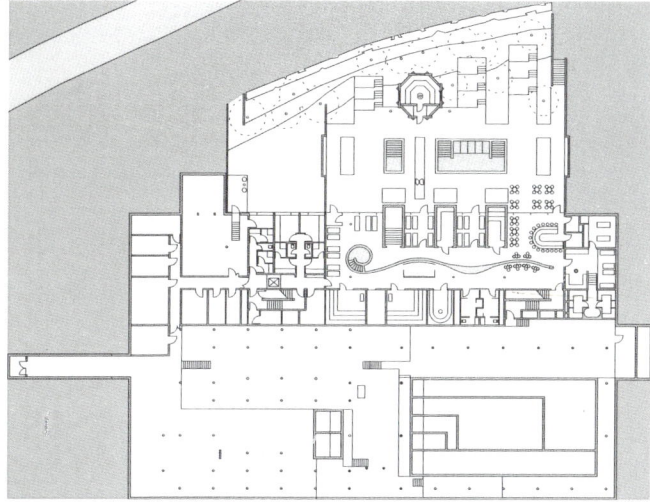

Basement

0   5   10

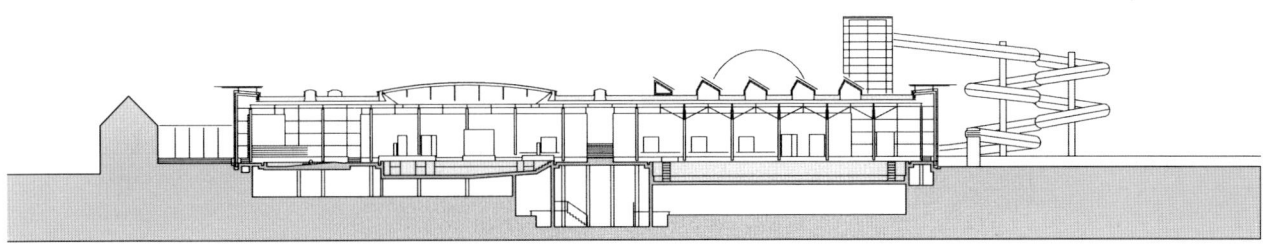

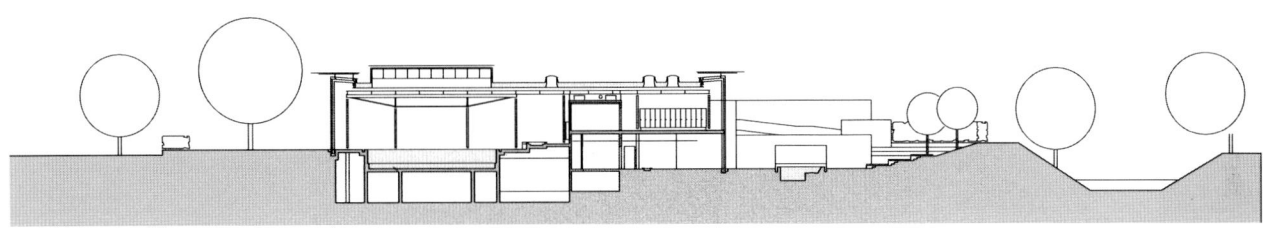

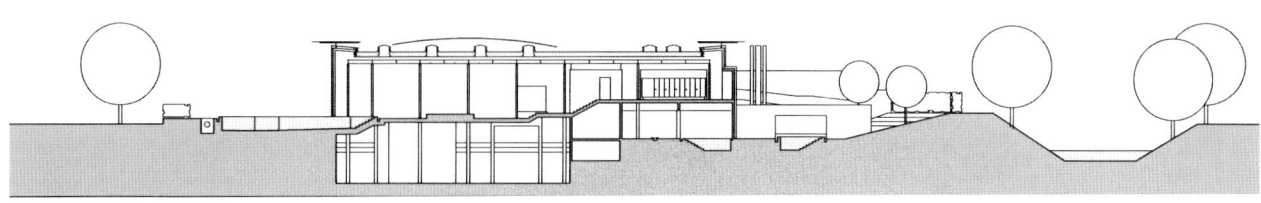

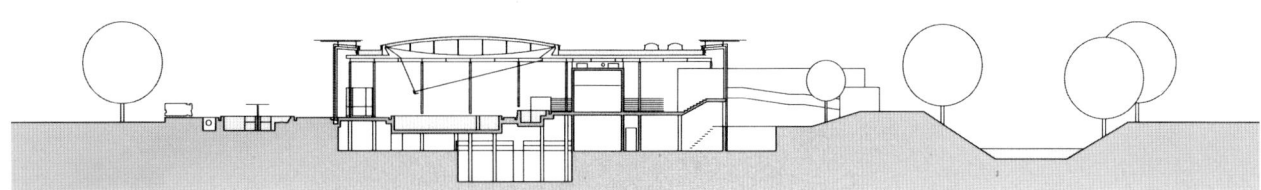

Sections

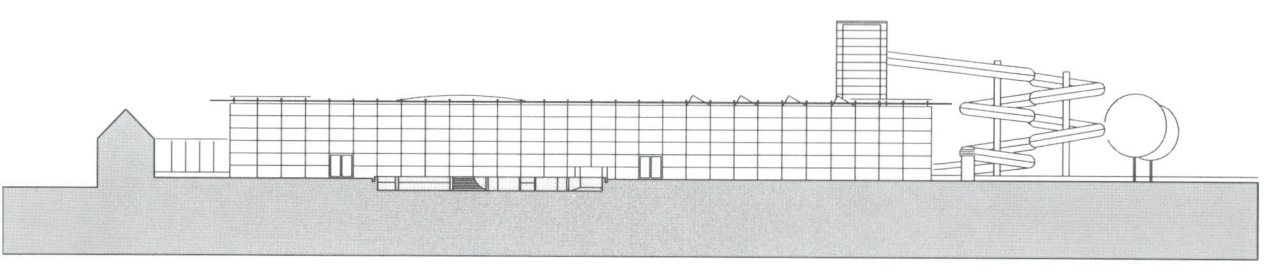

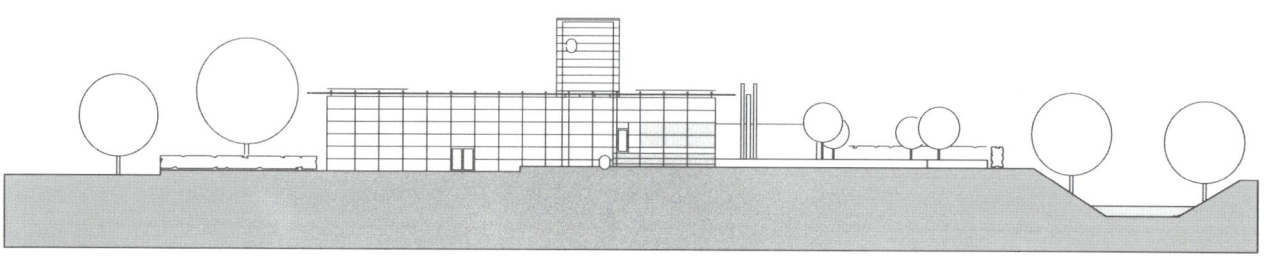

Elevations

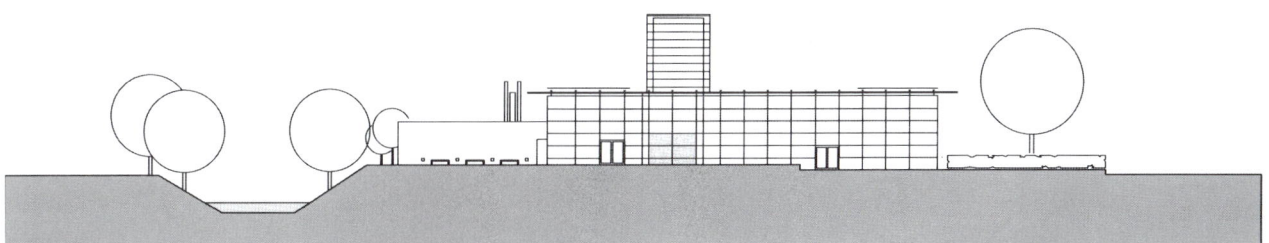

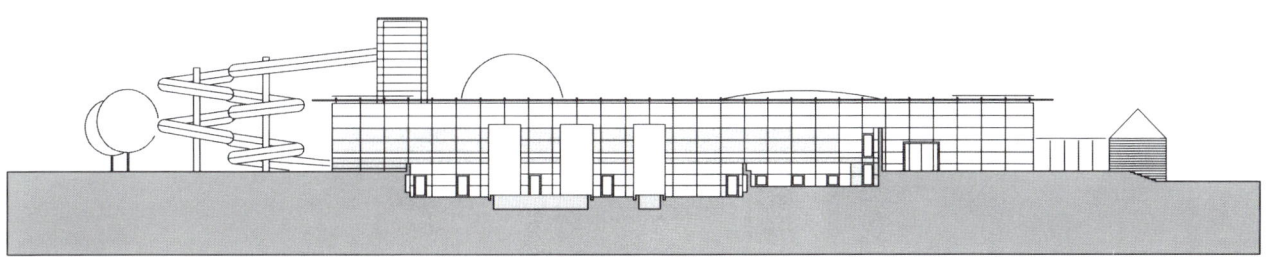

Elevations

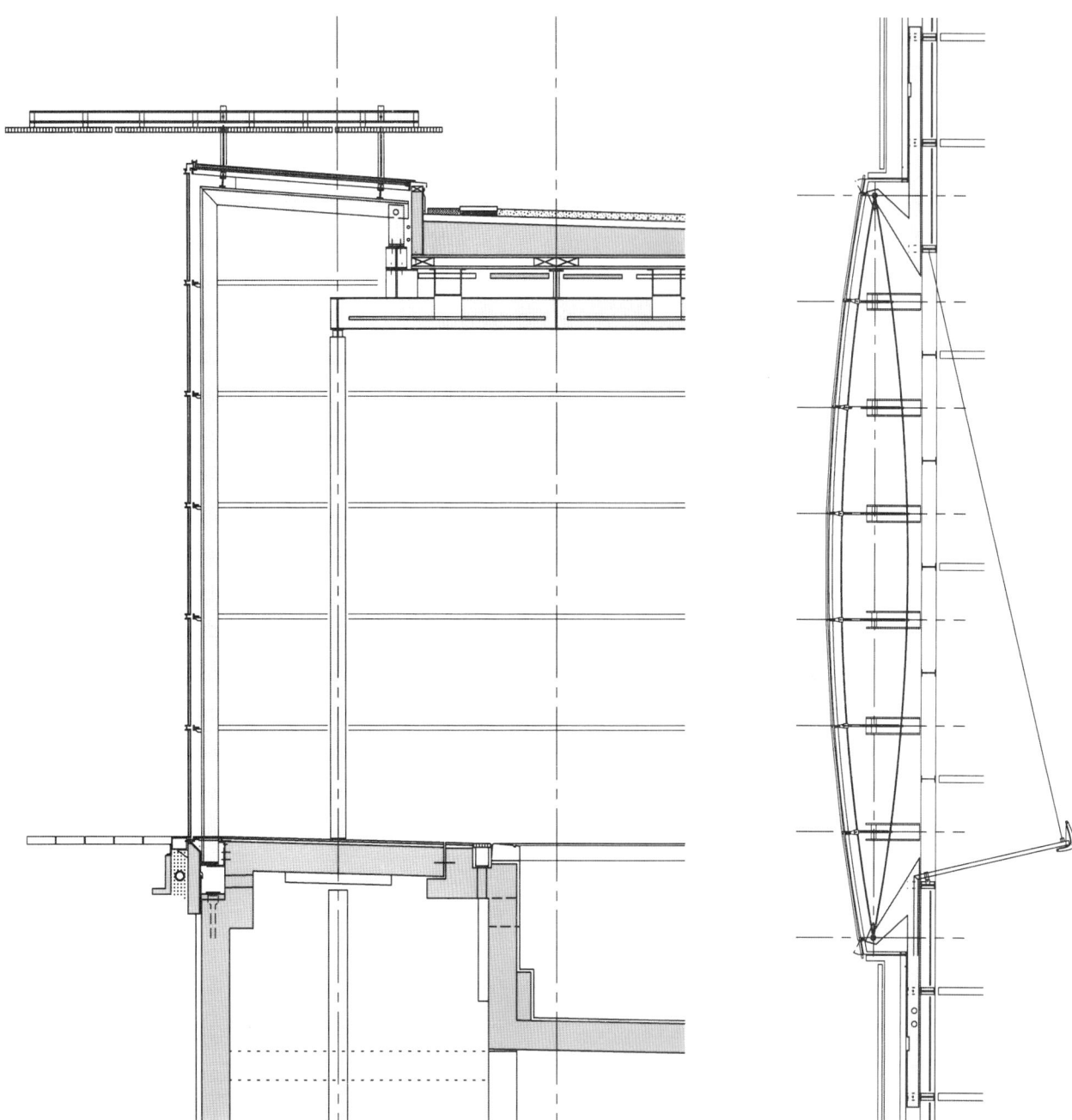

Roof construction detail

POOL AND SOCIAL CENTER

ARCHITECTS: JOHN FRIEDMAN & ALICE KIMM ARCHITECTS
COLLABORATORS: SEOUL ARCHITECTS & CONSULTANTS (ASSOCIATE ARCHITECTS)

PHOTOGRAPHS © HO KWAN PARK, SEOUL ARCHITECTS & CONSULTANTS

LOCATION: SEOUL, SOUTH KOREA
YEAR COMPLETED: 2002

THE POOL IS COVERED BY FLOATING PANELS AND THE REMAINING ELEMENTS IN THE PROGRAM ARE HOUSED TOGETHER BENEATH A CURVING SURFACE THAT SINKS INTO THE EARTH AT THE FAR WEST END OF THE SITE. A LARGE, OPEN-AIR SPACE LINKS THE SOCIAL CENTER TO THE VESTIBULE OF THE POOL AND SERVES AS AN ENTRANCE PORTICO TO THE PARK.

POOL AND SOCIAL CENTER

The headquarters and production plants of the SK Corporation, the largest refinery in South Korea, are located in the city of Ulsan. As it is one of the largest polluters in the area, yet also one of its largest employers, the SK Corporation decided to compensate the inhabitants of Ulsan by building a series of recreational facilities on one of the properties it owned in the city. Thus, the city was able to benefit from new, much-needed facilities, in addition to the additional income this would generate. The public pool and the social center, designed by John Friedman and Alice Kimm, form part of this new development.

The primary challenge to this commission was how to situate this new facility, which was to be located between the chaotic city limits and a large forest that had been declared a national park. The second challenge entailed combining numerous functions—a pool, administrative offices, and a social center—in a single, compact building that would not overwhelm the narrow site.

To minimize or magnify specific vistas from the building, the architects planned two highly different façades: an opaque façade made up of corrugated metal panels faces the city, while an almost entirely glass façade faces onto the park, as well as towards a small lake.

The structural system of beams and columns evokes the natural shapes and lighting of the adjacent forest, while another metaphorical gesture is the route taken by visitors from the entrance to the locker rooms, which is accompanied by views of the city. On the other hand, the journey from the locker rooms to the pool offers spectacular panoramic views out onto the nearby forest. One thus sheds one's city clothes as one makes one's way out towards nature.

Site plan

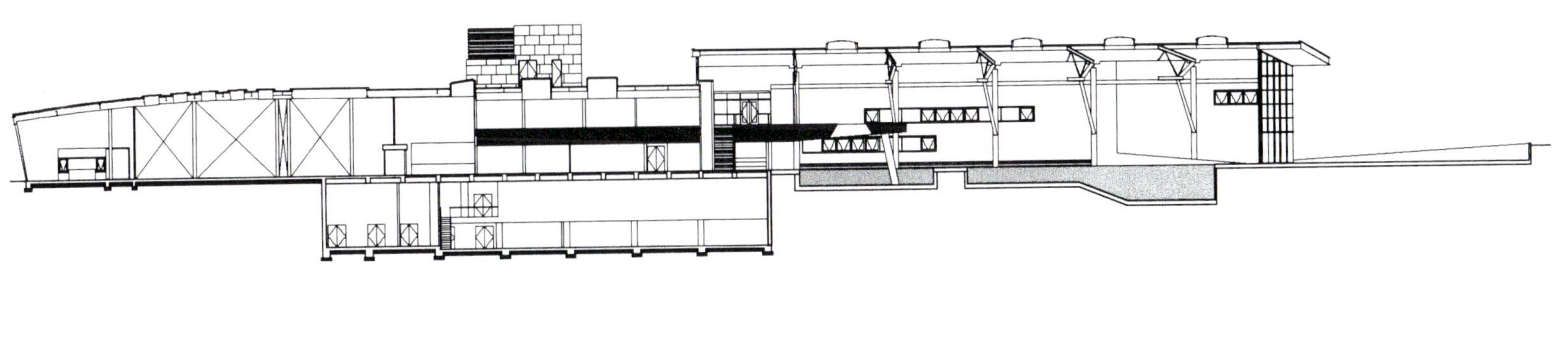

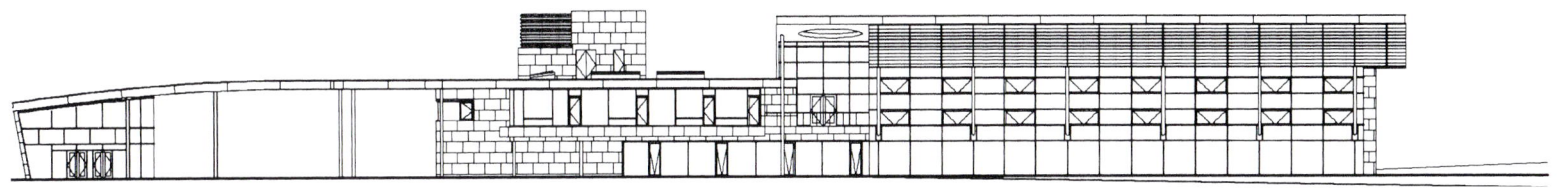

Sections

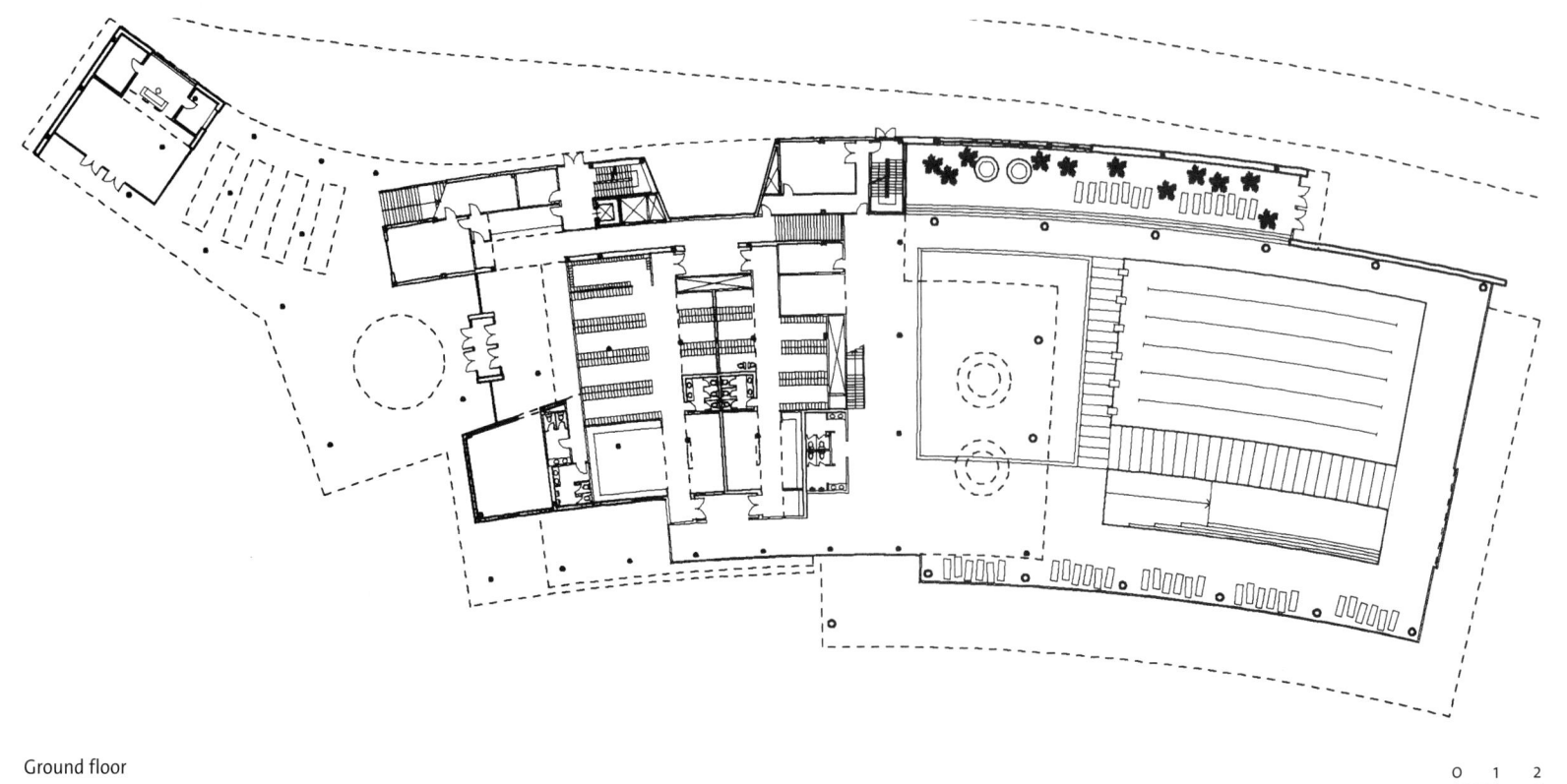

Ground floor

0   1   2

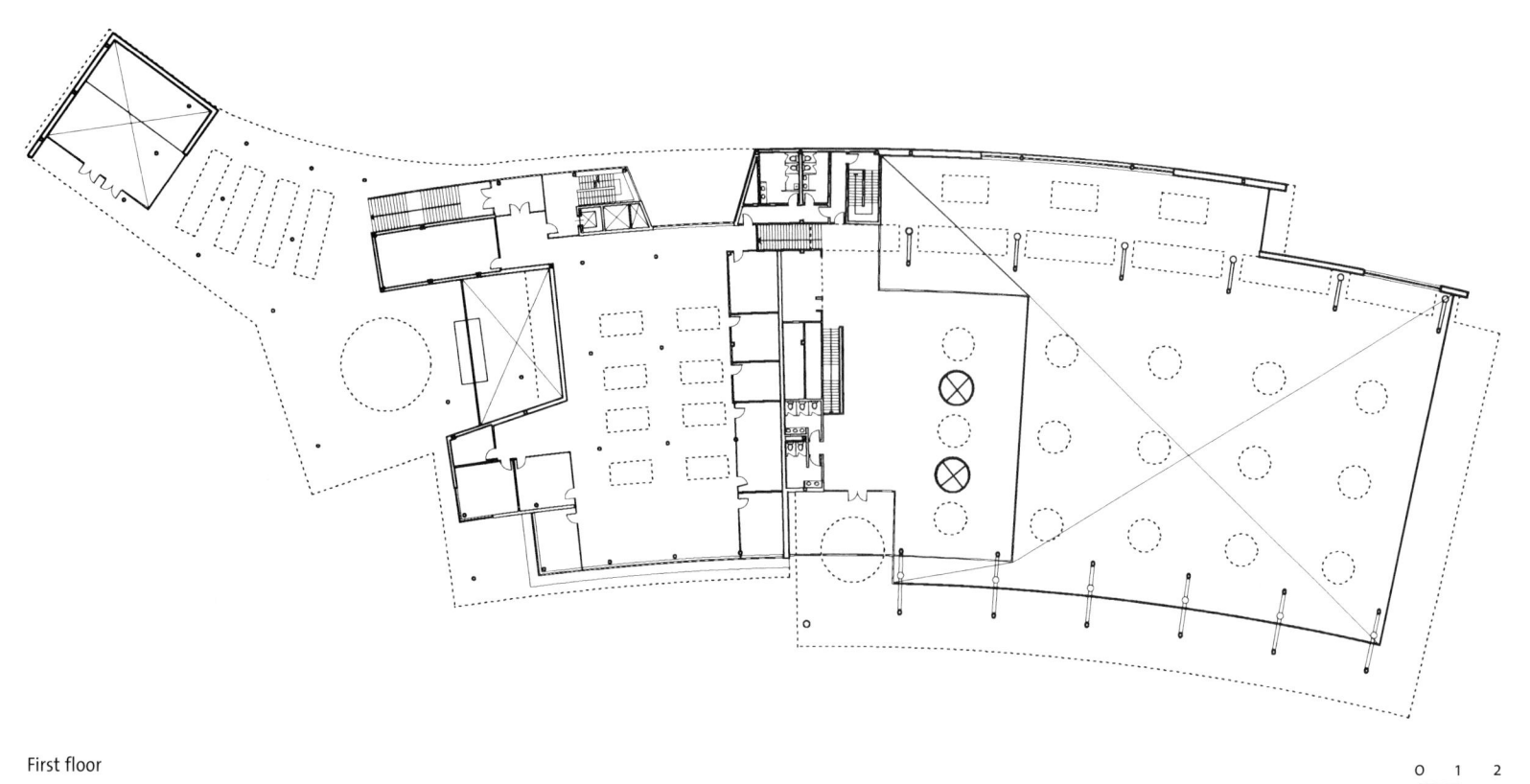

First floor

0   1   2

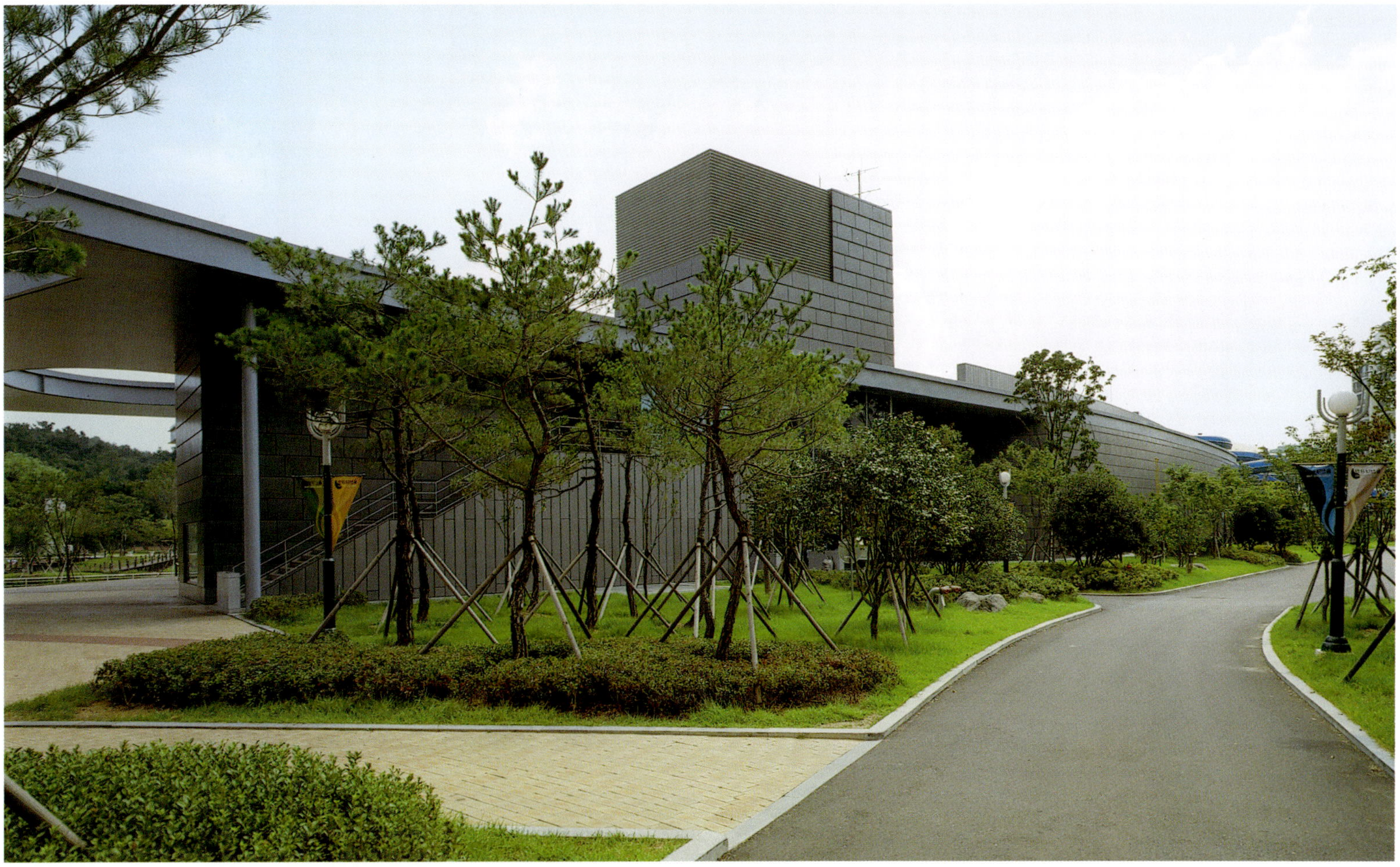

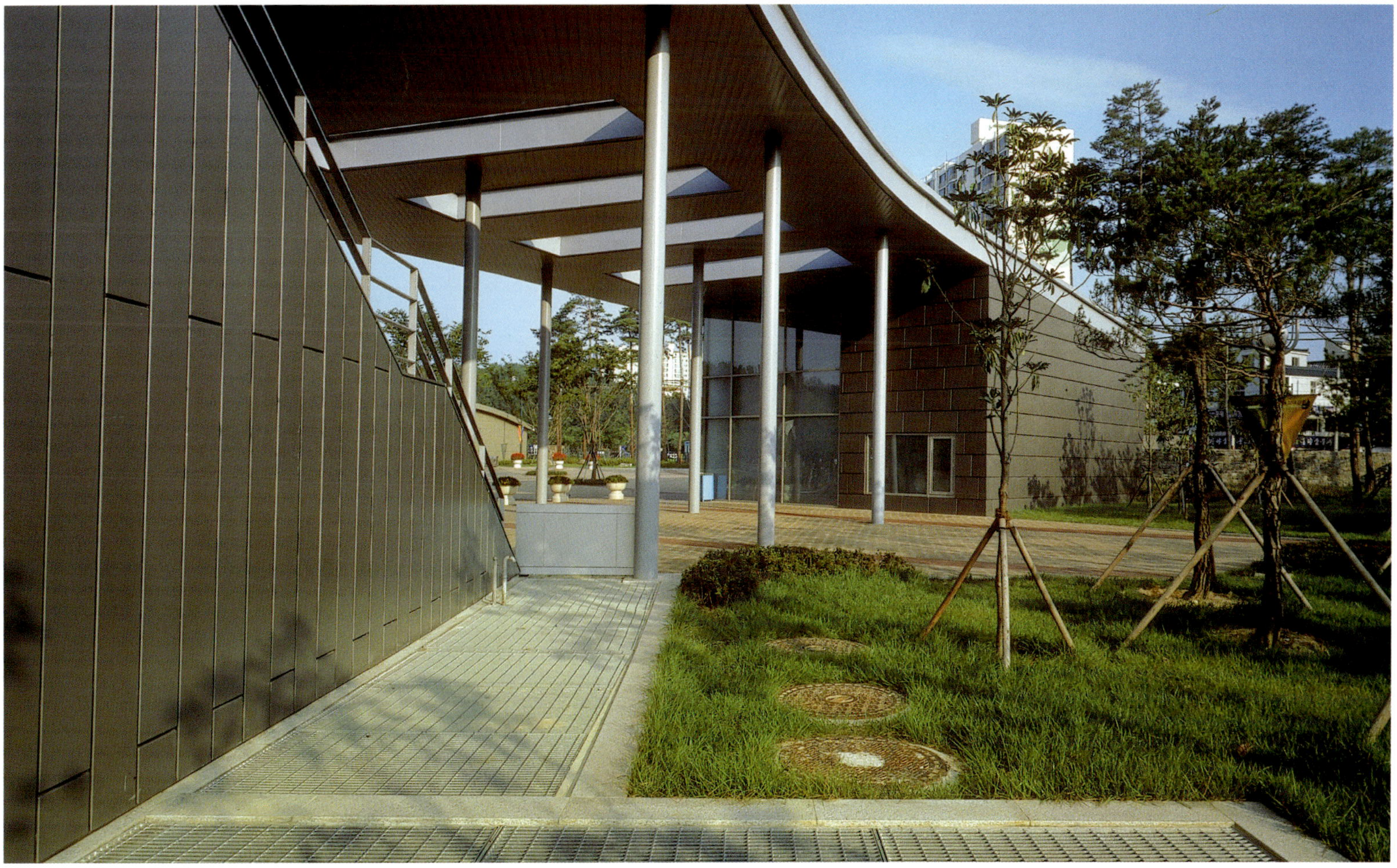

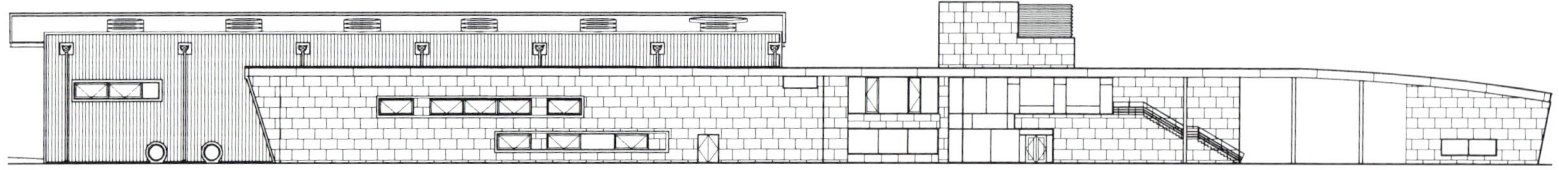

Elevation

0 1 2

BasketBar

Architects: NL Architects
Collaborators: Henry Betting and De Drie Musketiers (Interior Designers)

Photographs © Luuk Kramer

Location: Utrecht, the Netherlands
Year completed: 2003

A BAR, A BASKETBALL COURT, A SMALL AMPHITHEATER, AND A SPACE FOR SKATERS MAKE UP THIS ORIGINAL NEW MULTIFUNCTIONAL PROJECT DESIGNED BY NL ARCHITECTS, WHICH HAS GONE ON TO RECEIVE A NUMBER OF PRESTIGIOUS INTERNATIONAL PRIZES..

BasketBar

The campus of the University of Utrecht has evolved from a single-function environment that was solely dedicated to education into a small city in its own right: a rich amalgam of programs designed by OMA through an urban plan enhanced a variety of different areas and reinforced the qualities of the existing landscape. The strategy aimed to prevent the appearance of an excessive number of isolated and unconnected elements by situating all the newly added functions in pre-existing buildings: this allowed these new activities to grow within the perimeters of the existing campus.

As soon as the restrictions on on-campus housing were lifted and student apartments were converted into a real projects, new uses were made to transform some of these spaces into leisure areas. These included such spaces as restaurants and bars, which were designed to provide a relaxing environment in which students, professors, and researchers could meet. The young team of NL Architects was assigned the task of designing a bar in the Van Unnik building, by expanding the existing bookshop. Due to the location's low ceiling, it was decided to lower the floor and to insert the bar on a lower level, so that it would turn into a more private spot without sacrificing its views of the surrounding area. Handicapped access is possible through a small, orange amphitheater, which mediates the change in level between street and bar, in addition to offering patrons a place to sit outside, and even a place for skaters to practice. The roof of the bar, which offers a view out over the campus, was used to install a basketball court, which ties back in to the interior via a large, transparent skylight in the middle of the court.

Floor plan

0   4   8

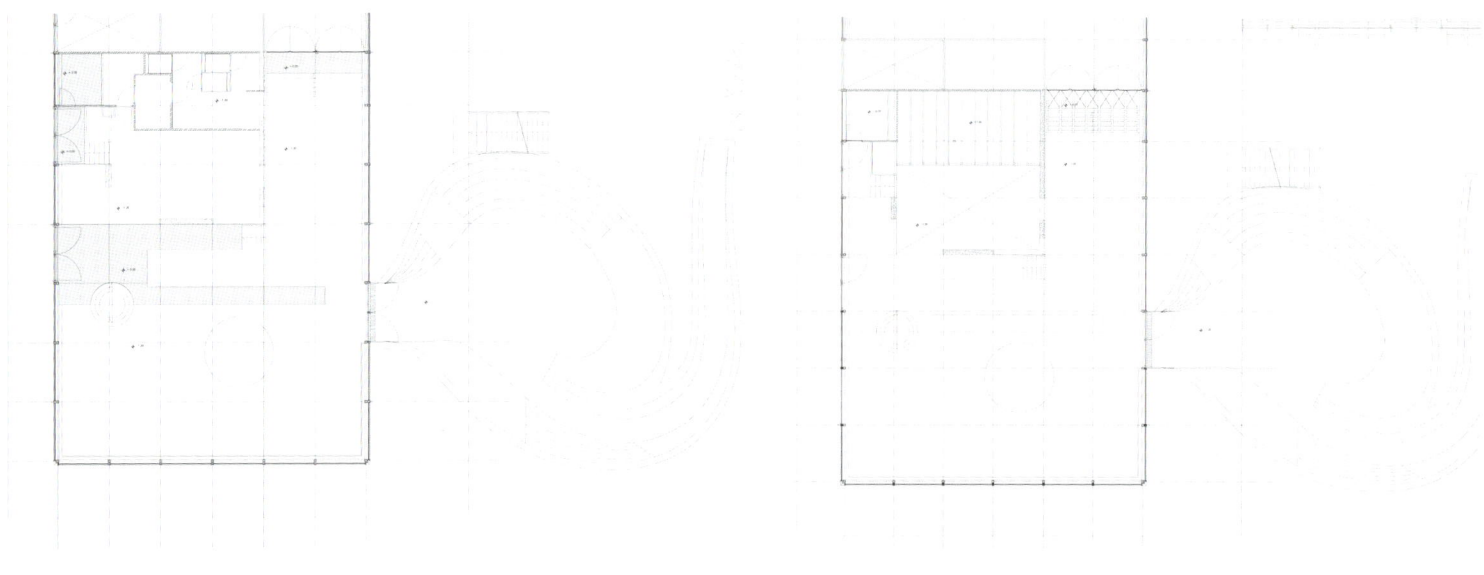

Level 0

Level 1

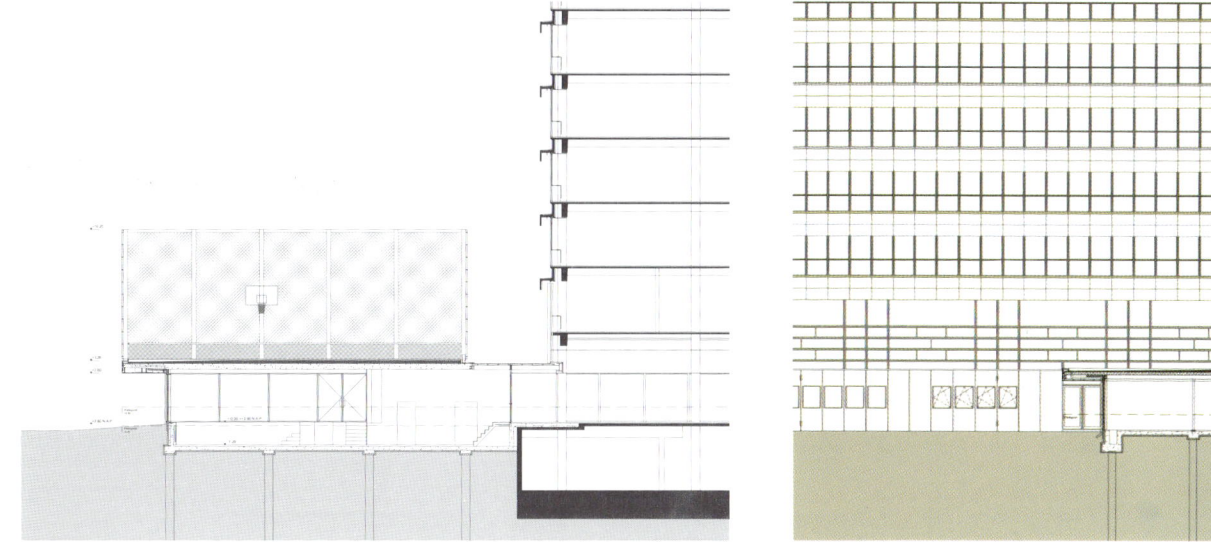

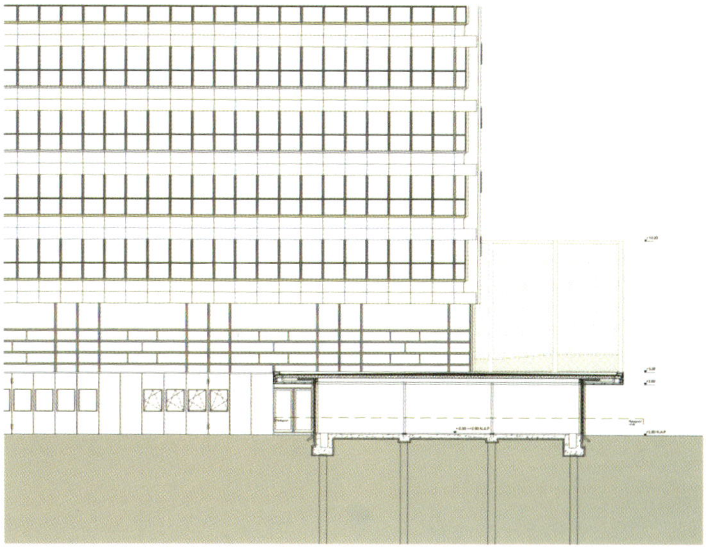

Sections

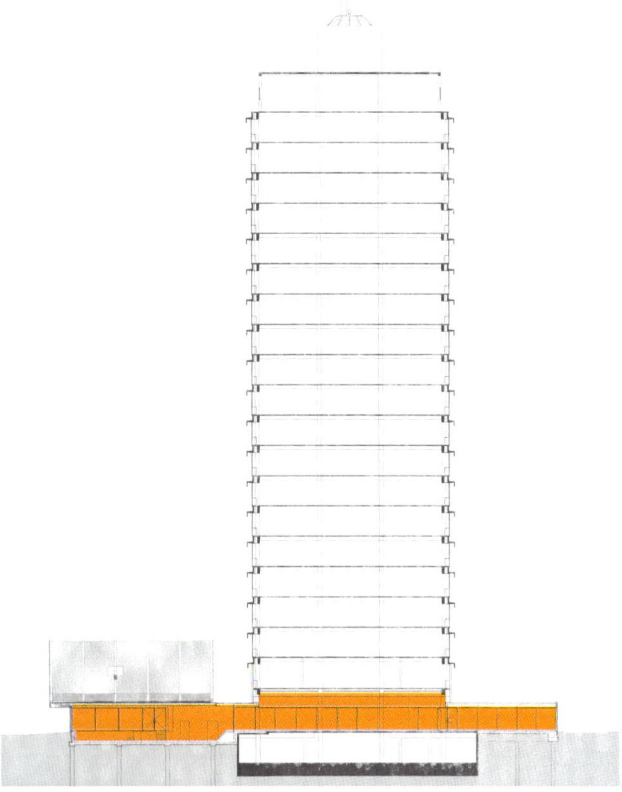

Section

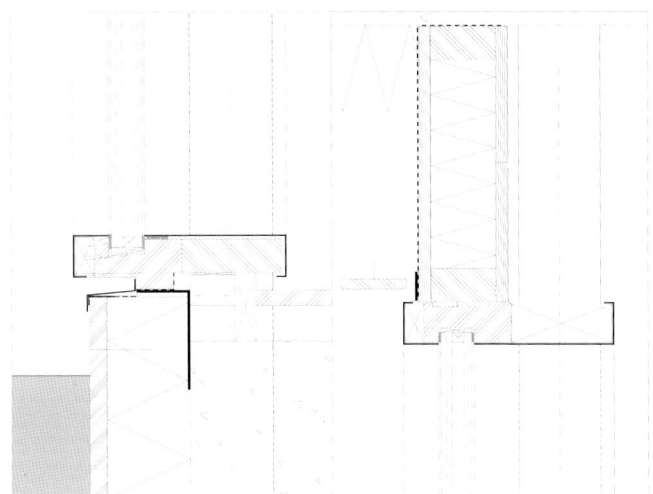

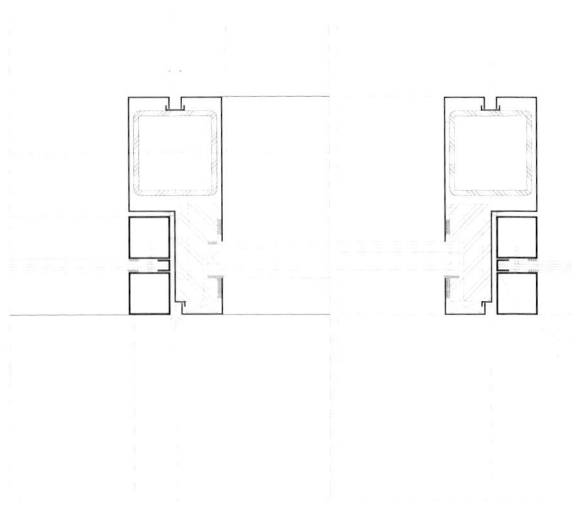

Construction details

WELLNESS 02 & CIMA

ARCHITECTS: ALONSO BALAGUER Y ARQUITECTOS ASOCIADOS

PHOTOGRAPHS © JOSEP MARIA MOLINOS

LOCATION: BARCELONA, SPAIN
YEAR COMPLETED: 2005

THIS FACILITY REPRESENTS A LANDMARK IN TERMS OF HEALTH AND SPORTING FACILITIES IN THE CITY, AS IT WAS THE FIRST TO MARRY HEALTH AND SPORTS. TRADITIONAL WEIGHTLIFTING MACHINES HAVE BEEN COMBINED WITH A MULTITUDE OF THERAPIES AND WATER-BASED ACTIVITIES.

WELLNESS O2 & CIMA

This project combines the Wellness O2 Sports Center and the International Center for Advanced Medicine (CIMA) under one roof in Barcelona's Sarriá neighborhood, immediately adjacent to Santa Amelia Park. The complex also entails an old country house that was rehabilitated to house the center's central administrative department, and came to represent the logistical nucleus of the facility. The renovation of the pre-existing historical building allowed the architects to establish a dialogue between traditional architecture and the technological innovations applied herein—this, of course, in addition to tying the complex into the history of the neighborhood.

The two main functions of the building have been separated: the medical services are housed in a glass box, which is open to the street, while the sports facilities are enveloped in an opaque volume with a stone façade whose only openings are towards the park next door.

Harmonic colors were meticulously sought after for the interior of the building, in addition to warm materials and excellent finishes. Marble and polished stone floors and acid-frosted or transparent glass partitions are yet more of the materials that were chosen to round out this serene and Minimalist décor. The lighting was also carefully designed to create a relaxing atmosphere, as well as to create sophisticated interplays of light and the iridescence that arises when light comes into contact with water.

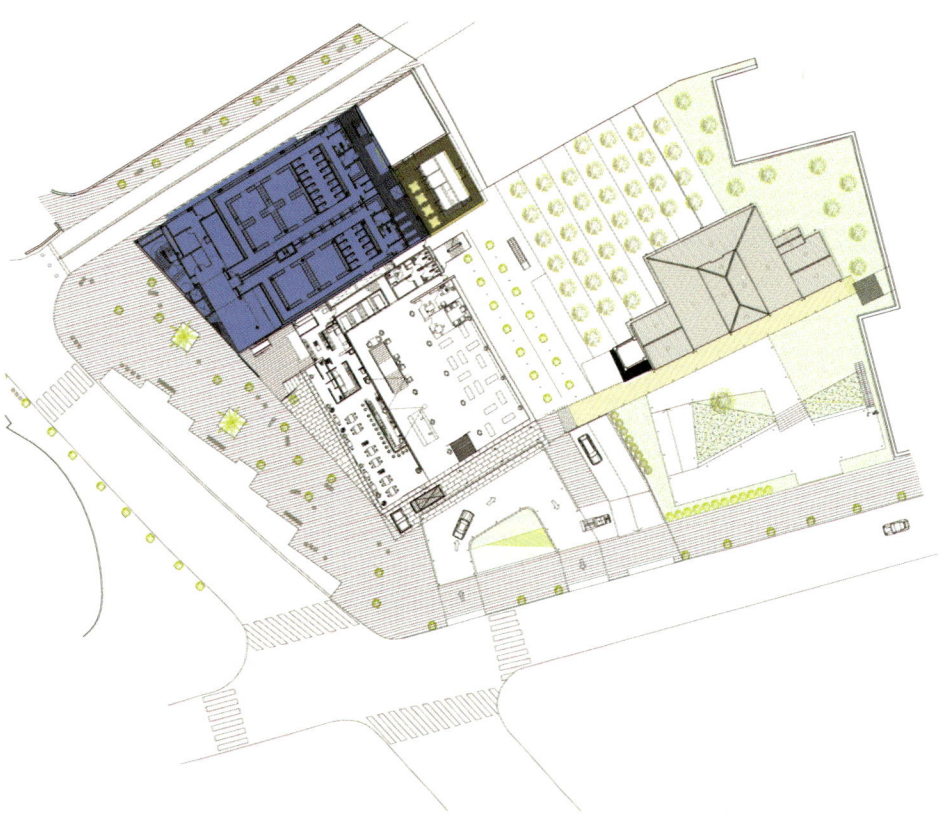

Floor plan

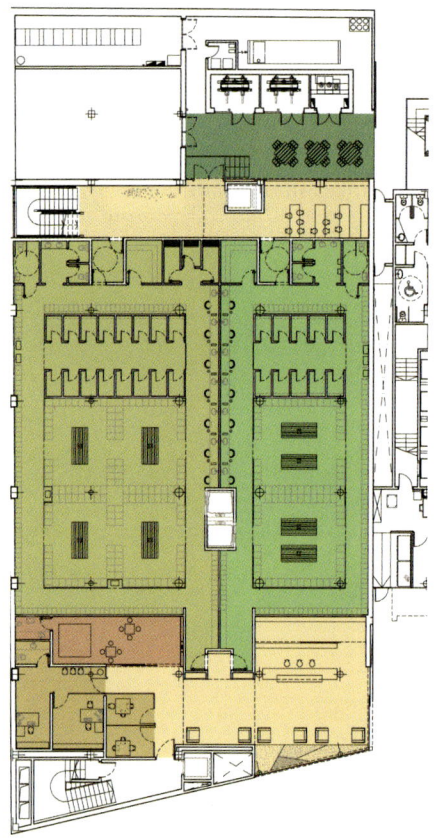

Ground floor

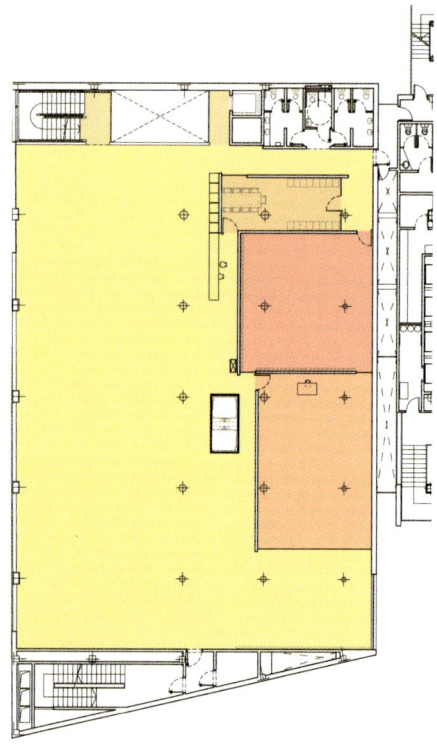

First floor

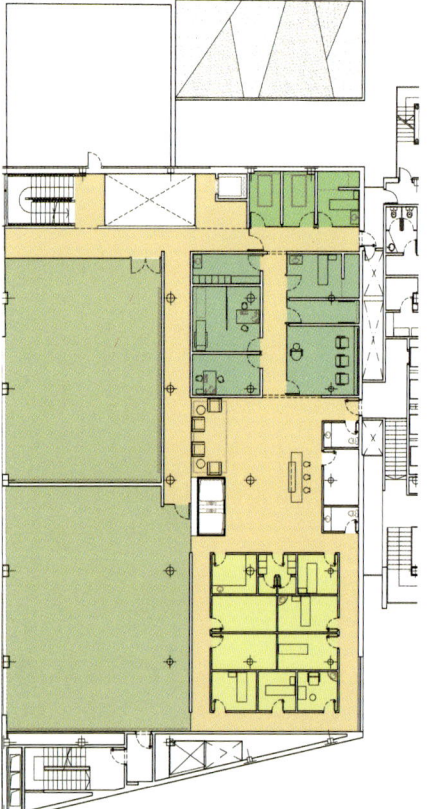

Second floor

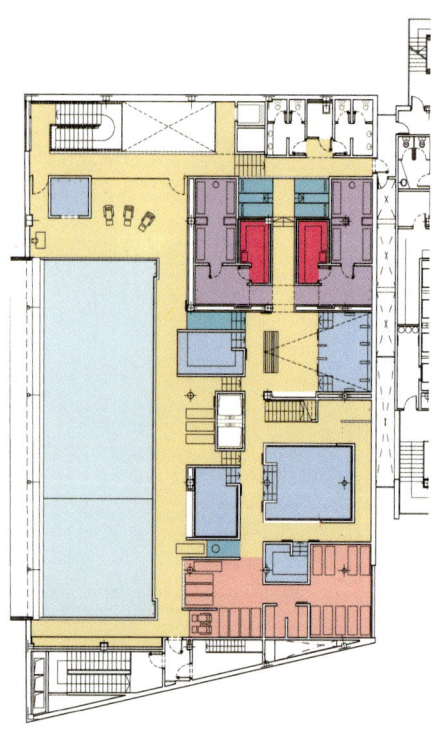

Third floor

0 2 4

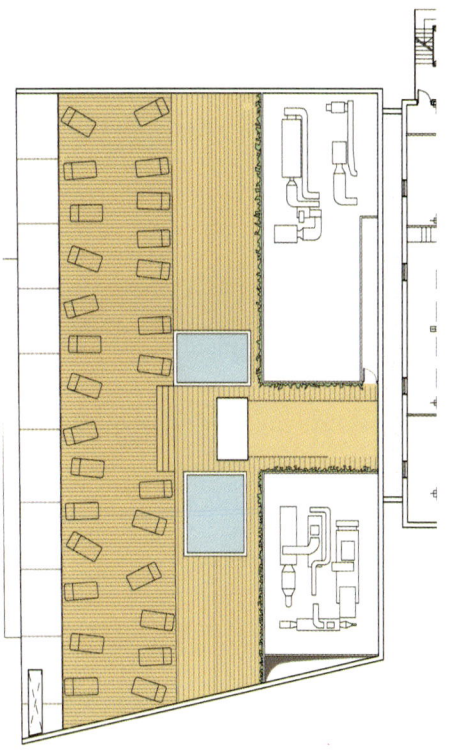

Roof floor

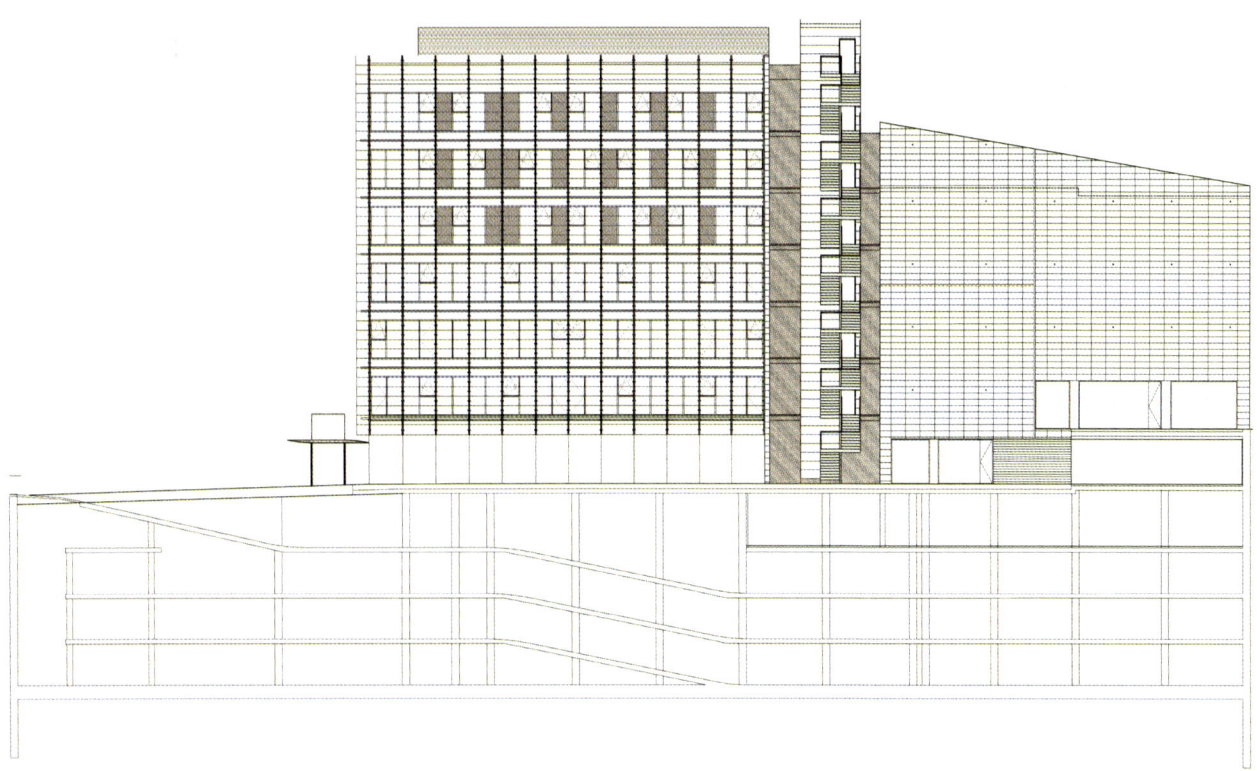

Section

El Sorrall Sports Complex

ARCHITECTS: PALLEJÀ–LEÓN ARQUITECTES
COLLABORATORS: BRUFAU, OBIOL Y MOYA (STRUCTURES), GRUPO JG (SERVICES), D. FABREGAT (DRAFTSMAN)

PHOTOGRAPHS © JORDI MIRALLES

LOCATION: MATARÓ, SPAIN
YEAR COMPLETED: 2003

El Sorrall Sports Complex

This project arose from the Mataró City Council's desire to create a new recreational and leisure center for the city, as well as to create a new urban façade along the highway that girds the city. This design of the complex kept to environmental and ecological criteria: it utilizes renewable sources of energy and construction systems that optimize energy savings. It is additionally a pioneer in using the heat emitted by wastewater treatment plants' drying of sludge to heat the building itself, as well as to heat its hot water supply.

One enters the facility through a large exposed concrete portico, which frames the entryway and the administrative area. The sheer size of the building and its marked horizontality mean that the area around the entrance form an emblematic part of the ensemble and serve as the link between the three volumes that make up the complex. These three volumes are as follows: the linear body of the story that contains the locker rooms and serves, the emerging volume of the workout area and gyms, and the water zone.

The volume that contains the gymnasiums was conceived of poetically as representing a link between the sea and the mountains, as though it were a beached ship. Thus, its roof exhibits a slight curvature with six skylights that recall the smokestacks of a steamship. The façade is clad in wooden planks and steel plates, and has three windows reminiscent of portholes as well as lightweight white metal banisters with a wooden handrail. However, the volume of the dressing rooms attempts to blend into the landscape through a roof garden that can be seen from the street.

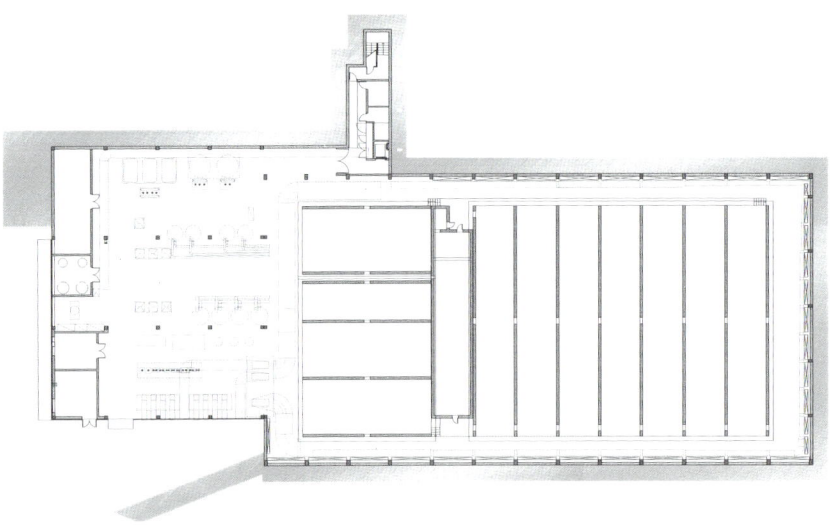

Second basement

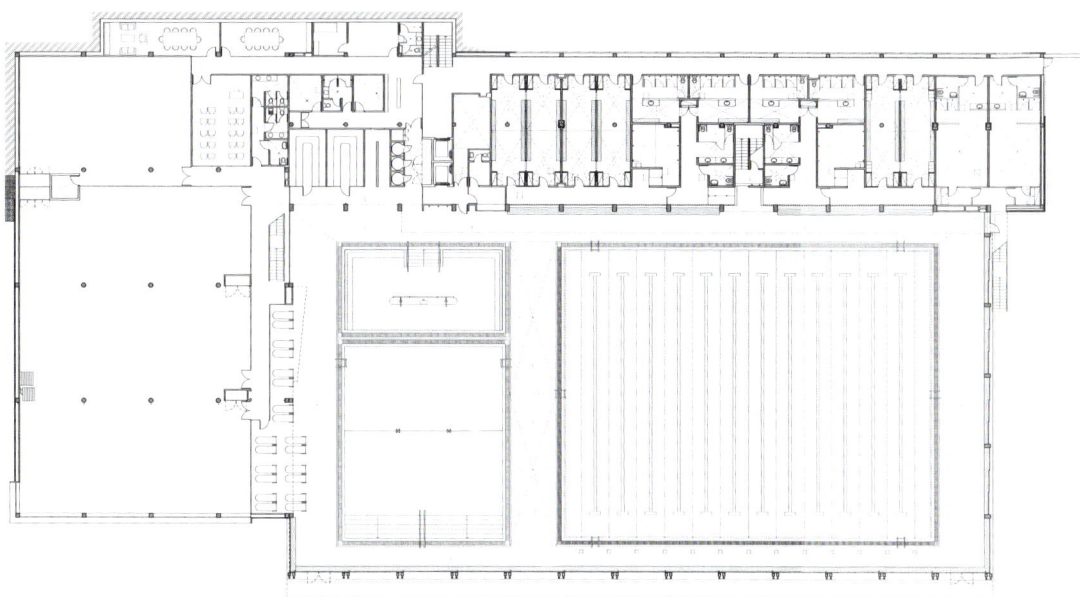

First basement

0   4   8

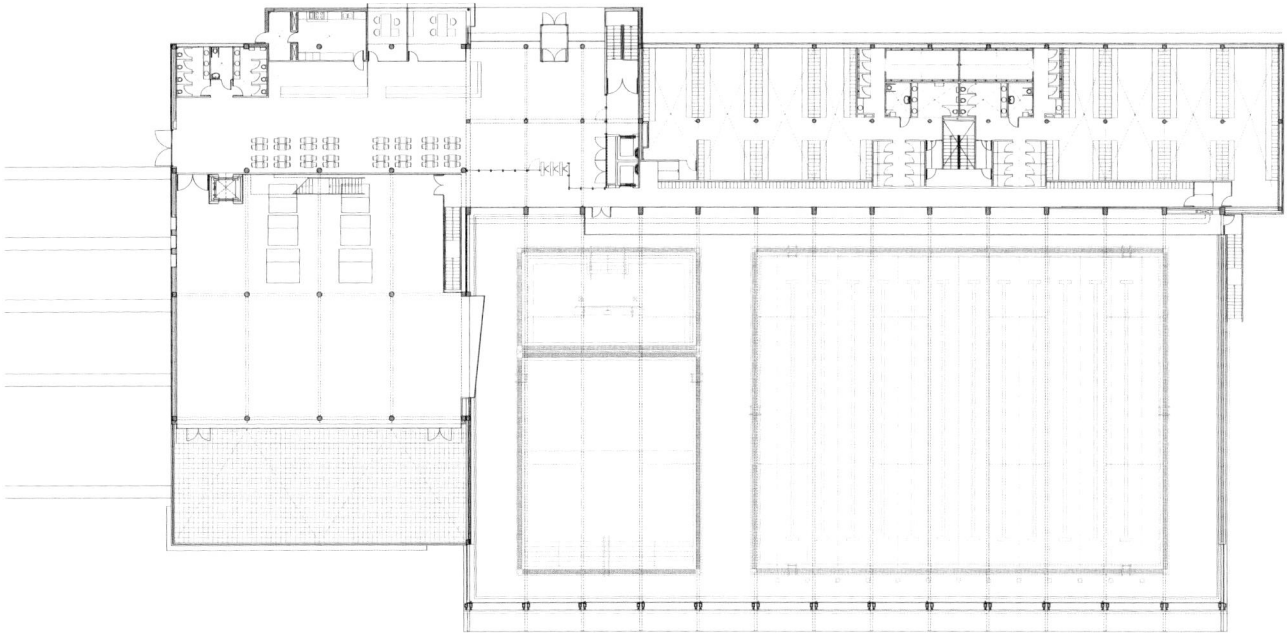

Ground floor

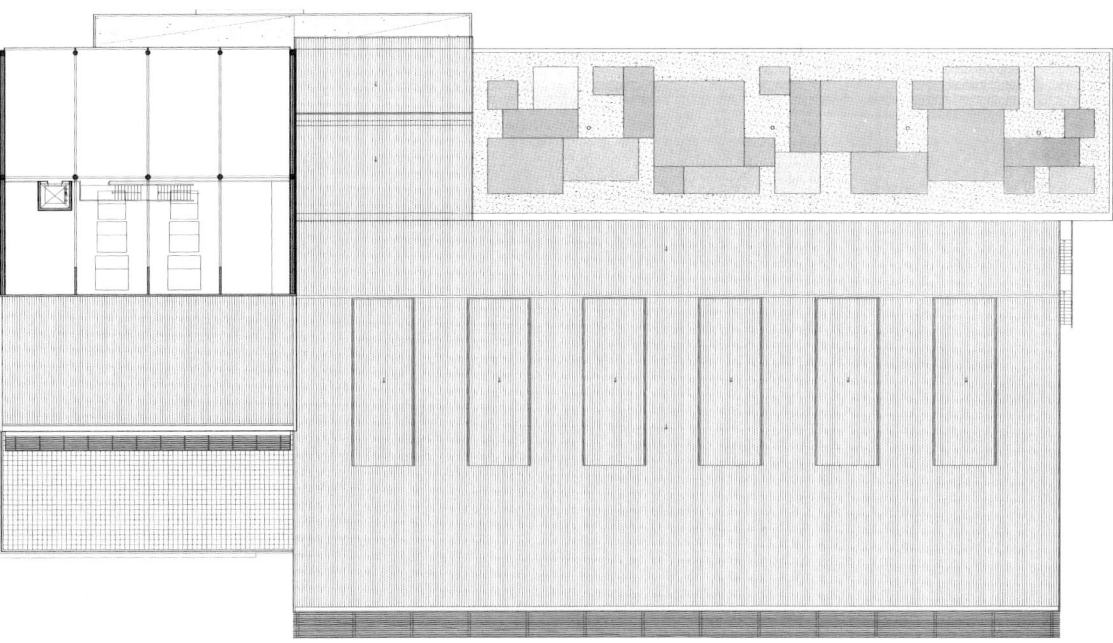

Roof plan

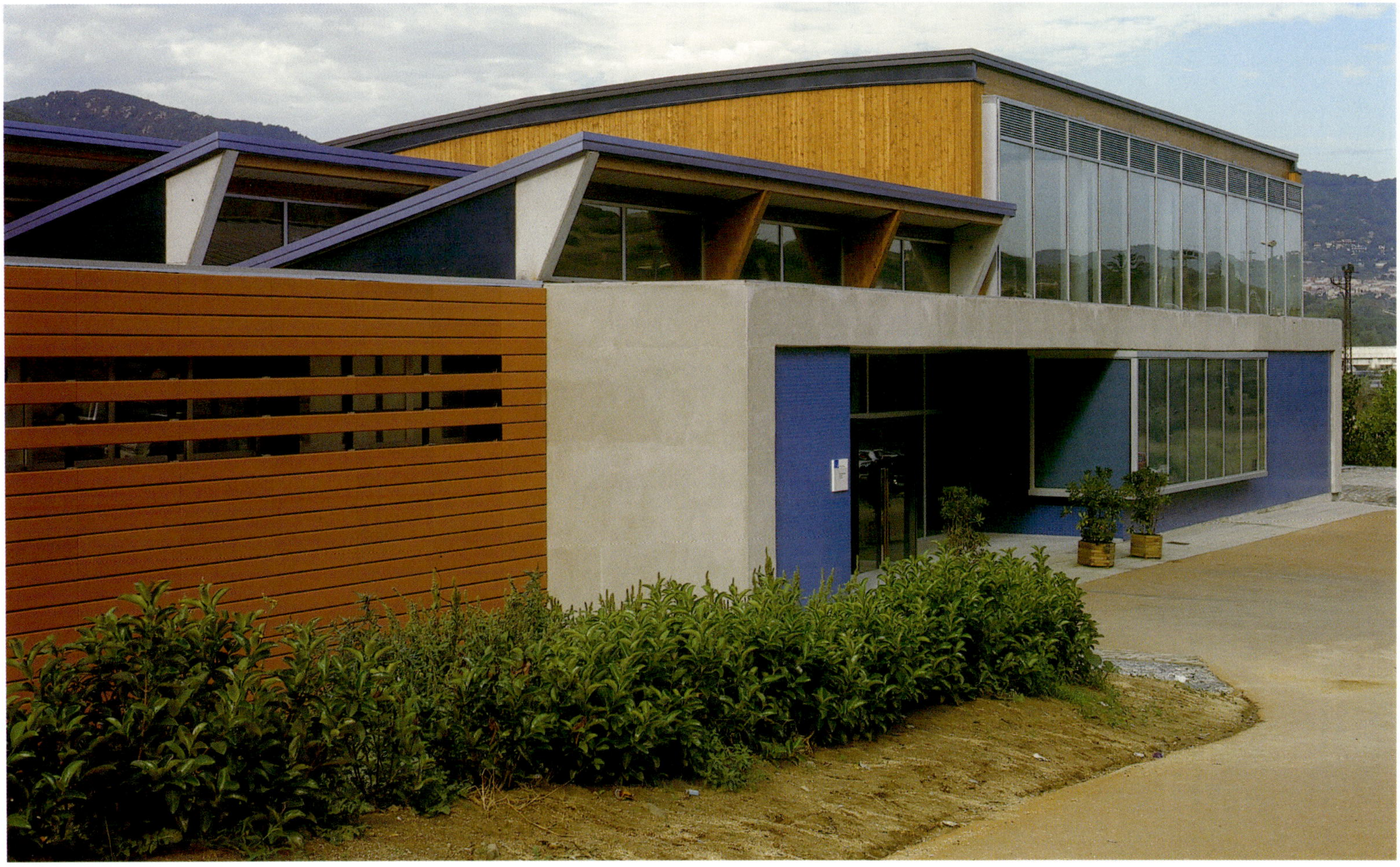

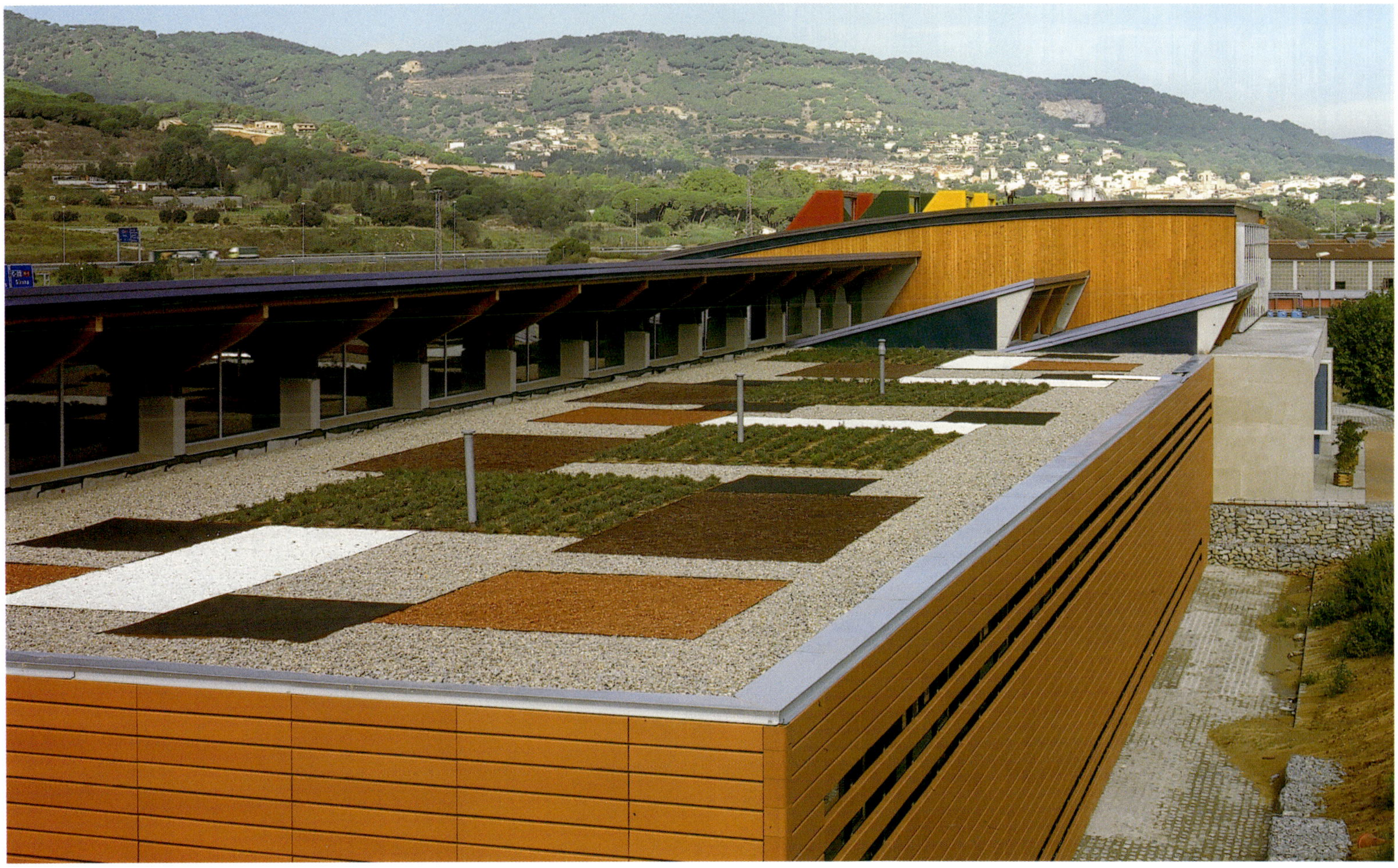

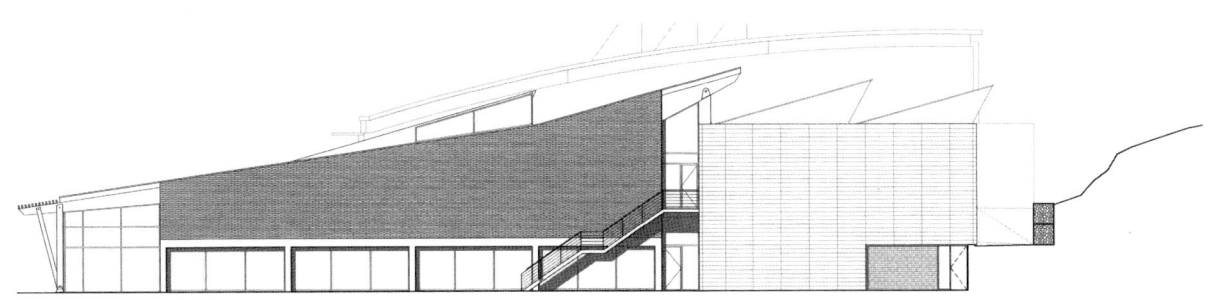

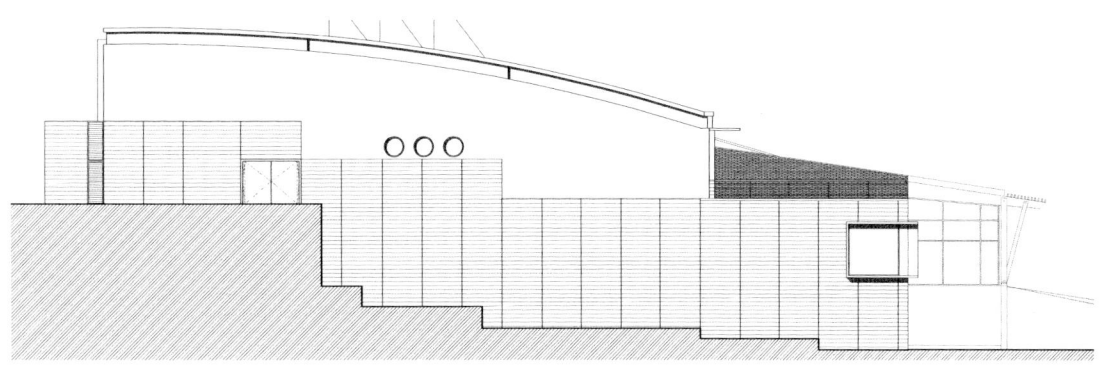

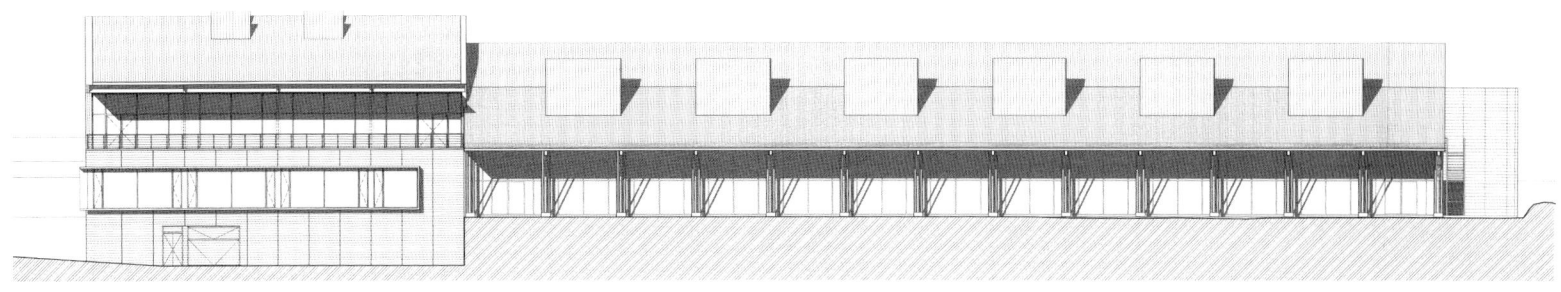

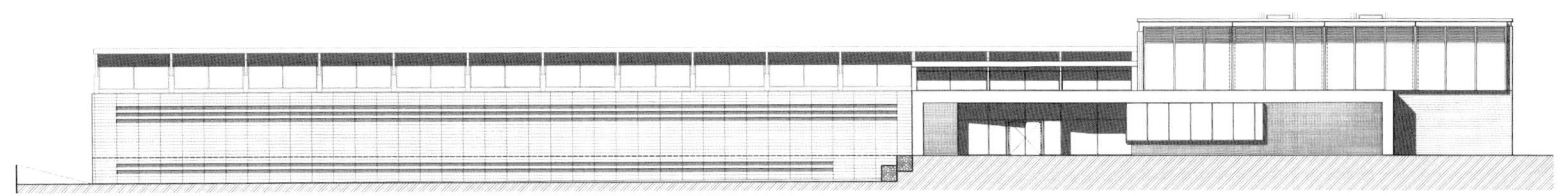

Elevations

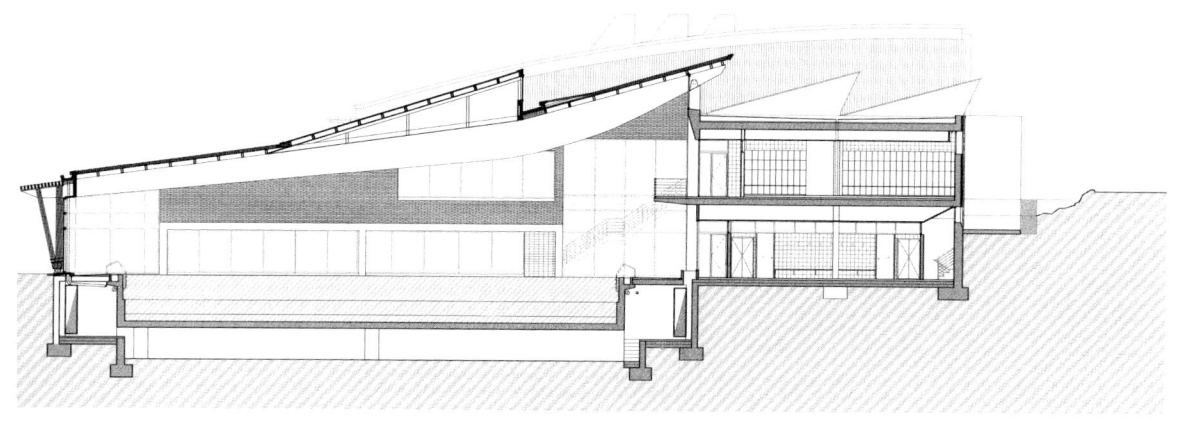

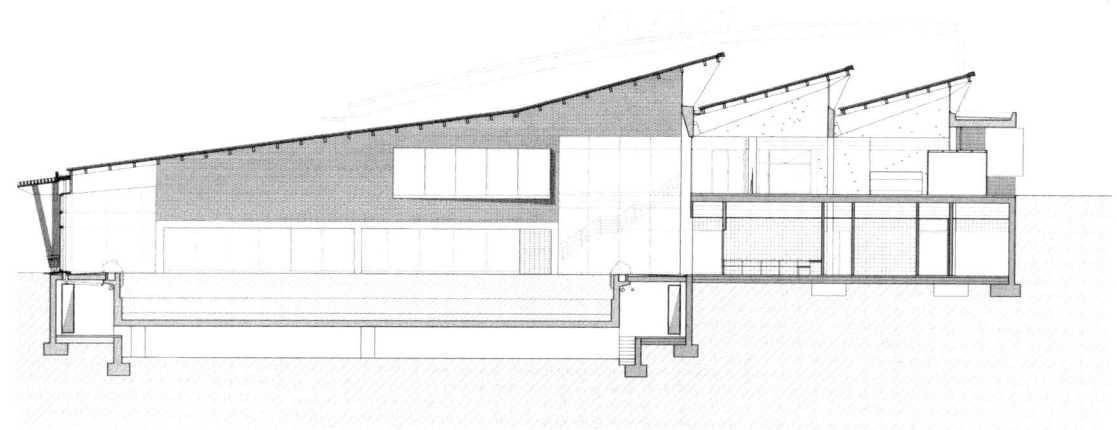

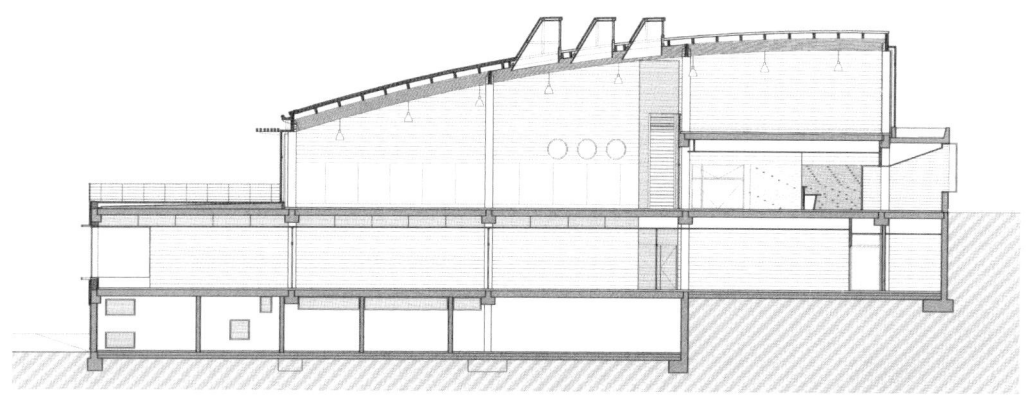

Cross sections

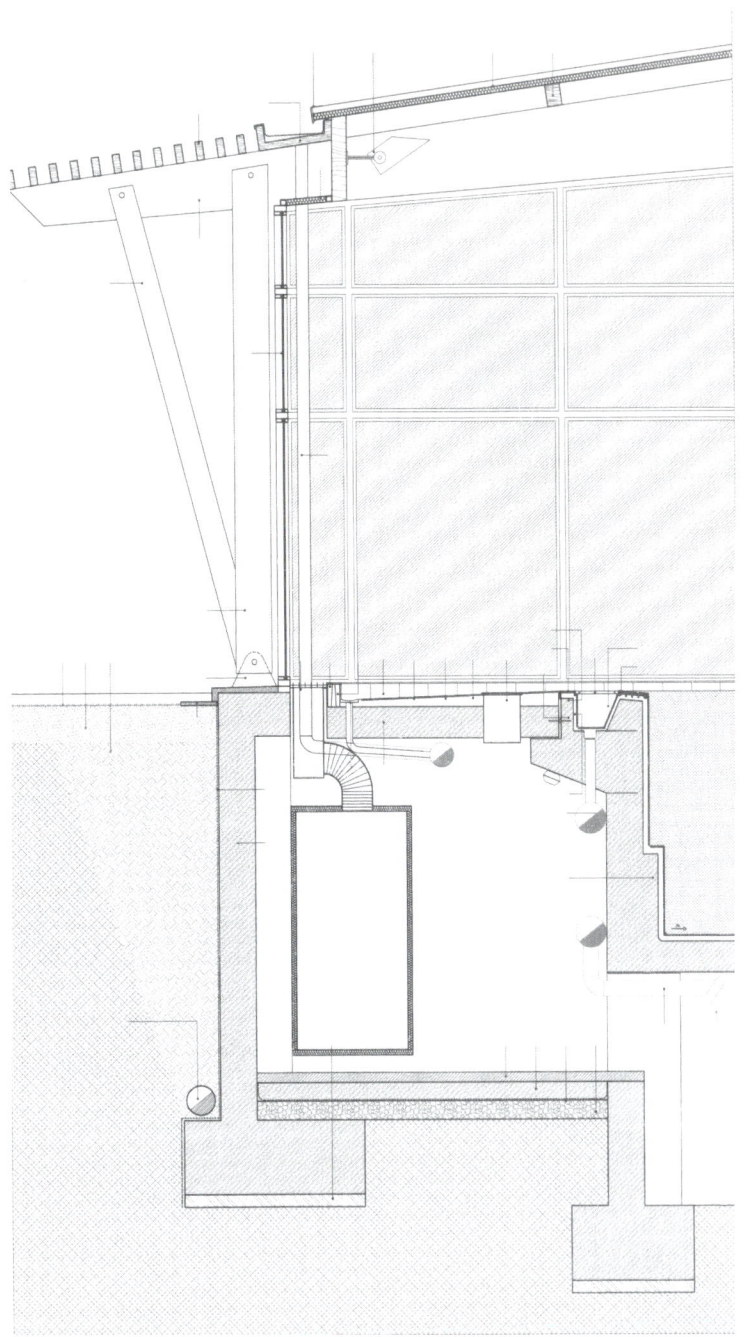

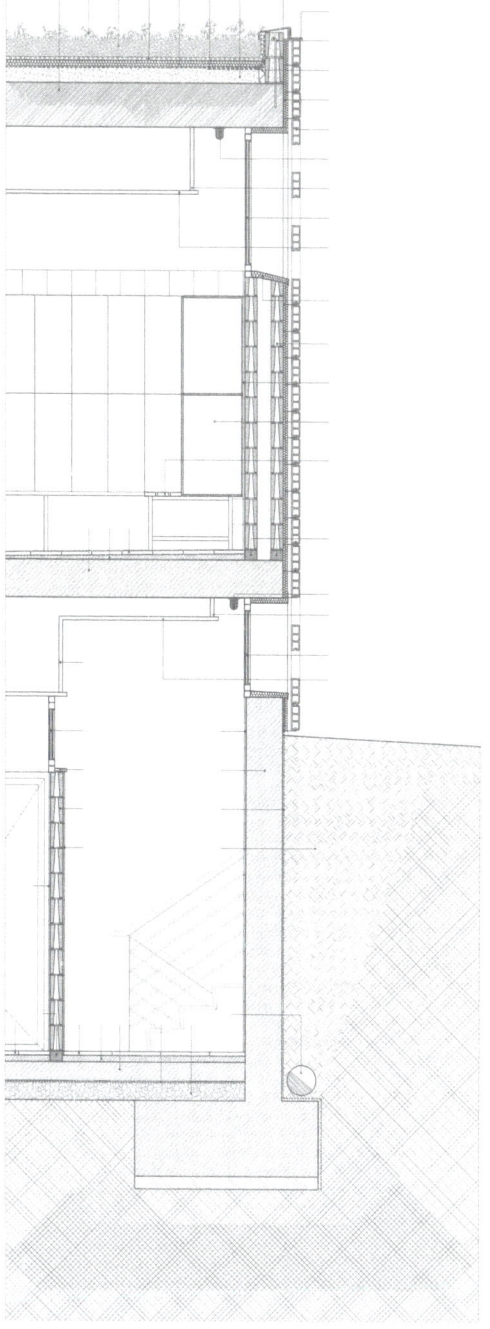

Cosntruction details

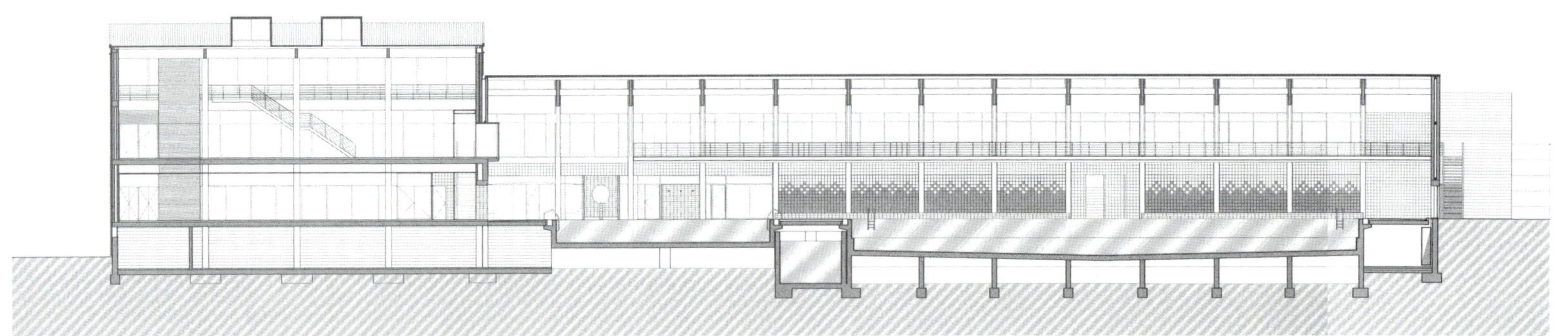

Longitudinal section

JUBILEE SPORTS CENTER

ARCHITECT: RICK MATHER ARCHITECTS

PHOTOGRAPHS © BENEDICT LUXMOORE

LOCATION: SOUTHAMPTON, UNITED KINGDOM
YEAR COMPLETED: 2003

THE FORMAL LANGUAGE DEFINED ON THE EXTERIOR OF THIS CENTER IS REPEATED INSIDE ITS POOL THROUGH THE CREATION OF AN INTERESTING COMPOSITION OF GEOMETRIC VOLUMES USED TO TIE TOGETHER THE DIFFERENT ACTIVITIES OFFERED AT THE CENTER.

JUBILEE SPORTS CENTER

This building is located at the center of the campus of the University of Southampton - Highfield, in the UK, and houses a wide range of indoor sporting activities in competition-grade facilities. The program of the center includes a six-lane, 25-meter pool, a badminton court and a 4,850 sq. foot gymnasium. Both the pool and the badminton court have stands alongside them, which can house spectators for both national and international events; furthermore, there is an ample lobby, cafeteria and staff office area.

Near this sports center one finds the University's Botanical Gardens, which ended up having a decisive influence on the design of the project. The volume of the building was designed to be as low as possible, and the program of activities was furthermore designed along a long, horizontal line. Additionally, the structure was designed in such a way that the roof surface would be as slender as possible.

The resulting volume stems from a clear and simple scheme that responds to the diverse characteristics of the environments that surround it, yet in a subtle fashion—this is achieved by the use of light forms that affect the volume itself or the use of a wide range of materials. The glass main façade allow us to gaze out on the panorama outside and extends the activities taking place inside outward. The soft curve of the north façade, which faces the university library, is clad in brick, and is mostly without openings. It contains the gymnasium and office. The south and west facades are covered in steel panels that act as the backdrop to the surrounding gardens and landscape.

UNIVERSITY ROAD
BUS STOP
STUDENT UNION SPORTS HALL
SERVICE BAY
LOADING BAY
B37
47
45
43
41

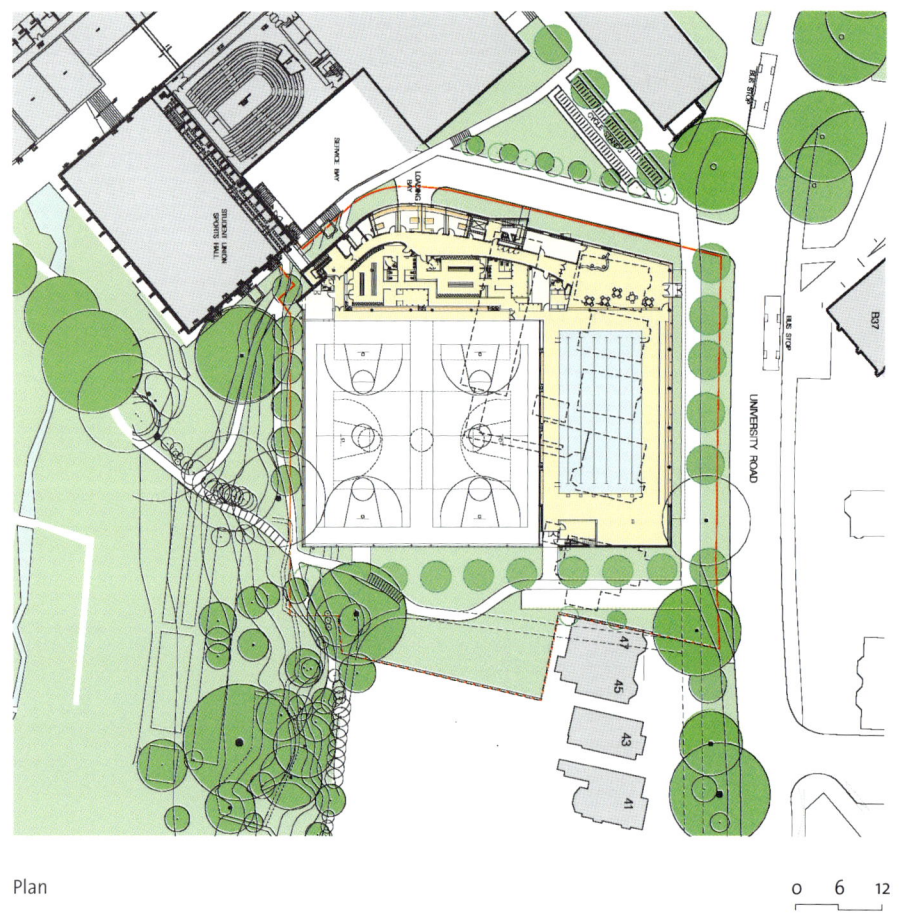

Plan

0 6 12

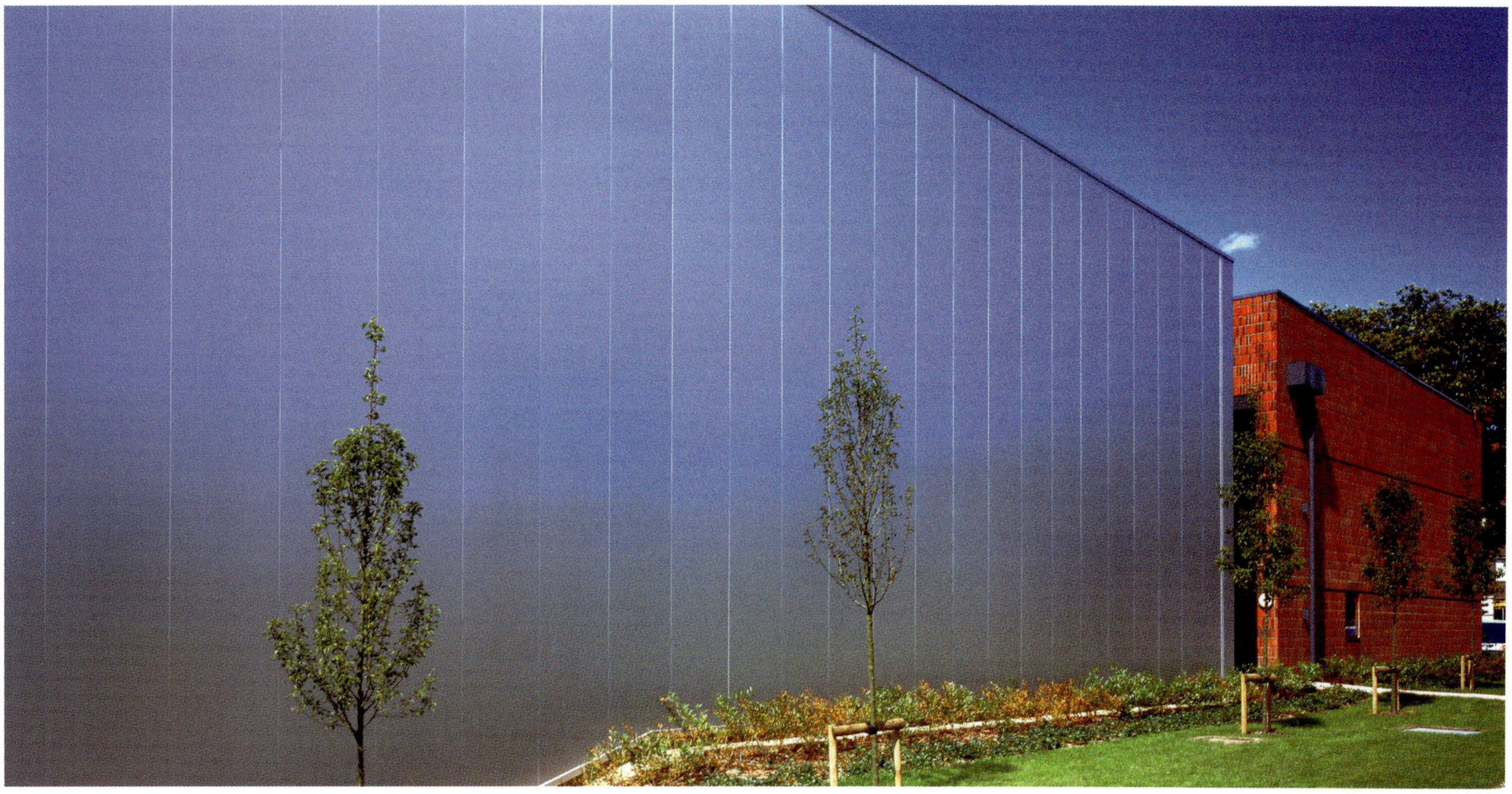

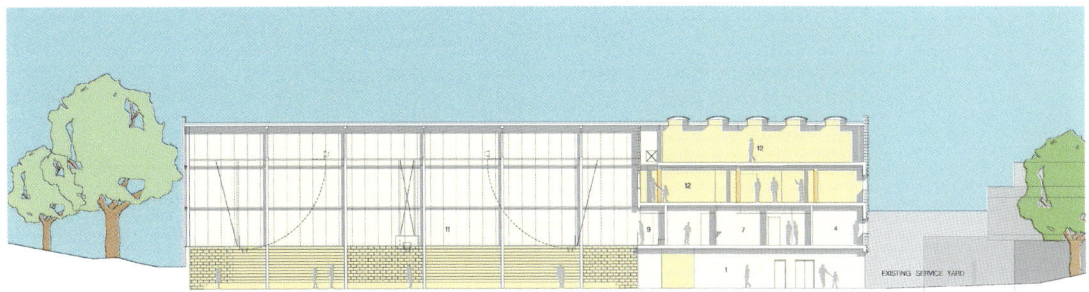

Sections

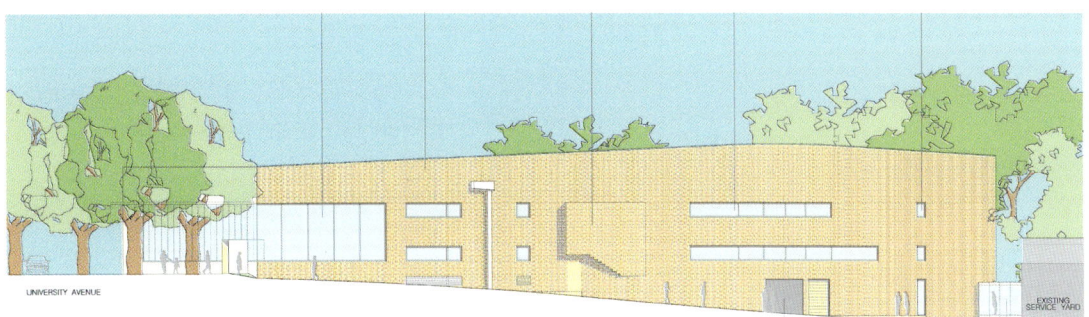

Elevations

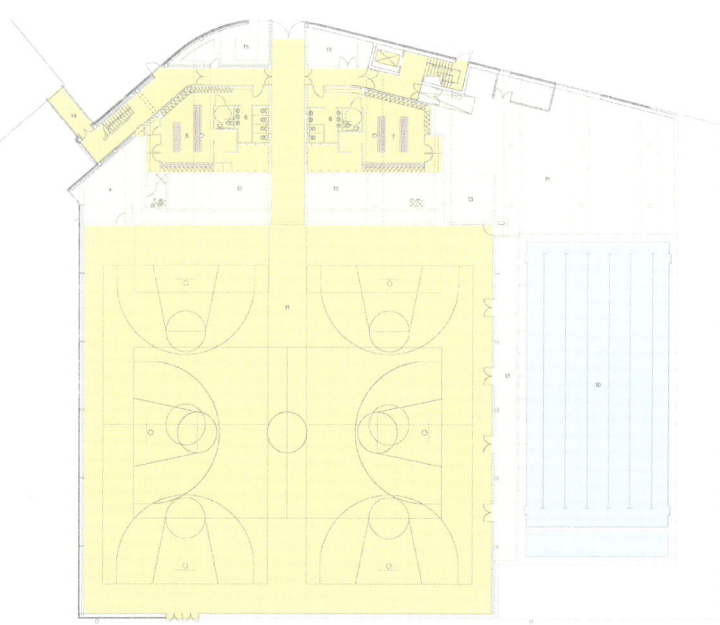

Basement

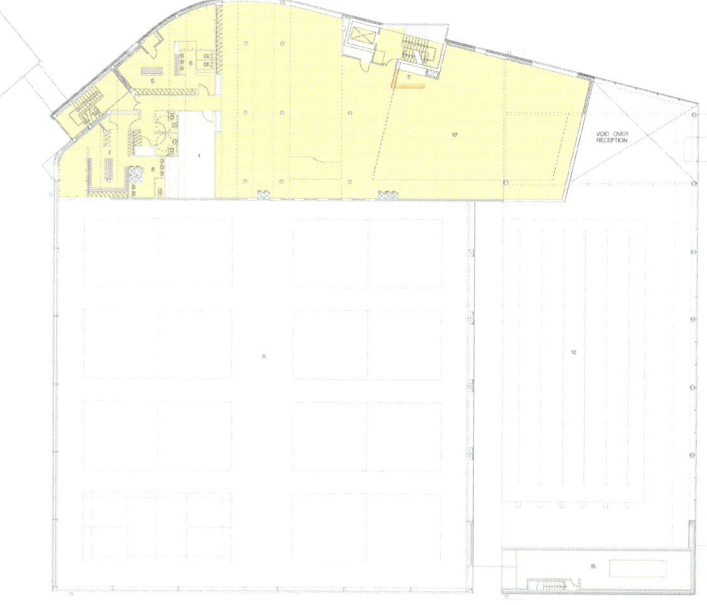

Mezzanine

Ground floor

Mezzanine

0 1 2

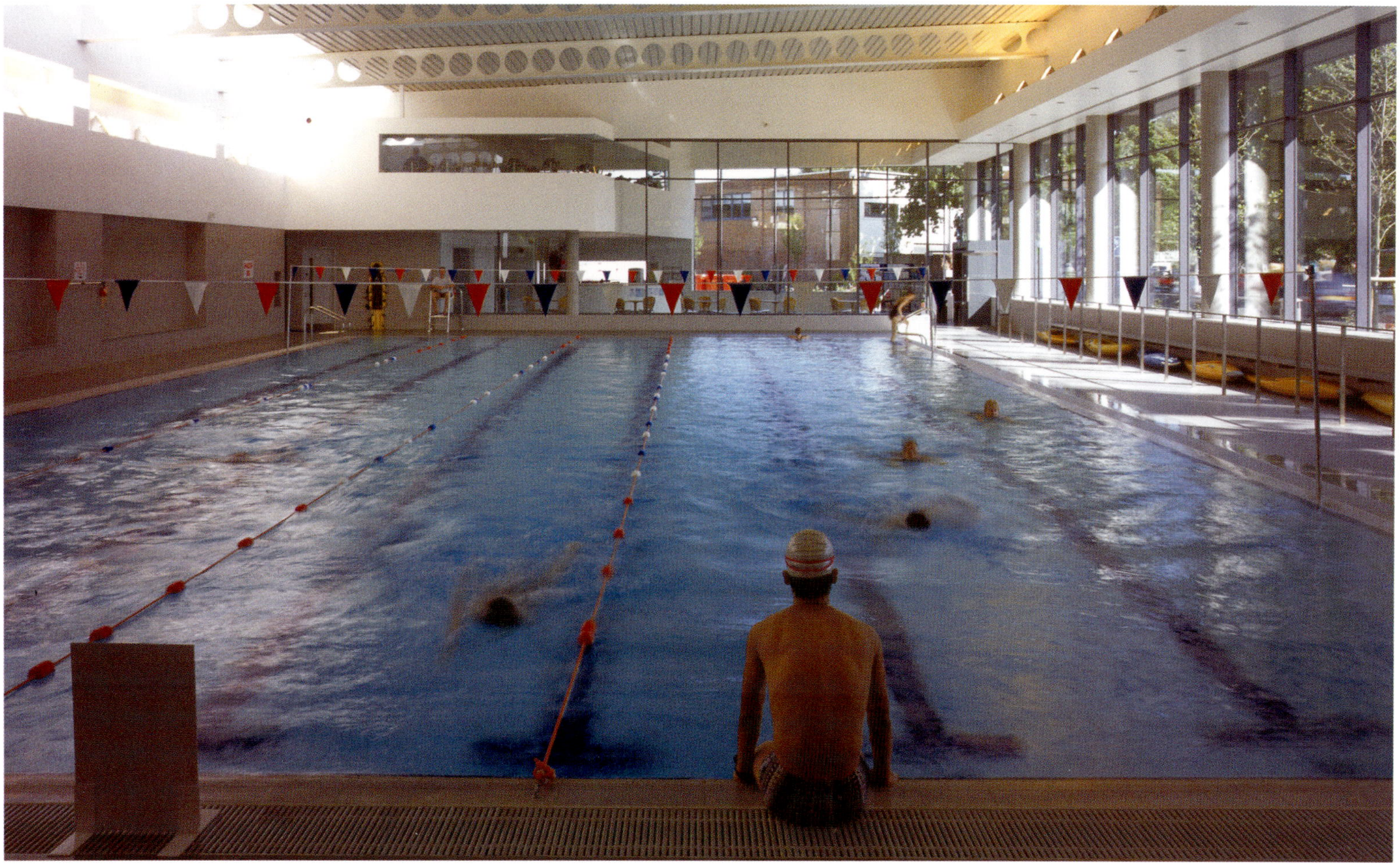

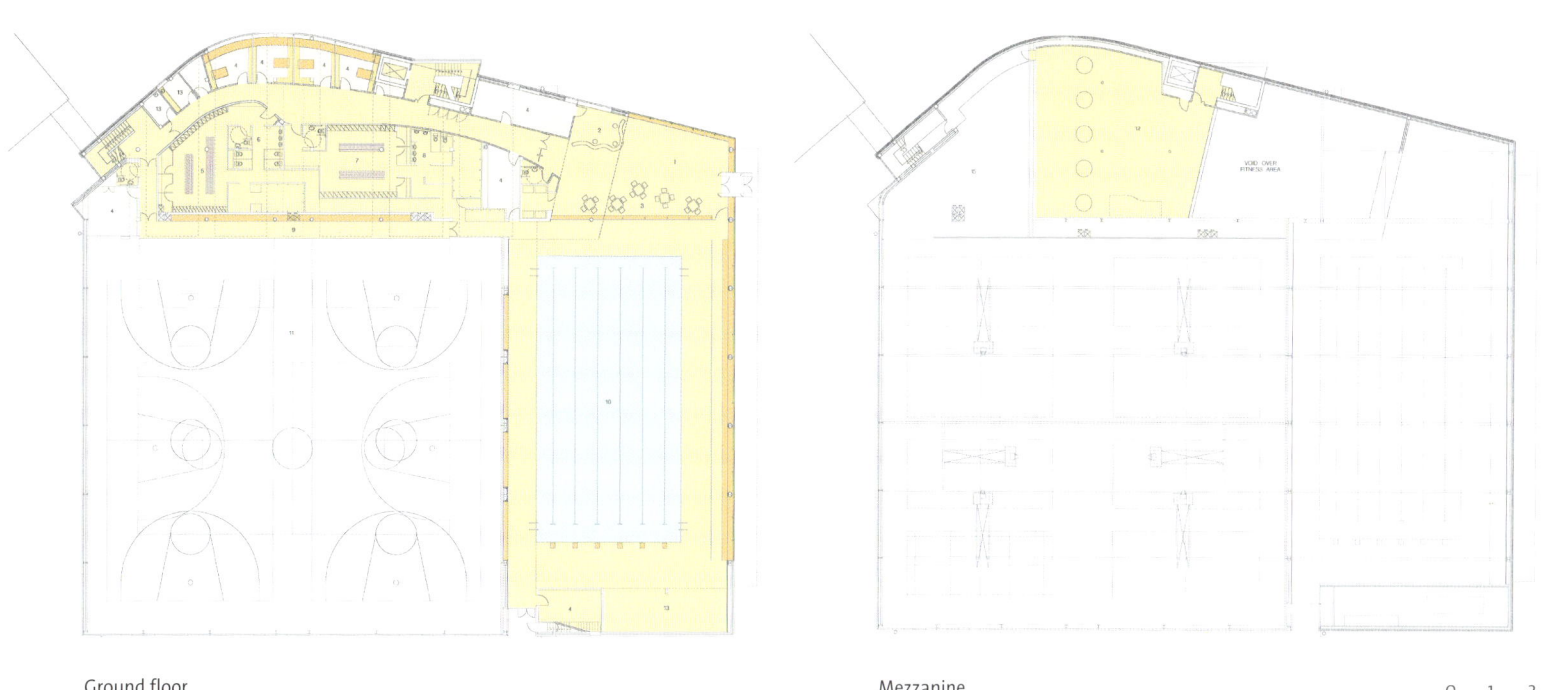

New Sports Pavillion for Latymer Upper School

Architects: Van Heyningen Haward Architects

Photographs © Sue Barr

Location: London, United Kingdom
Year completed: 2002

DESPITE THIS BUILDING'S HERMETIC EXTERIOR, ITS INTERIOR IS BRIGHT THANKS TO THE HIGH WINDOWS AND THE USE OF LIGHT COLORS ON THE WALLS AND FINISHES.

NEW SPORTS PAVILLION FOR LATYMER UPPER SCHOOL

This triangular pavilion complements the sporting facilities of this school, which is located to the west of London. It occupies a prominent corner on the campus and houses locker rooms, storage space, offices and spacious exterior balconies that serve as an ideal meeting point. The balconies extend all along the building, so as to offer a maximum of panoramic views out over the school's sporting fields. The simple volume of the building is finished off with a flat roof that covers the balcony and extends towards the corners of the triangle, signaling the two main entrances to the building and protecting the two outdoor concrete staircases located at these two points.

The program of activities the building would house, which mainly entailed showers and locker rooms, resulted in a building that was hermetically closed off from the outside, yet benefits from strategically placed windows that allow natural light in and ventilate the interior. A screen was built into the main façade of the building to display the scores of ongoing cricket matches, which are played in a field adjacent to the pavilion. The reception area, which doubles as a clinic, is located on the lower floor, directly behind the main entrance to the building. A longitudinal bench, just behind the balcony, serves as a area for people to unwind, and also conceals the laundry room for shoes, which is located directly across from the entrance to the building. The predominant use of black plywood paneling on the façade evokes the traditional architecture of English cricket pavilions, while other materials—such as the exposed concrete on the façade, the metal banisters, and the rubber floors—were chosen based on criteria of strength and durability.

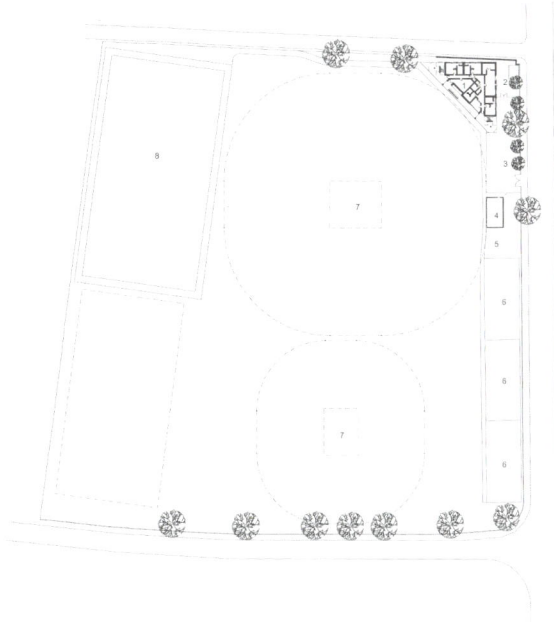

Location plan

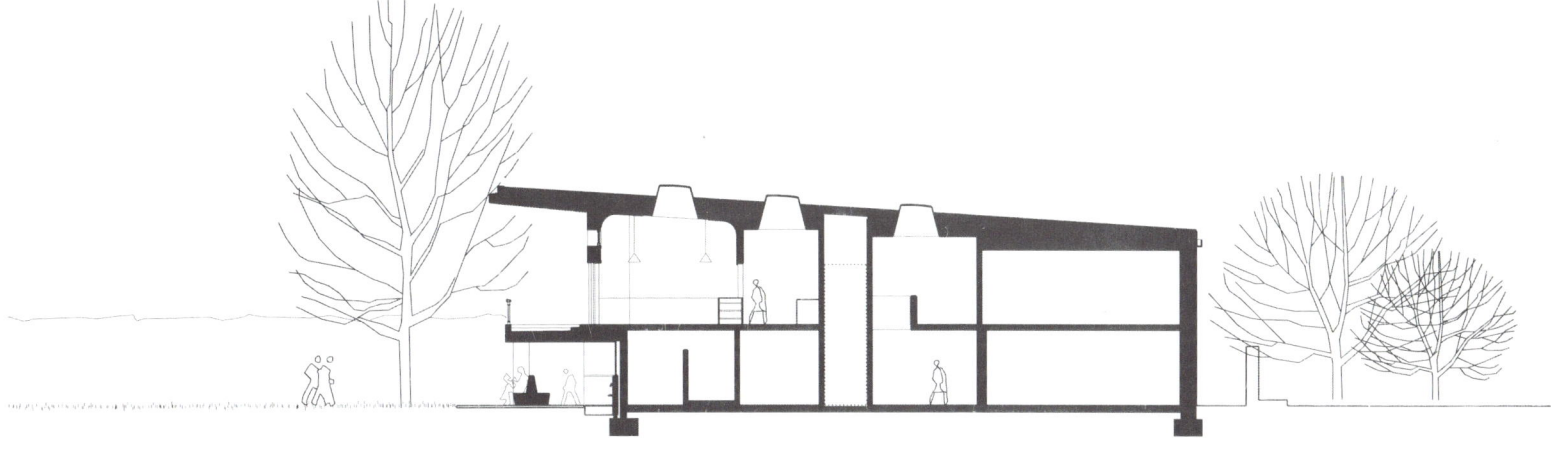

Section

Elevation

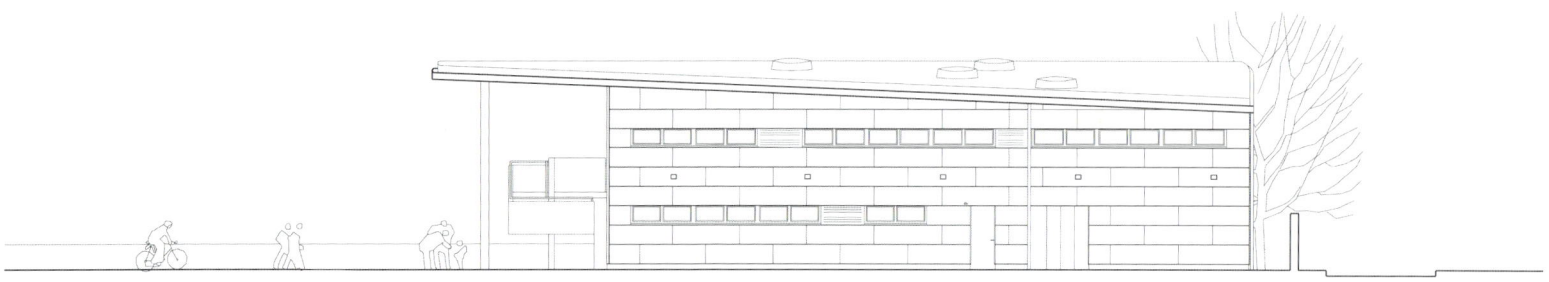

Elevation

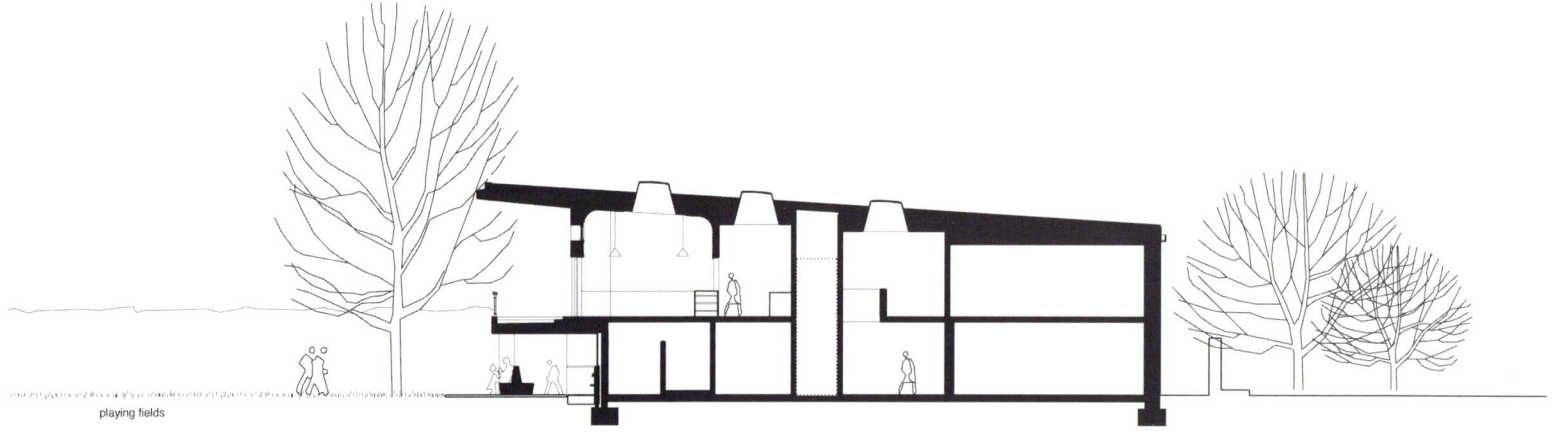

playing fields

Section

TOTAL   WKTS   OVERS   LAST MAN   1ST INNS

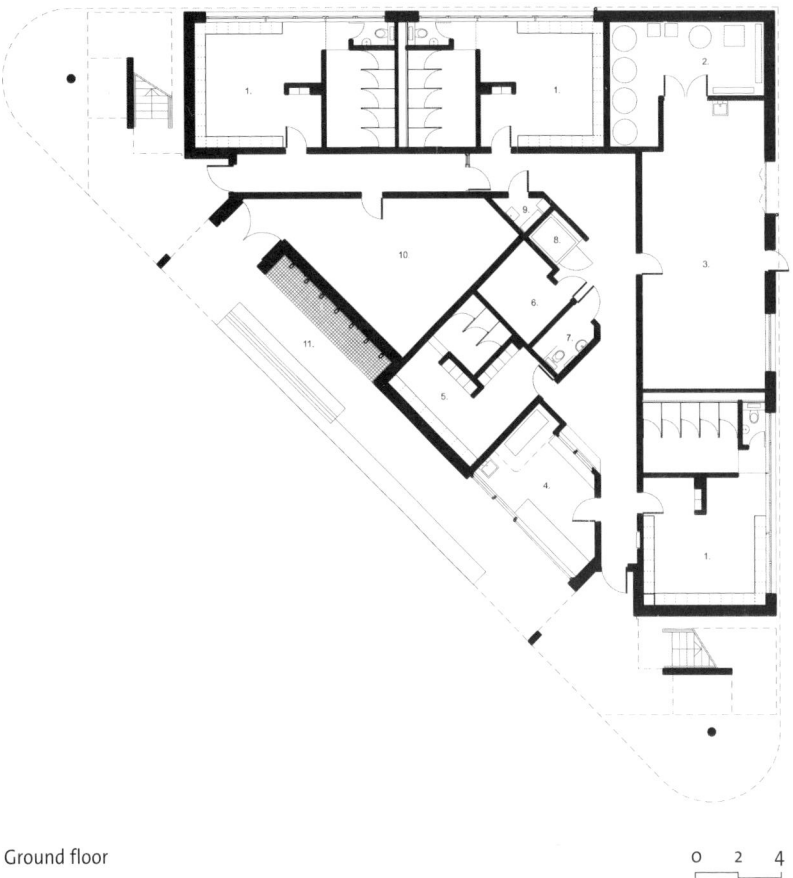

Ground floor

0   2   4

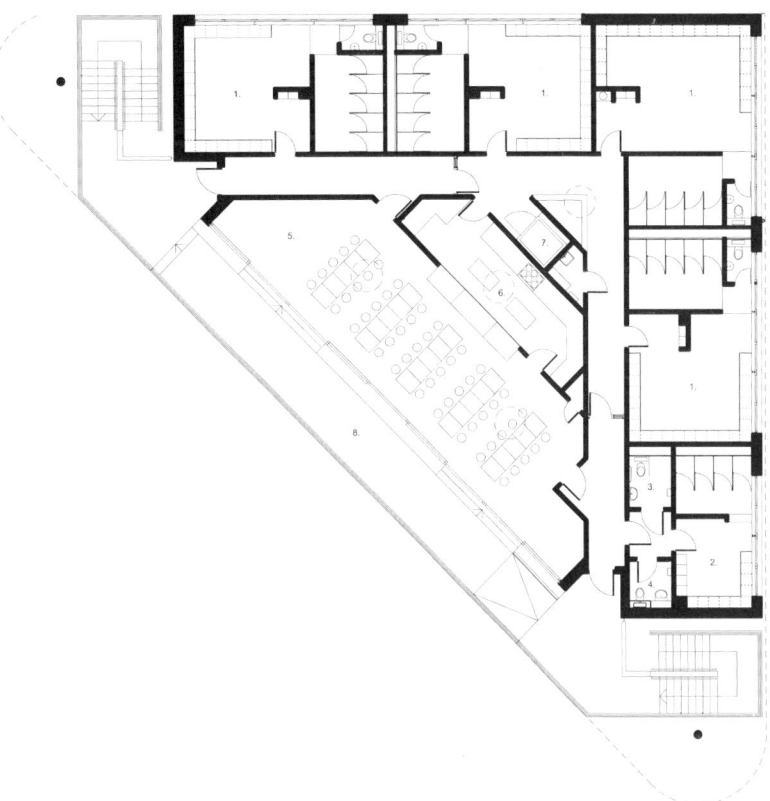

First floor

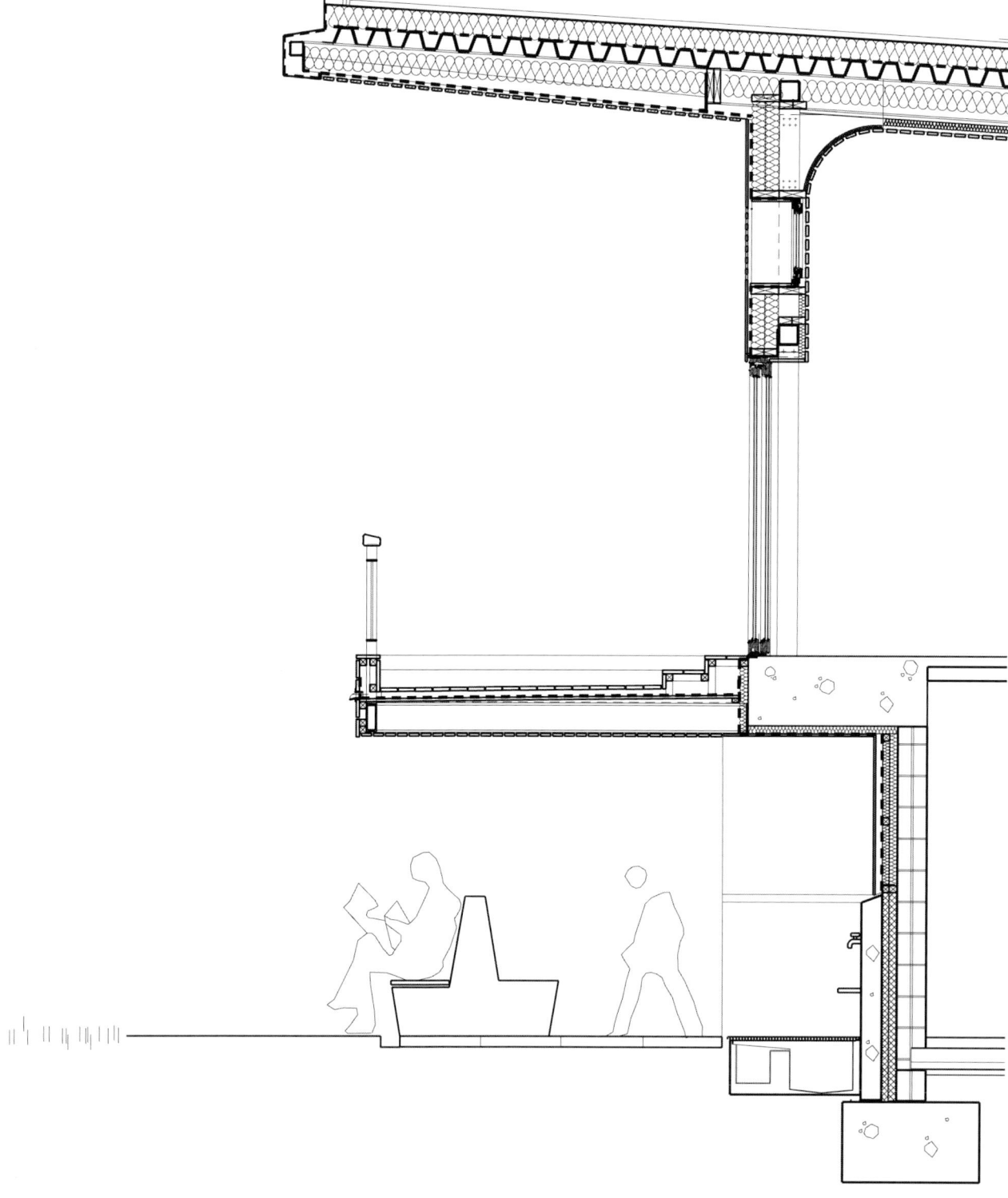

Construction detail

RECONSTRUCTION OF BERLIN'S OLYMPIC STADIUM

ARCHITECTS: VOLKWIN MARG, HUBERT NIENHOFF /ARCHITEKTEN VON GERKAN, MARG & PARTNER

PHOTOGRAPHS © HEINER LEISKA

LOCATION: BERLIN, GERMANY
YEAR COMPLETED: 2004

THIS INTERVENTION STANDS OUT FOR THE EQUILIBRIUM IT ACHIEVED THROUGH REWORKING A BUILDING OF HISTORICAL AND INSTITUTIONAL IMPORTANCE WHILE SIMULTANEOUSLY RENOVATING IT, PROVIDING IT WITH MODERN EQUIPMENT AND INCORPORATING A NEW ICONIC ELEMENT INTO IT—AN ILLUMINATED ROOF.

RECONSTRUCTION OF BERLIN'S OLYMPIC STADIUM

This project entailed the reconstruction, renovation and expansion of the historical sporting complex built for the 1936 Olympics. As Werner March's monumental building is a listed building, the intervention instead focused on bringing out the qualities of the original structure and modernizing the stadium to meet current-day needs.

These modifications focused on a number of different areas: interventions ranged from renovating and repairing limestone façades and columns—a meticulous task in which each piece was individually dismantled and cleaned—to the construction of removable VIP booths. All the service and maintenance facilities, in addition to a training field and a parking lot, were located underground and outside the perimeter of the complex. Inside the stadium, the level of the courts and the football field were lowered some eight and a half feet, which allowed two rows to be added to the lower part of the stand, and the stadium's capacity to be increased to 76,000 spectators.

However, the most important intervention was that of the roof: this consists of a lightweight cantilevered steel structure, which was wrapped in a double membrane. To maintain the façades of the building as unchanged as possible, the height of the roof was reduced to as low a height was feasible—it is thus almost invisible from the outside. Inside the stadium, the ceiling rests atop twenty low-profile steel columns, which in turn distribute the load to bear to lower columns that are hidden in the structure of the upper level of the stands. In keeping with the sober and simple lines of the buildings, the acoustical and lighting equipment were integrated into the roof, which is completely illuminated and creates a characteristic and easily recognizable image for the interior of the stadium.

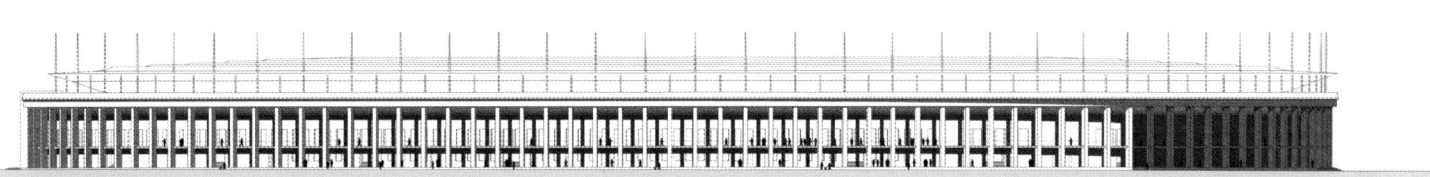

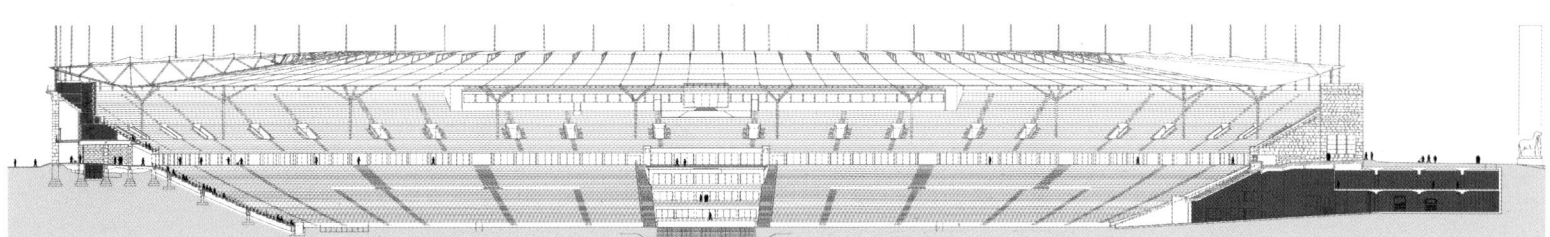

Elevations and sections

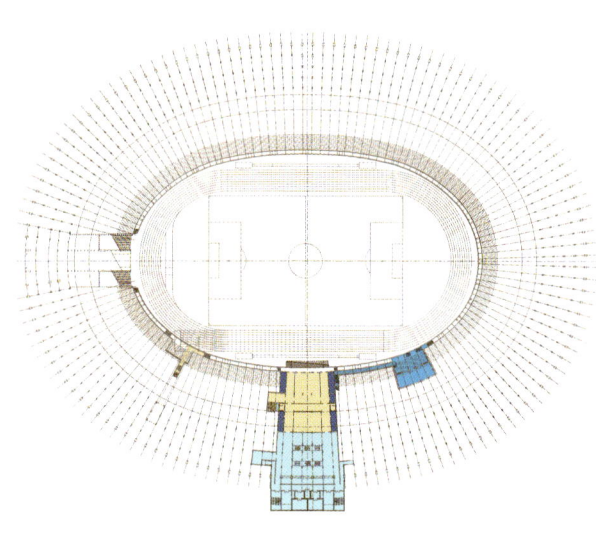

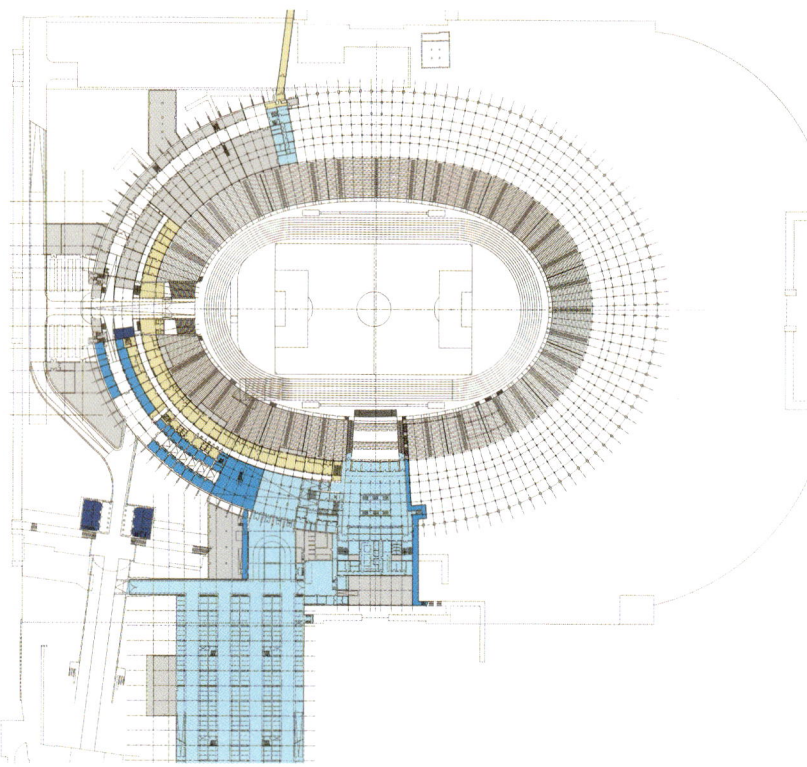

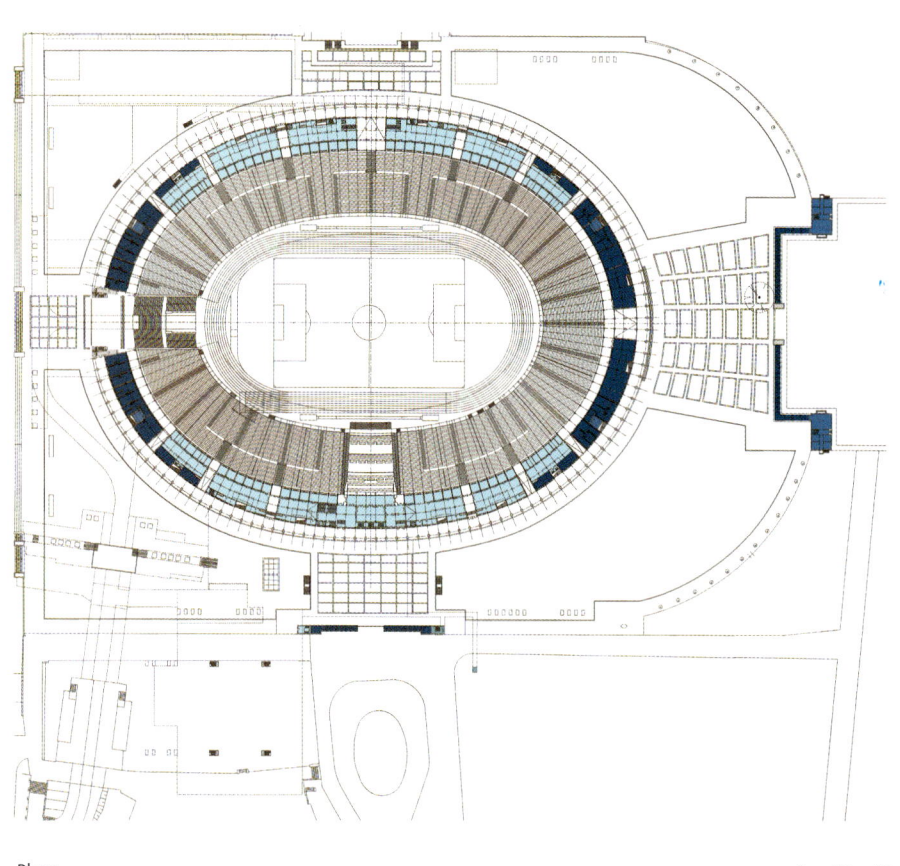

Plans

0   10   20

WALTERSDORFER CHAUSSEE SPORTS CENTER

ARCHITECTS: DIRK ALTEN/ALTEN ARCHITEKTEN

PHOTOGRAPHS © HANS-CHRISTOPH BRINKSCHMIDT, ORTWIN HEIPE, HANS JOOSTEN

LOCATION: BERLIN, GERMANY
YEAR COMPLETED: 2001

THIS SPORTS CENTER HAS TURNED INTO A BUSY CENTER OF
SOCIAL LIFE IN ONE OF BERLIN'S SUBURBS, THANKS TO ITS
WIDE OFFERING OF INDOOR SPORTS AND THE RANGE OF
ACTIVITIES CARRIED OUT IN THE ADJACENT OUTDOOR SPACES.

WALTERSDORFER CHAUSSEE SPORTS CENTER

The peculiar location of this project—between a
very busy street and a small pedestrian thoroughfare
in the suburbs of Berlin—gave way to a dialogue of
contrasts, based on which the design of the various
elements making up the building took shape.
Everything, ranging from the structure to the
selection of the materials and the definition of the
construction details, was affected by this dialogue.
The large, multi-purpose room can be used in its
entirety or subdivided into three courts, and its
stands can seat up to two hundred spectators. The
courts were placed four and a half feet below ground
level, and this change in elevation was used to
provide floor space for the locker room and access
ramps.

Furthermore, different types of paving materials
were used around the building to demarcate a wide
variety of activities related to the sports center and
the neighborhood, and from which one can peer into
the busy interior through glass stretches in the
façade. The building was conceived of as
representing a small urban landscape comprised of a
sequence of sports fields, ramps, walls, and terraces.
A thin aluminum veneer covers part of the building
and grants it visual continuity. In contrast, some of
the panels of the façade were constructed in
exposed concrete or plywood paneling.

Inside, a system of large metal beams and columns
hold up the aluminum roof that stretches across the
expansive indoor courts. The stands, made up of
concrete benches, are finished in wooden planks.

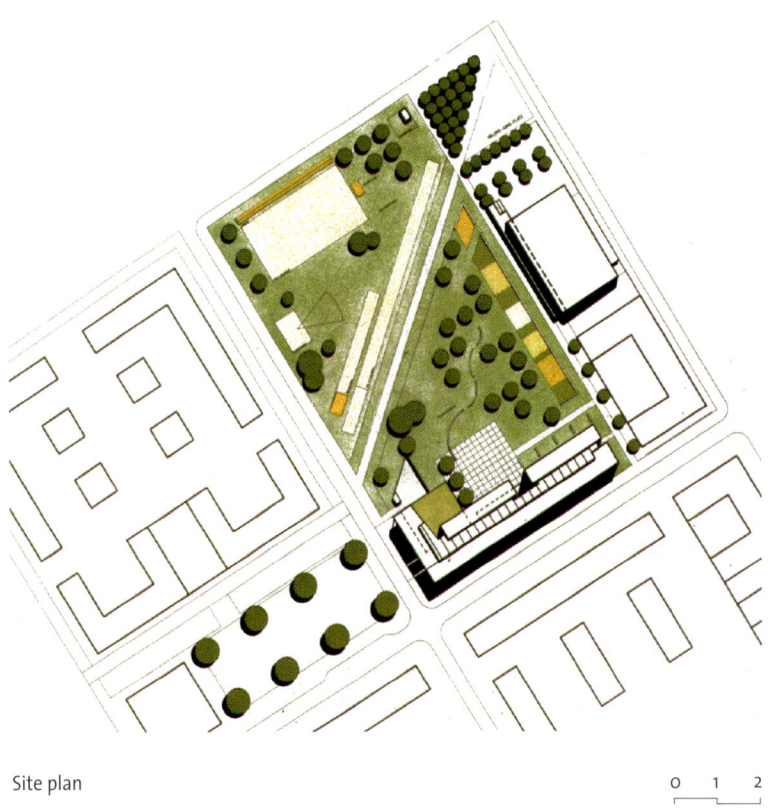

Site plan

0 1 2

Elevation

Sketches

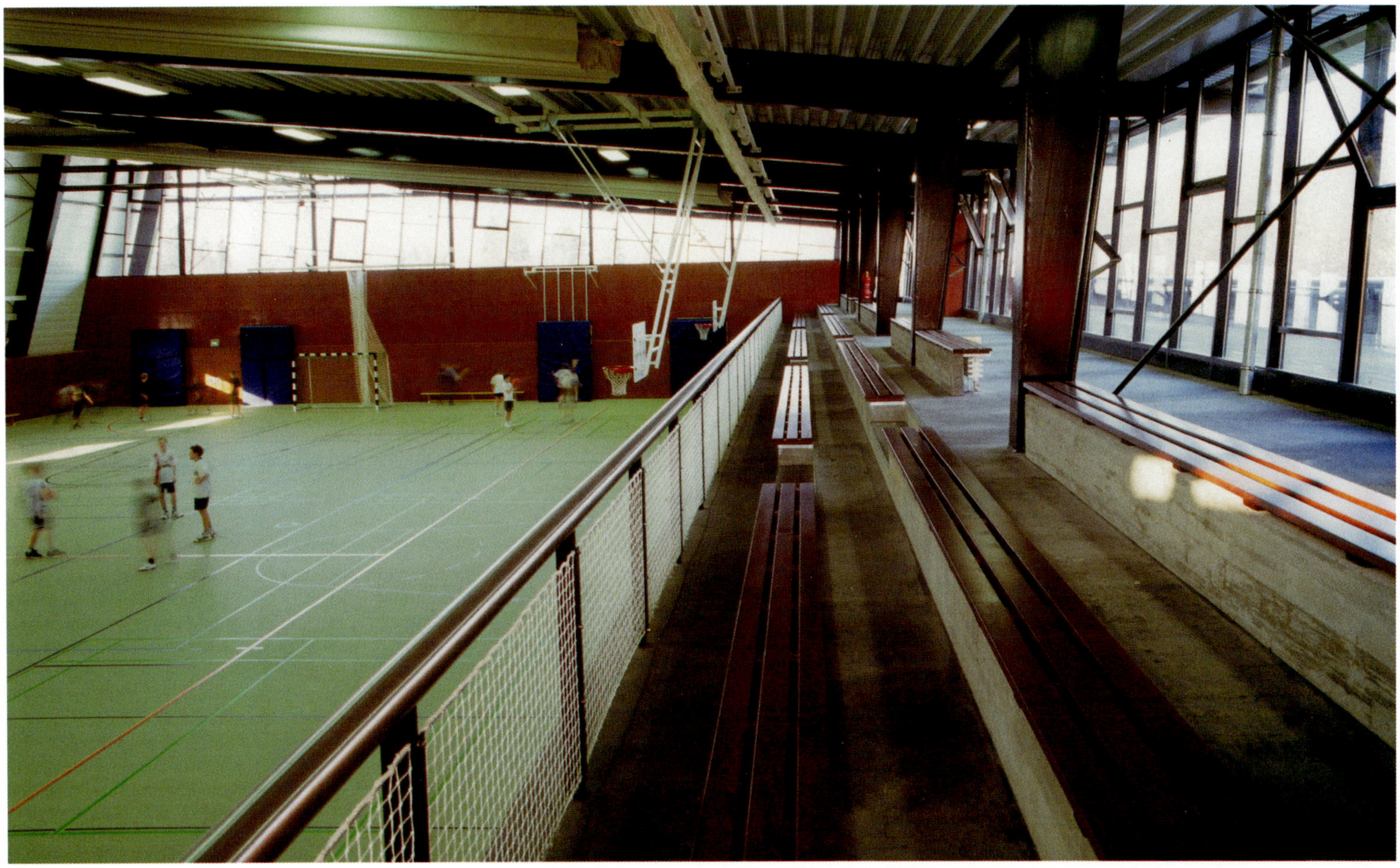

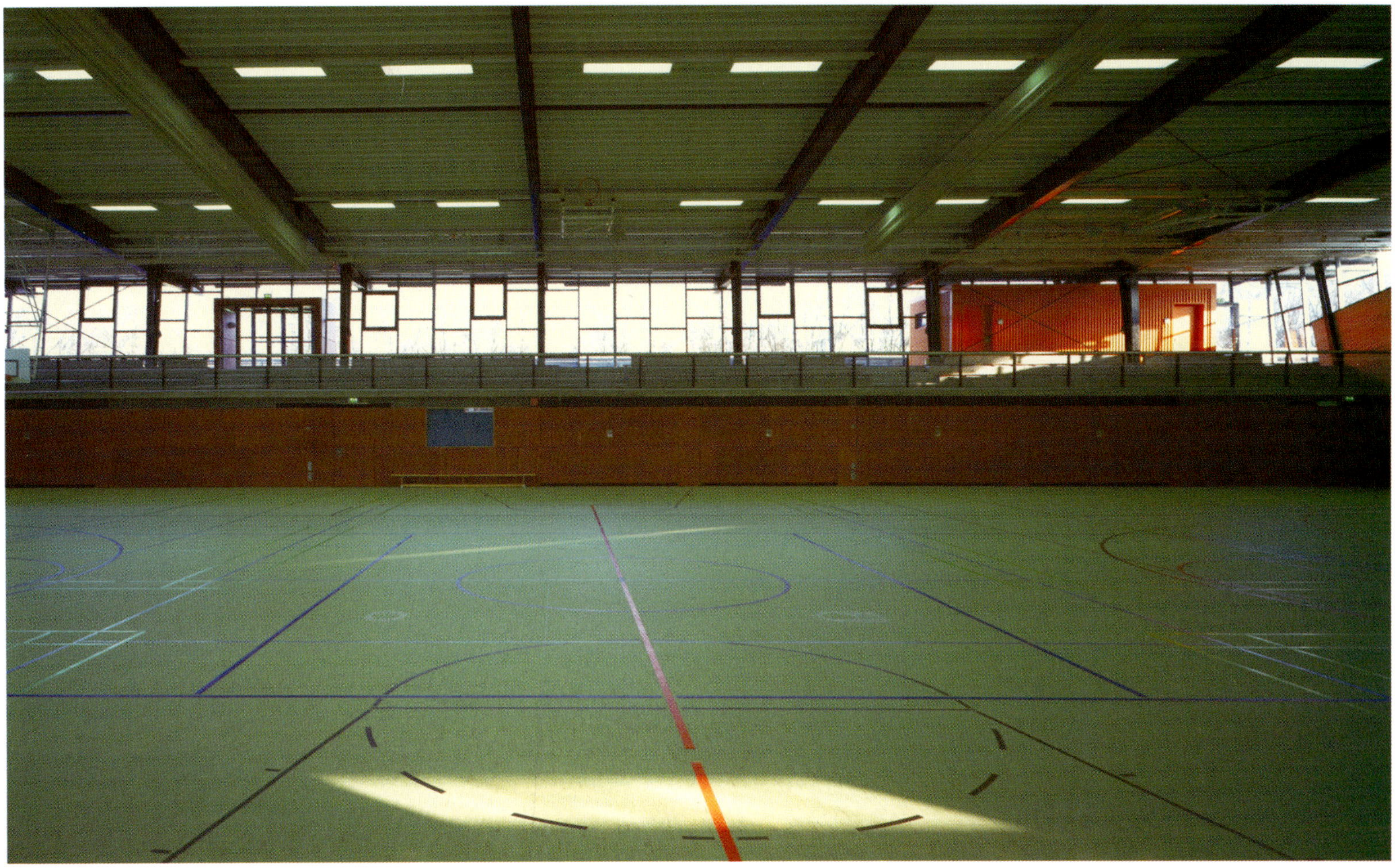

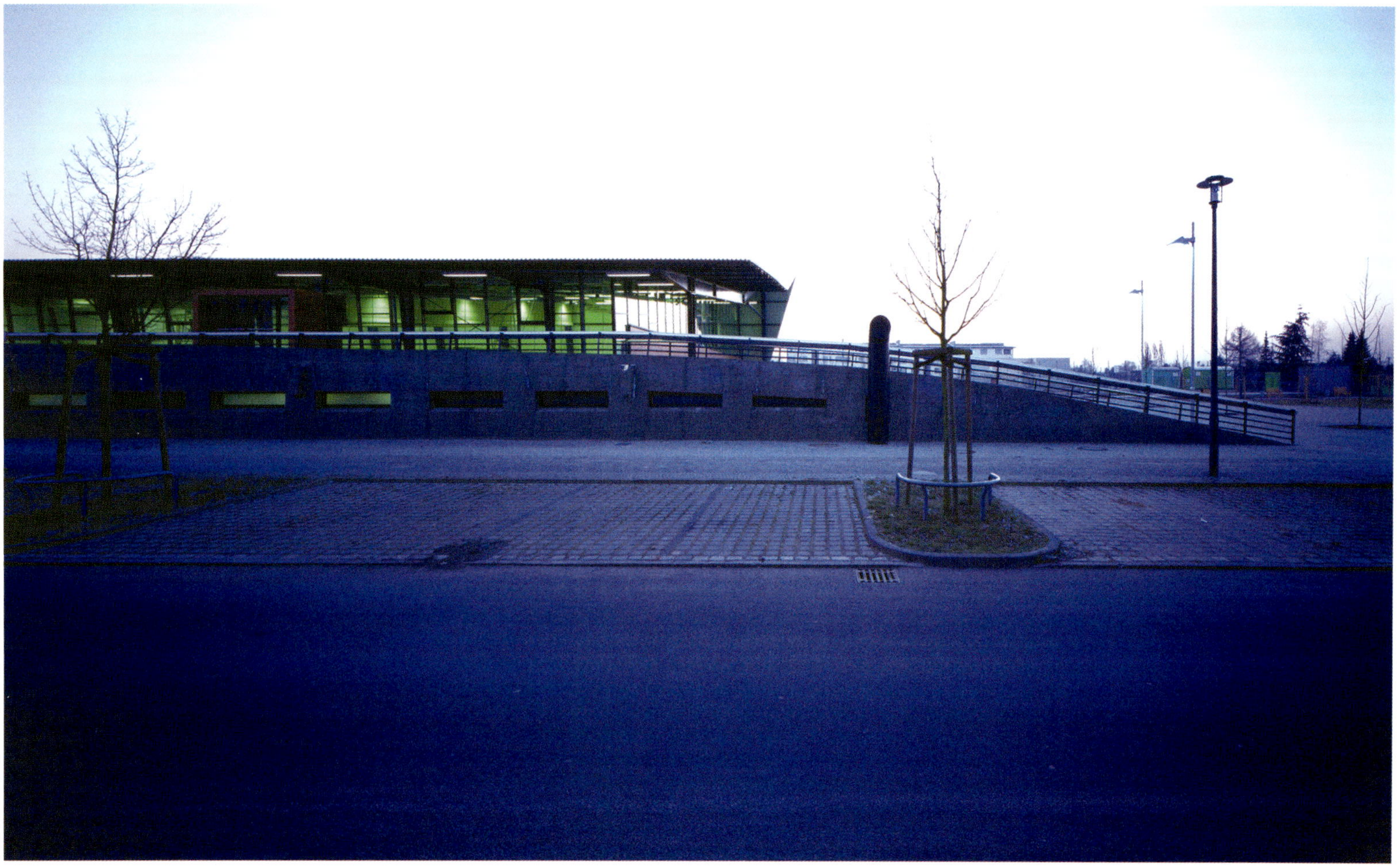

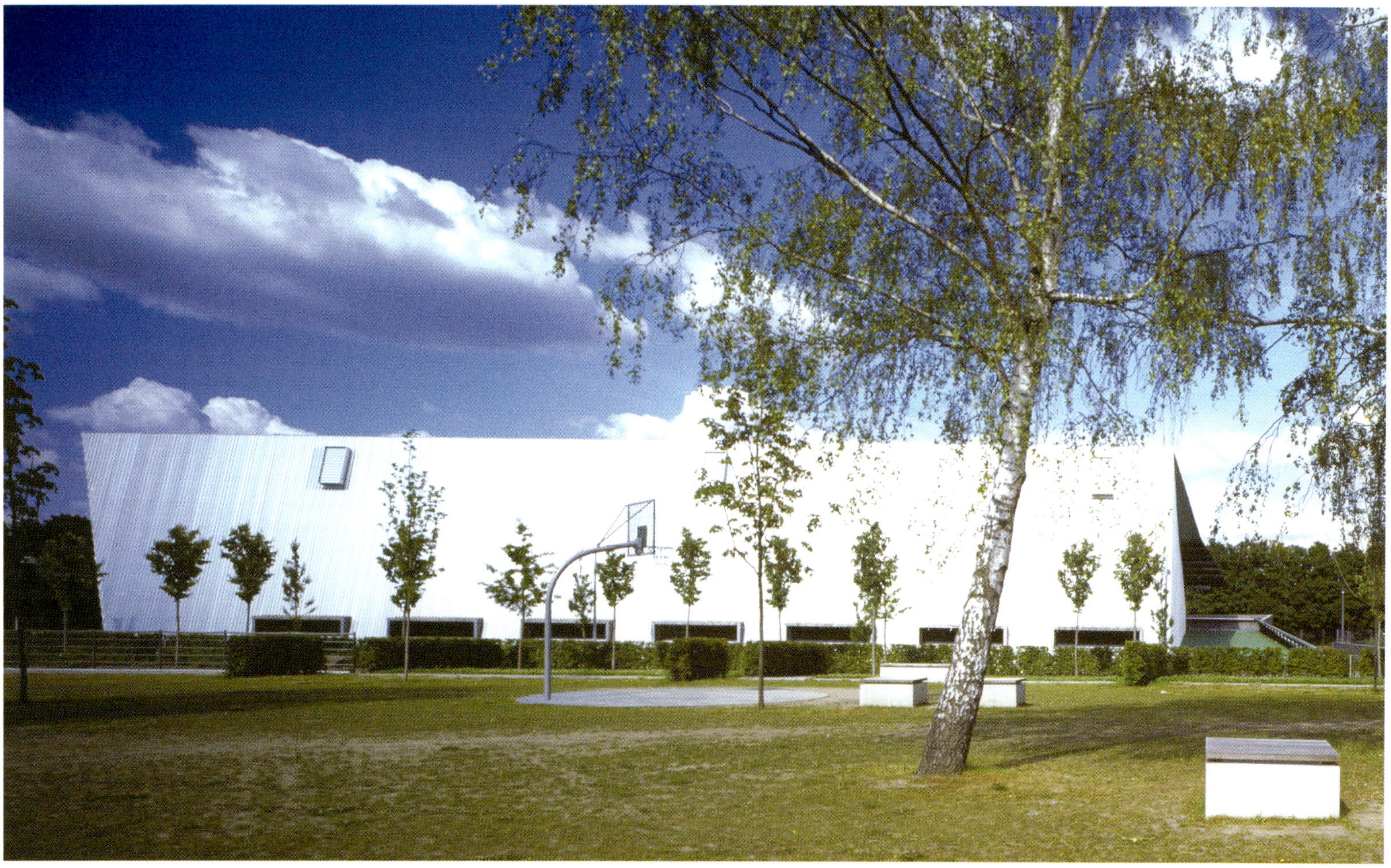

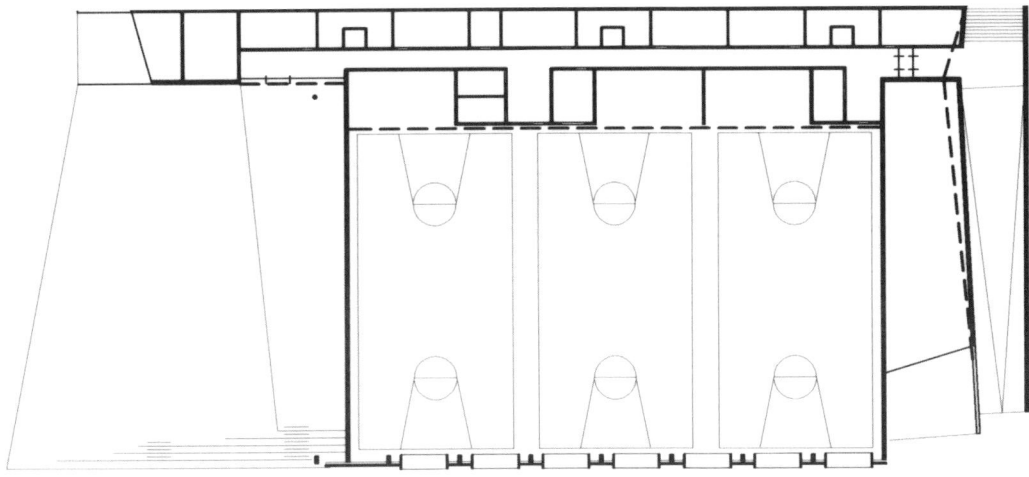

Basement

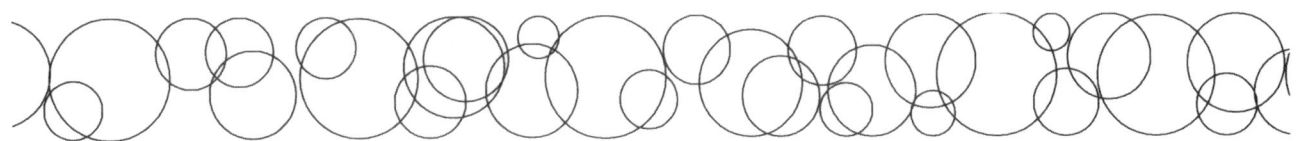

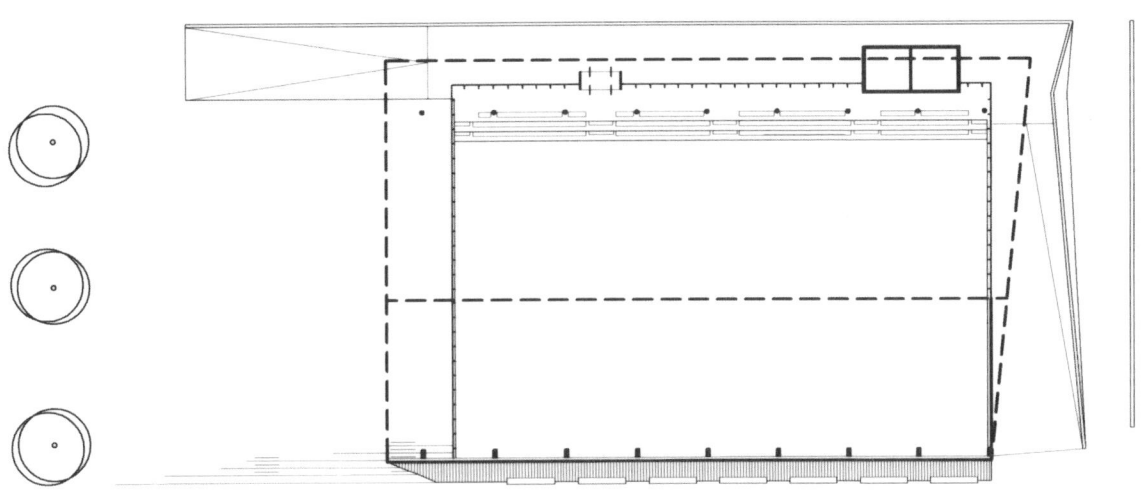

Ground floor

0　5　10

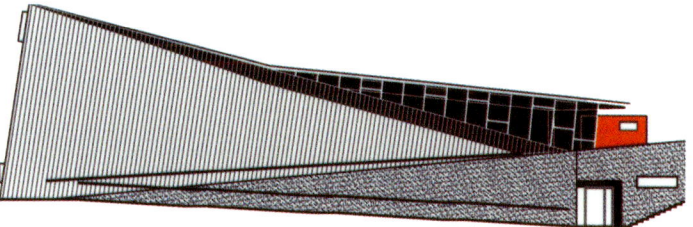

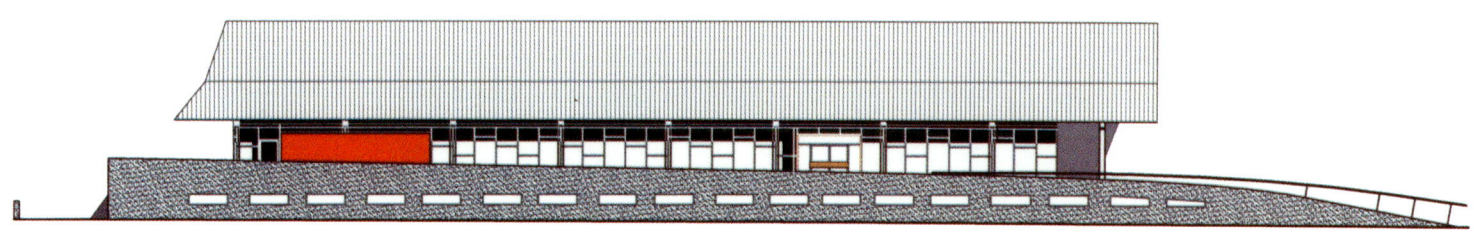

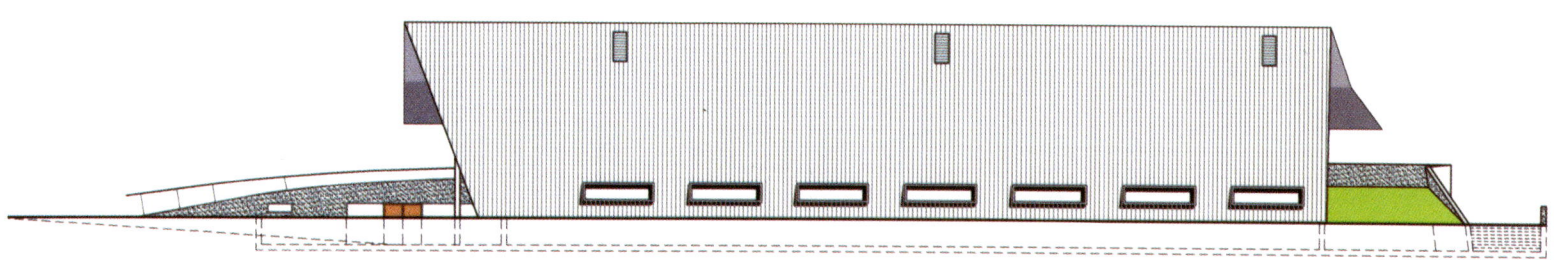

Elevations

CLUB DUET

ARCHITECT: ALONSO BALAGUER Y ARQUITECTOS ASOCIADOS

PHOTOGRAPHS © JOSEP MARIA MOLINOS

LOCATION: TIANA, SPAIN
YEAR COMPLETED: 2003

THE LARGE EXPANSES OF GLASS ON THE FAÇADES THAT COVER THIS BUILDING AND DIVIDE ITS INDOOR SPACES ALLOW VISITORS TO ENJOY PANORAMIC VIEWS OF THE SURROUNDING NEIGHBORHOODS AS WELL AS TO DRAW VISUAL CONNECTIONS BETWEEN THE DIFFERENT AREAS OF THE CLUB.

CLUB DUET

After the 1992 Barcelona Olympic Games, the city's town hall came up with a strategic plan that entailed the construction of sports centers in the centers of each of its neighborhoods, in order to promote residents' use of these municipal facilities. This sports center is yet another that was promoted by this policy, and whose design was used in another region of the country in which all available sports facilities were still located in the outer ring of cities. In addition to serving as a sports complex, this center also provides the important social function of serving as a meeting point for local residents. Stemming from the idea of promoting these social benefits, this sports club was designed so as to promote a close relationship between interior and exterior. In order to achieve this, the architecture employed in its design uses clear geometric lines and makes reference to the local architecture of the town. Additionally, it exhibits a visual transparency, both from inside out, as well as between the various areas that make up the center. The different functions are divided into three main areas—a water area, the general service area, and the gymnasium—and are all fitted into a rectangular, two-story building.

The sober geometry of the overall composition is emphasized on the exterior through the use of materials such as concrete, metal plating and glass. In contrast, the interior puts off a warmer and happier air thanks to the use of vivid colors in the areas of circulation, service, and lobbies.

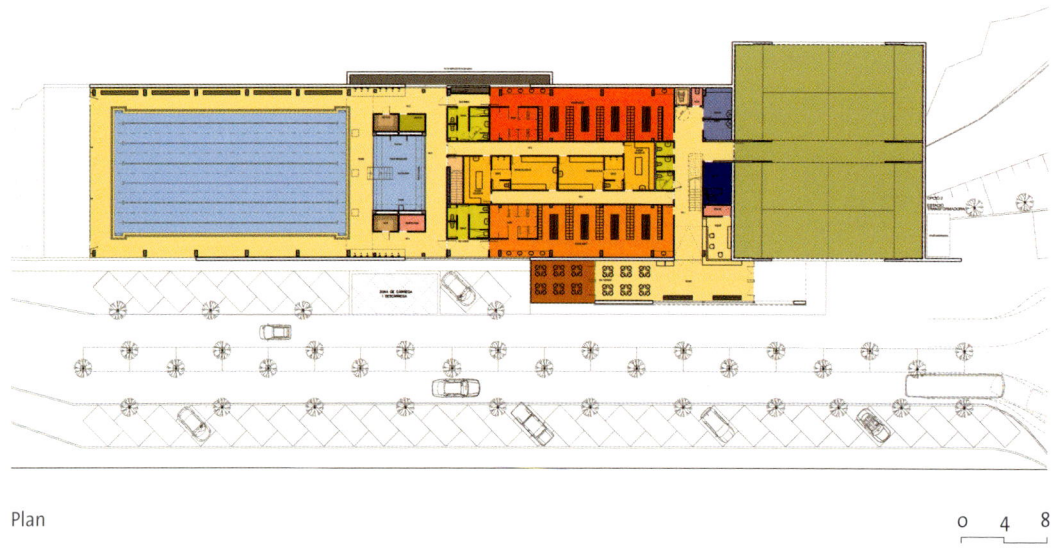

Plan

0 4 8

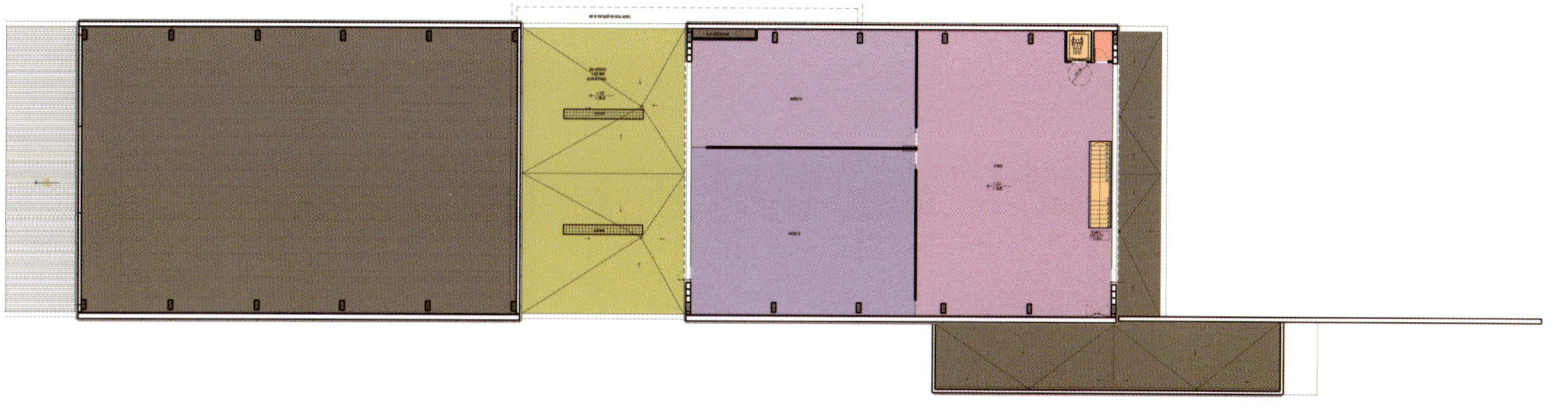

First floor

0   1   2

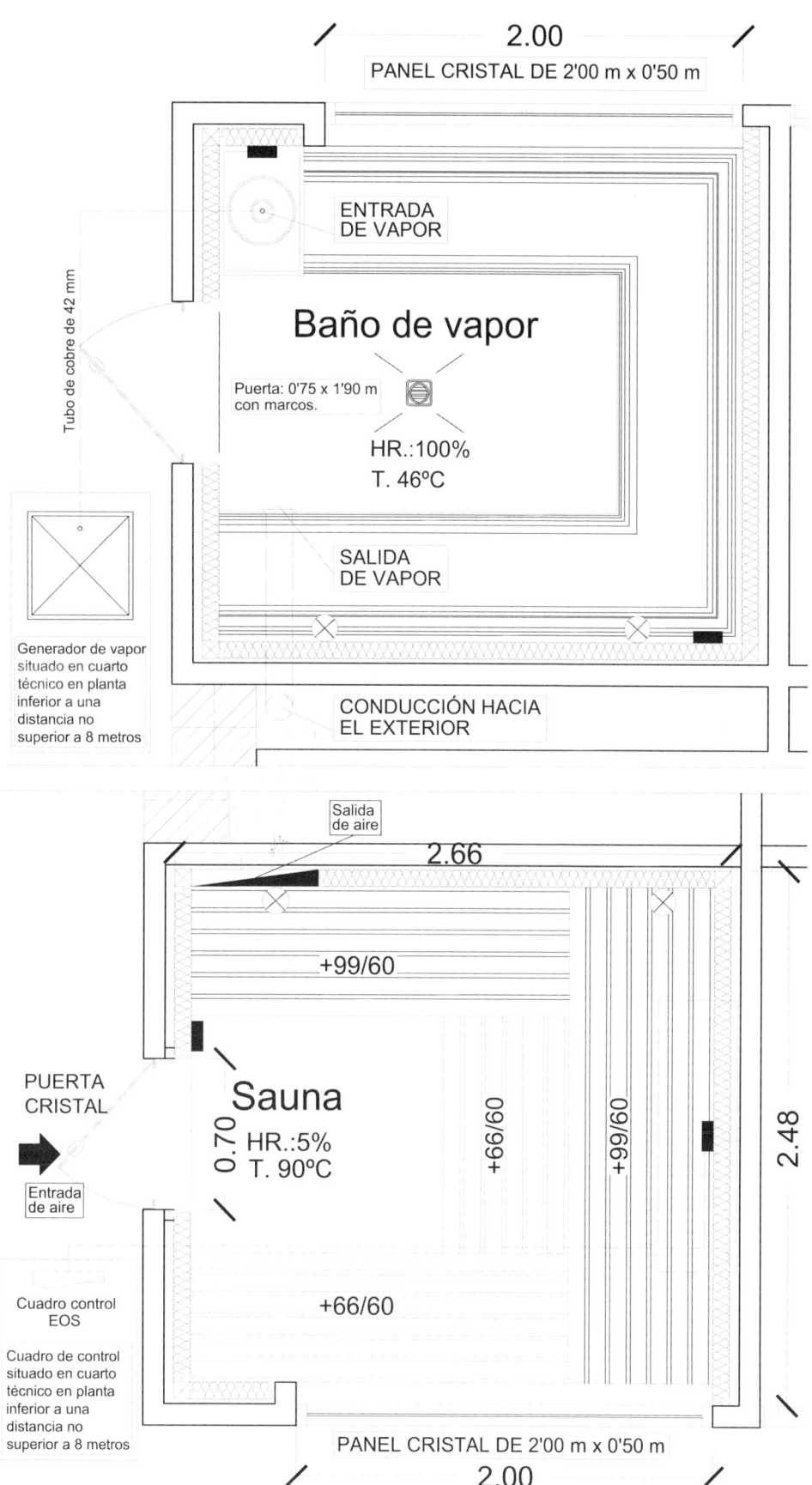

2.00
PANEL CRISTAL DE 2'00 m x 0'50 m

Tubo de cobre de 42 mm

ENTRADA
DE VAPOR

Baño de vapor

Puerta: 0'75 x 1'90 m
con marcos.

HR.:100%
T. 46ºC

SALIDA
DE VAPOR

Generador de vapor
situado en cuarto
técnico en planta
inferior a una
distancia no
superior a 8 metros

CONDUCCIÓN HACIA
EL EXTERIOR

Salida
de aire

2.66

+99/60

PUERTA
CRISTAL

Sauna

0.70
HR.:5%
T. 90ºC

+66/60

+99/60

2.48

Entrada
de aire

Cuadro control
EOS

Cuadro de control
situado en cuarto
técnico en planta
inferior a una
distancia no
superior a 8 metros

+66/60

PANEL CRISTAL DE 2'00 m x 0'50 m

2.00

Installation details

BUDOKAN IN EHIME

ARCHITECTS: ISHIMOTO ARCHITECTURAL & ENGINEERING FIRM, INC.
COLLABORATORS: VAN STRUCTURAL DESIGN STUDIO

PHOTOGRAPHS: ATSUSHI NAKAMICHI/NACÁSA & PARTNERS INC.

LOCATION: MATSUMAYA CITY, JAPAN
YEAR COMPLETED: 2003

WITH ITS SPECTACULAR WOODEN STRUCTURE, ITS STEEPLY SLOPING ROOF AND ITS USE OF LOCALLY-FOUND MATERIALS —CEDAR, GRANITE, AND CLAY—THIS PROJECT REPRESENTS A CONTEMPORARY REINTERPRETATION OF TRADITIONAL JAPANESE ARCHITECTURE.

BUDOKAN IN EHIME

From karate to kendo, traditional martial arts in Japan (collectively known as budo) enjoy immense popularity in Japan, and local governments incentivize citizen participation in them by building martial arts academies (known as budokan). Here, the prefecture of Ehime sought to build a sports center that would enjoy a strong physical presence, attract visitors, stimulate the local economy, and draw recognition for the region on both the national and the international level. Destined not only to teaching and publicizing the martial arts, this center was also designed to house events, and represents a collaborative effort between client and architect. The two new buildings are built entirely out of materials found or produced locally—cedar, granite, and roof tiles—which meant that the design is the natural result of the possibilities offered by these elements. The design centers on two enormous pitched roofs that cover a 58,000 sq. foot space and a 29,600 sq. foot space, respectively. These rest atop a colossal structure crafted in cedar wood, whose steel screws and joints are practically invisible. To maintain the visual continuity between the two roofs both on the inside and the outside, the buildings were enclosed by curtain walls, which allow for a complete transparency, in addition to accentuating the large size of the pavilions. The latticework of the diamond-shaped structure is reminiscent of the shapes used in traditional dressing rooms, which roots these buildings even more strongly in the past. Five months after the project was finished, the complex had already housed over twenty sporting and cultural events, and the number of visitors to the region had multiplied by a factor of six.

Elevation

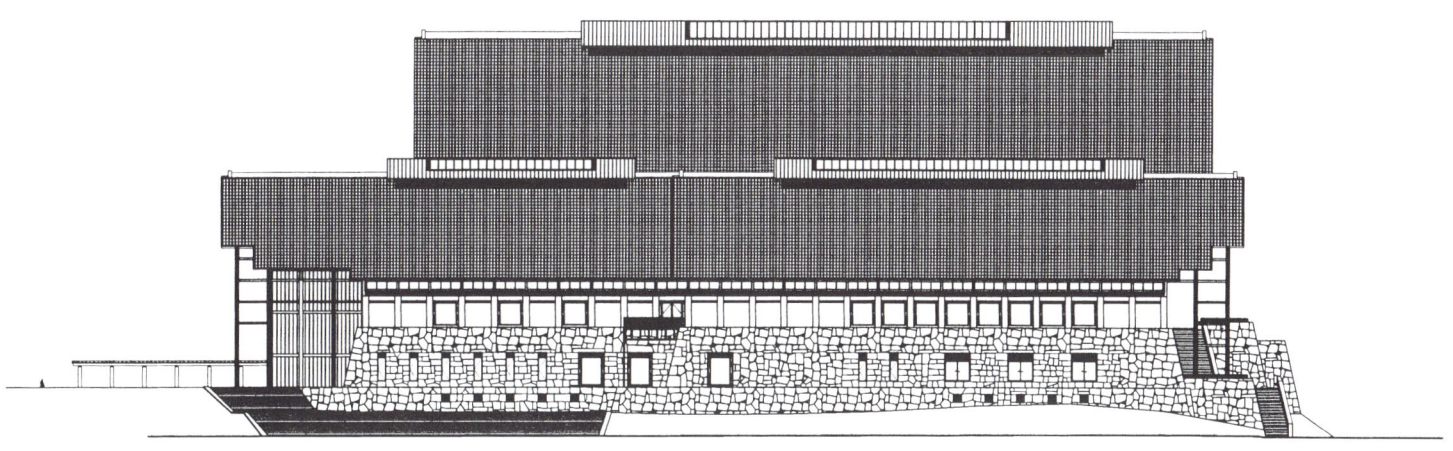

Elevation

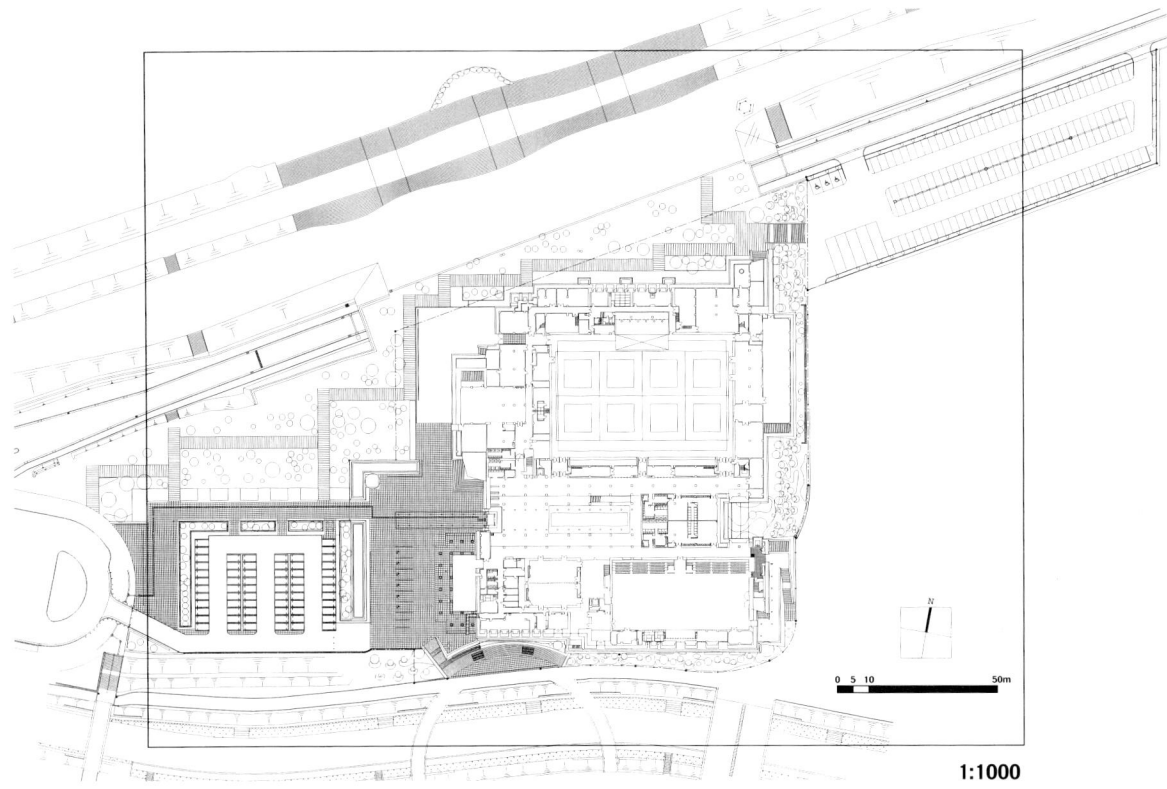

1:1000

Site plan

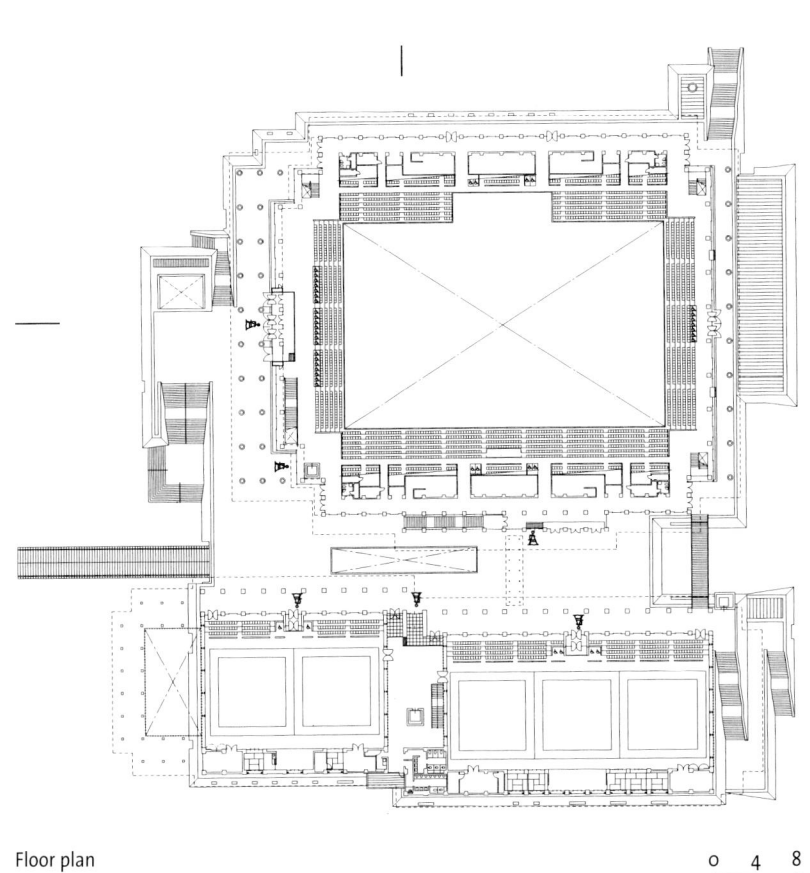

Floor plan

0 4 8

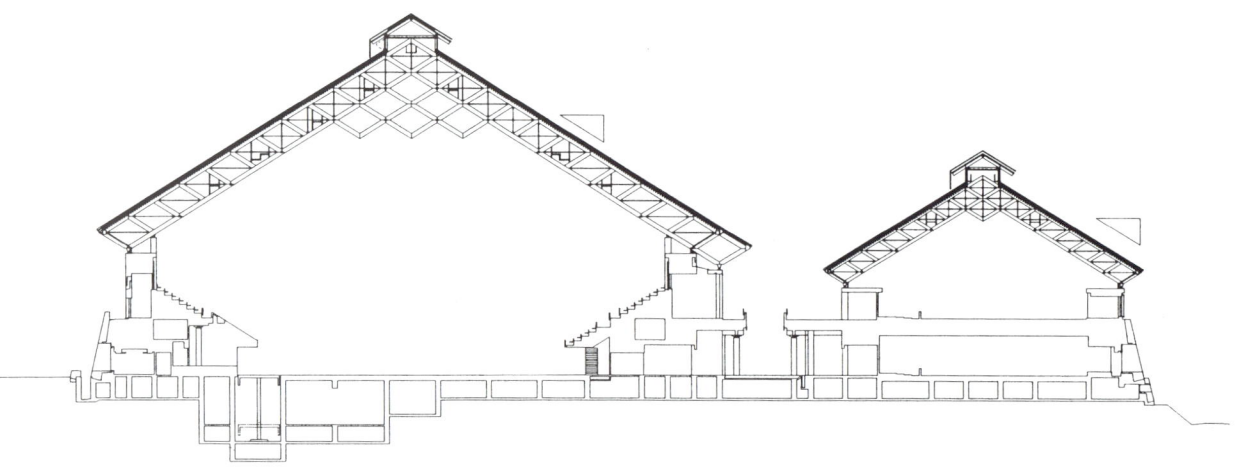

Section

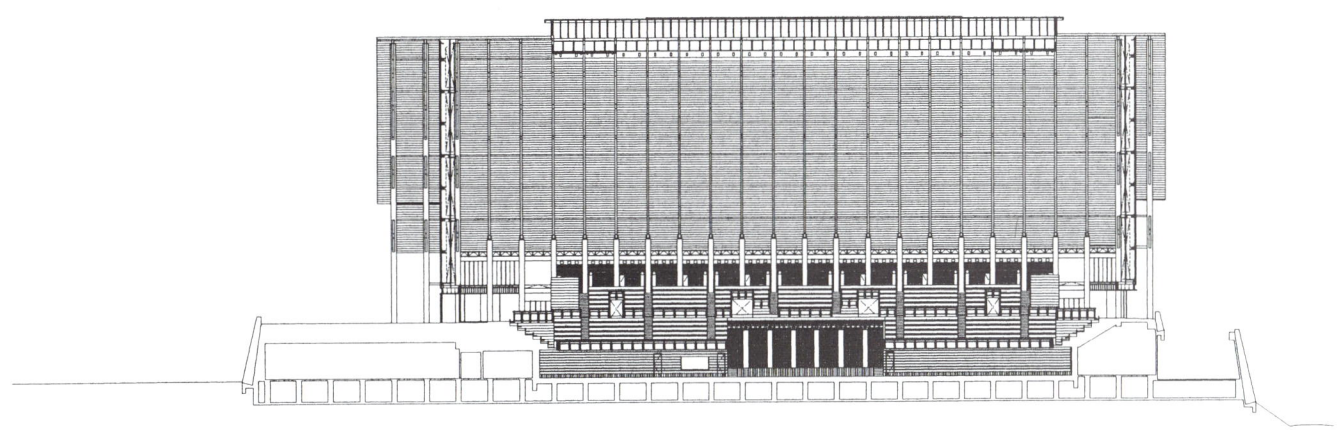

Section

AMERICAN AIRLINES STADIUM

ARCHITECTS: ARQUITECTONICA (ARQ)
COLLABORATORS: HEINLEIN & SCHROCK (ASSOCIATE ARCHITECTS), THRONTON-
TOMASETTI AND DONNELL-DUQUESNE-ALBAISA (STRUCTURES)

PHOTOGRAPHS © SCOTT B. SMITH, ARQUITECTONICA

LOCATION: MIAMI, UNITED STATES
YEAR COMPLETED: 2000

The basketball stadium built for the Miami Heat was designed as a dynamic and attractive building that would serve as an architectural reference point for the city. In addition to the architects, a number of artists also participated in the project, which converted it into one of the most distinguished of all the NBA's stadiums in the country.

AMERICAN AIRLINES STADIUM

The client for this project, the Miami Heat basketball team, hired the Arquitectonica studio to designed a unique stadium on a site that was rather unique itself: a flat parcel in the middle of Miami's harbor. Previously occupied by dry docks, the site enjoys stunning views of the bay and can also be seen from different locations around the port, from the water, and also from the various bridges that connect the city's main thoroughfares. As the extensive spread of the site also allows the stadium to be seen as a free-standing object, the architects sought to design a building that would possess sculptural qualities. In addition, they aimed to depart from the typical conception people had of these types of buildings (as being large, closed, opaque boxes made of concrete), and to create an attractive and avant-garde building, whose large openings would provide natural light and open up to views of the city.

The results of these ideas and requirements is an elliptical stadium that evokes the arenas of ancient Rome, though it has a slightly modified perimeter that brings to mind the sails of a ship. The façade is made from curving metal panels painted white—which cut across the sky—and large expanses of glass. These transparent parts allow some of the activities taking place inside to be seen from the exterior.

The lighting and some of the decorative motifs inside the stadium allude to the team colors. Thus, yellow, orange and red are alternated on the various floors, as well as in the colors chosen for the seats in the stadium. Still, different colored additional lighting systems are being planned should the stadium also come to house professional hockey matches or rock concerts.

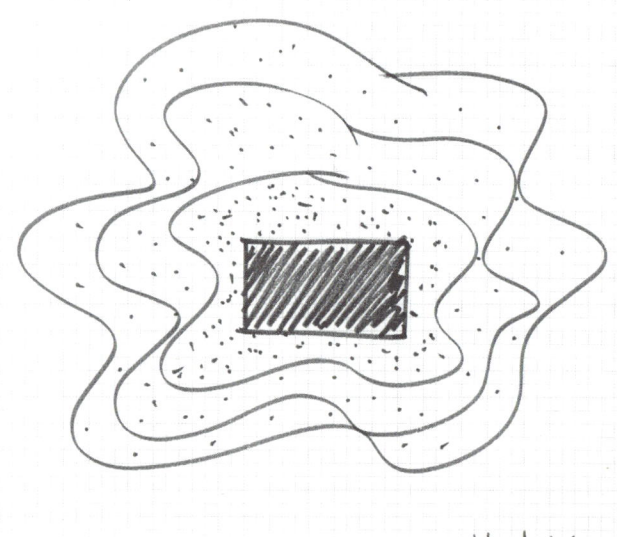

Heat Wave

Sketches

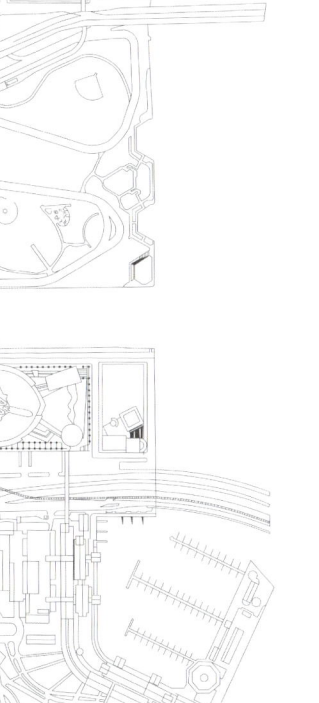

Site plan

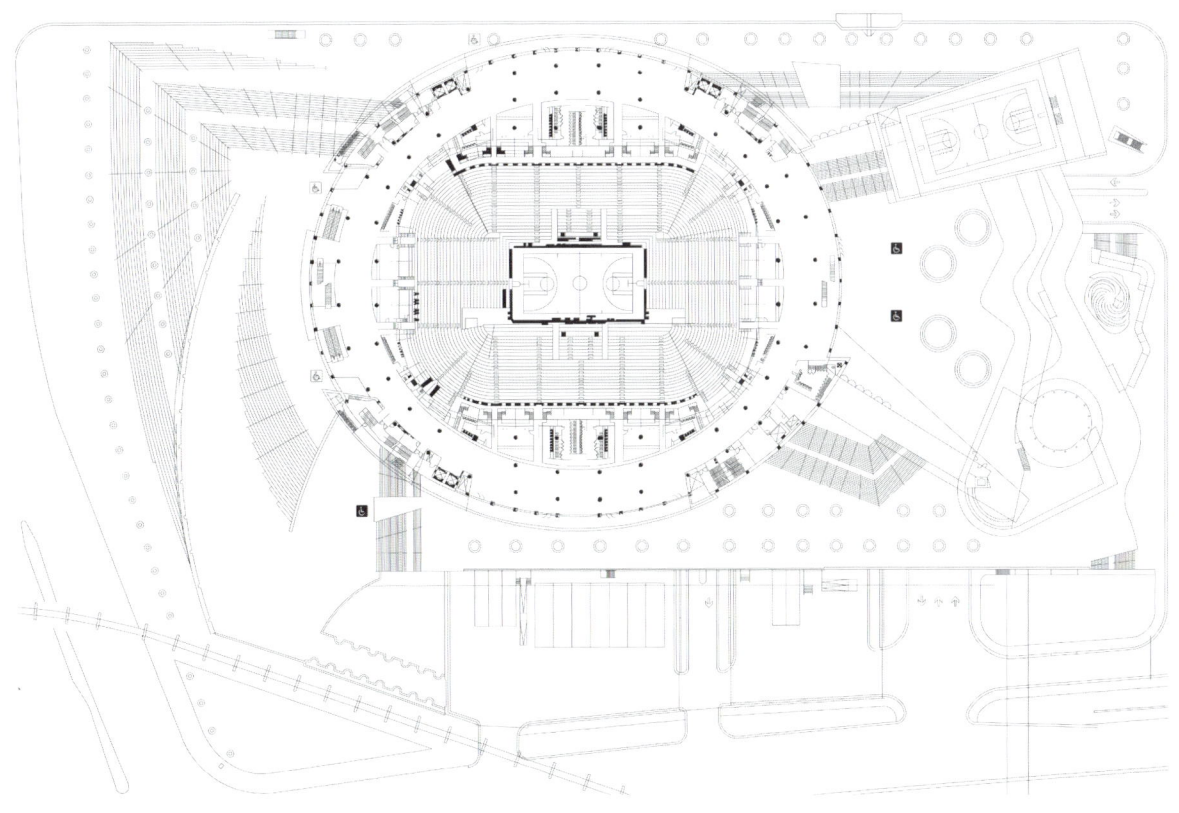

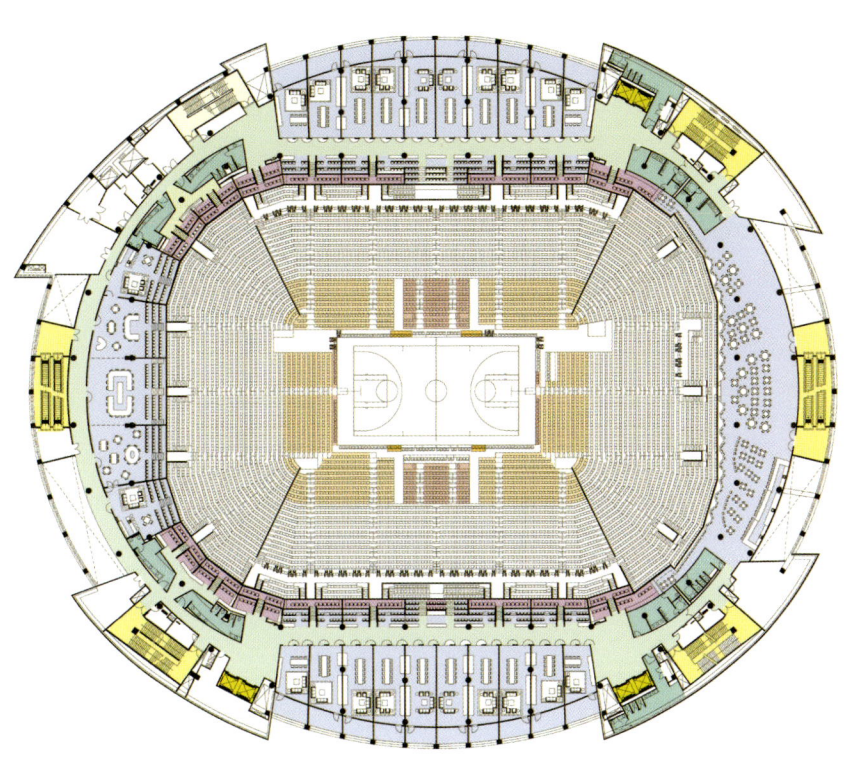

Plans

0   5   10

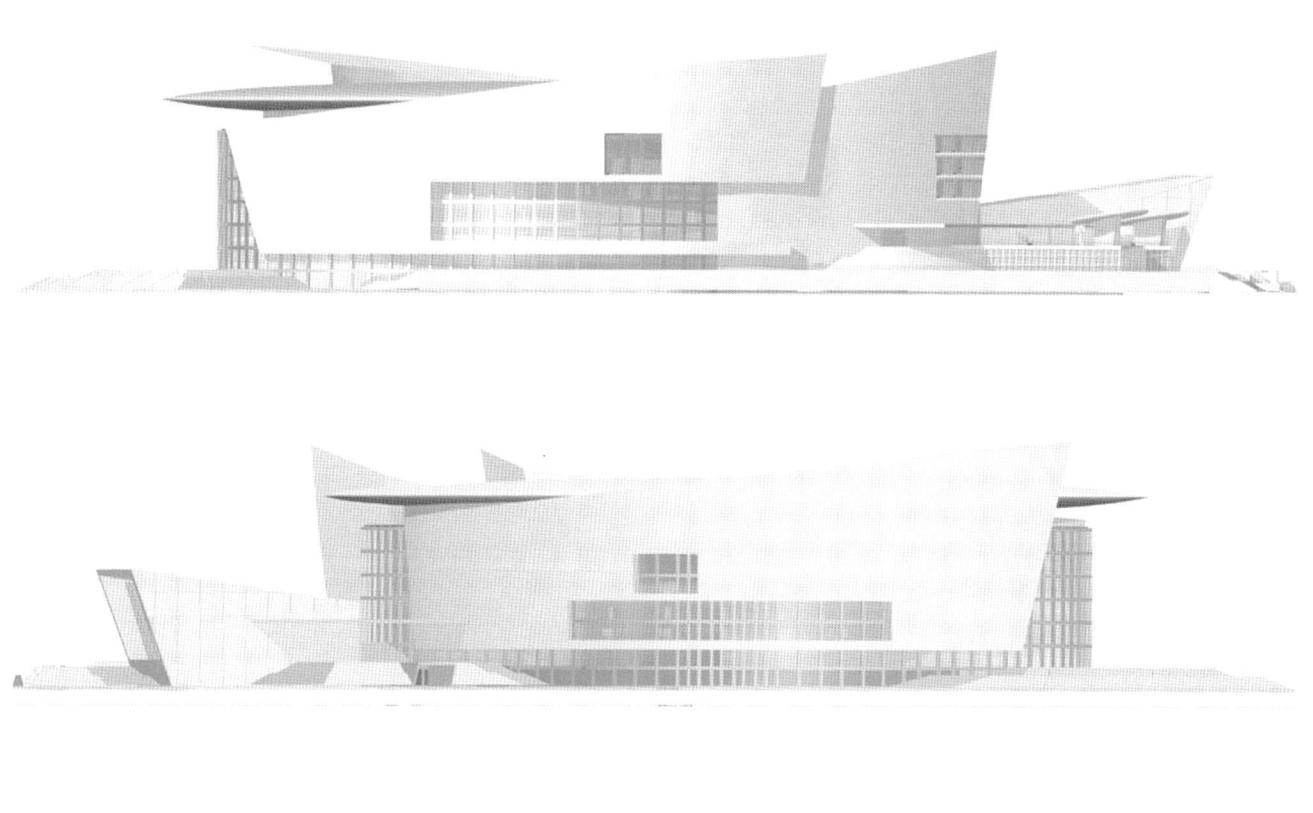

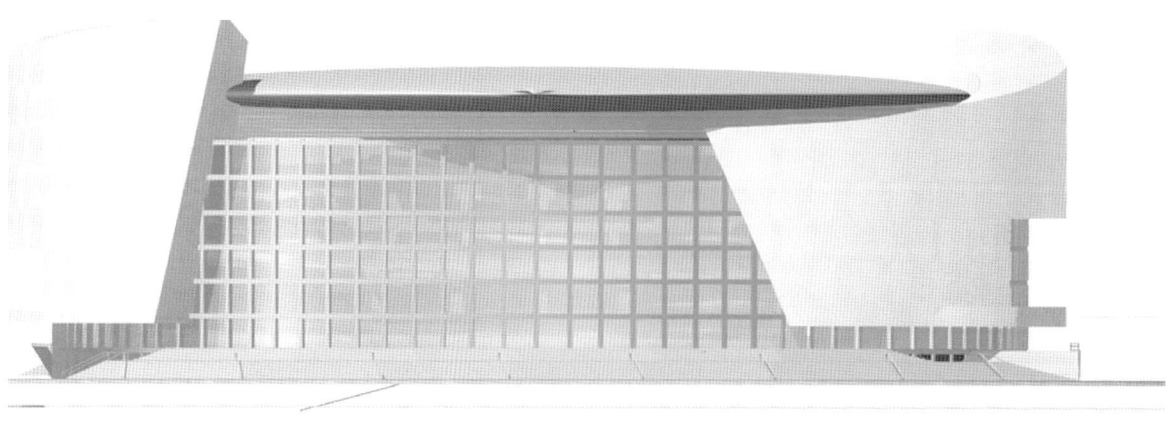

Elevations

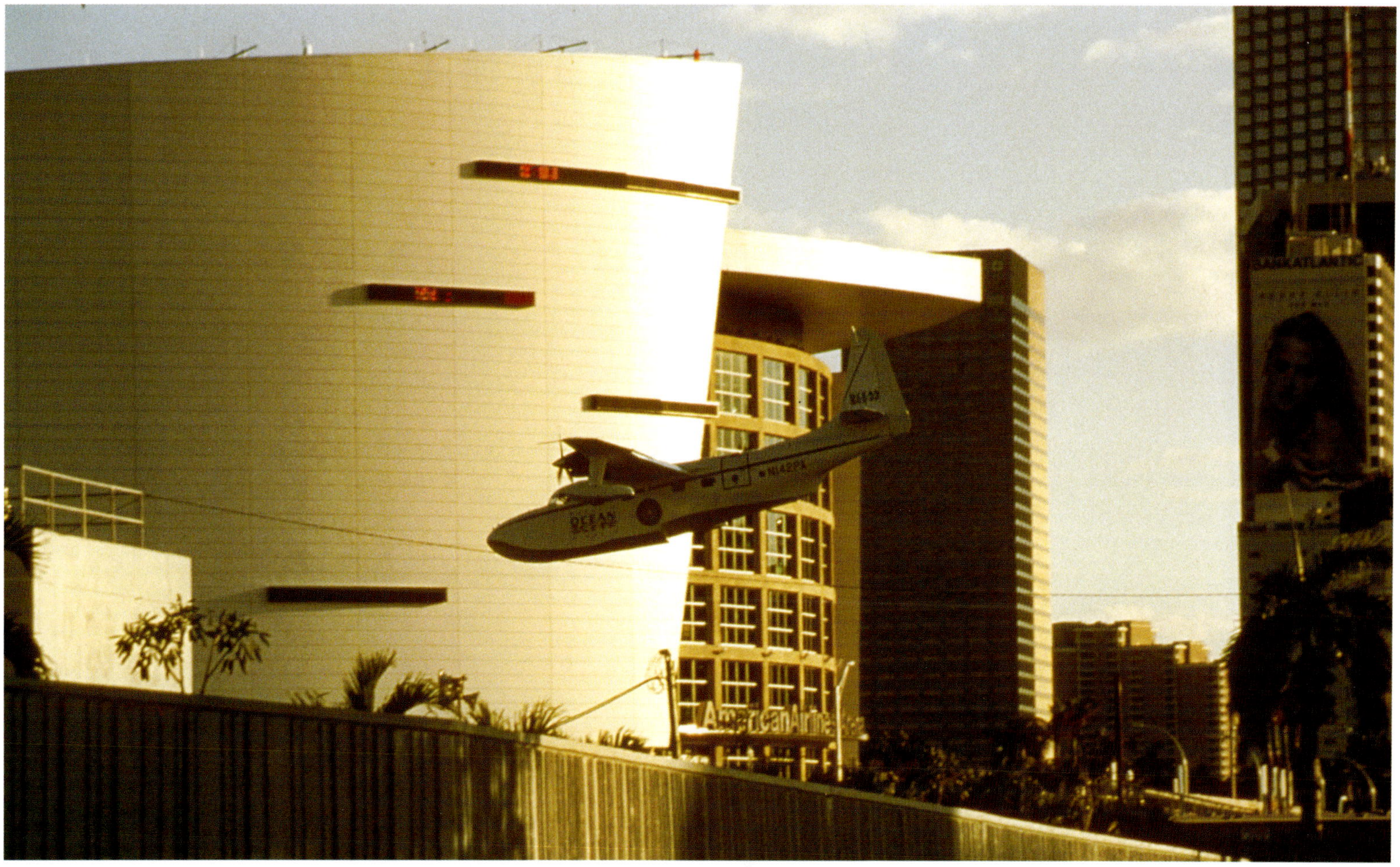

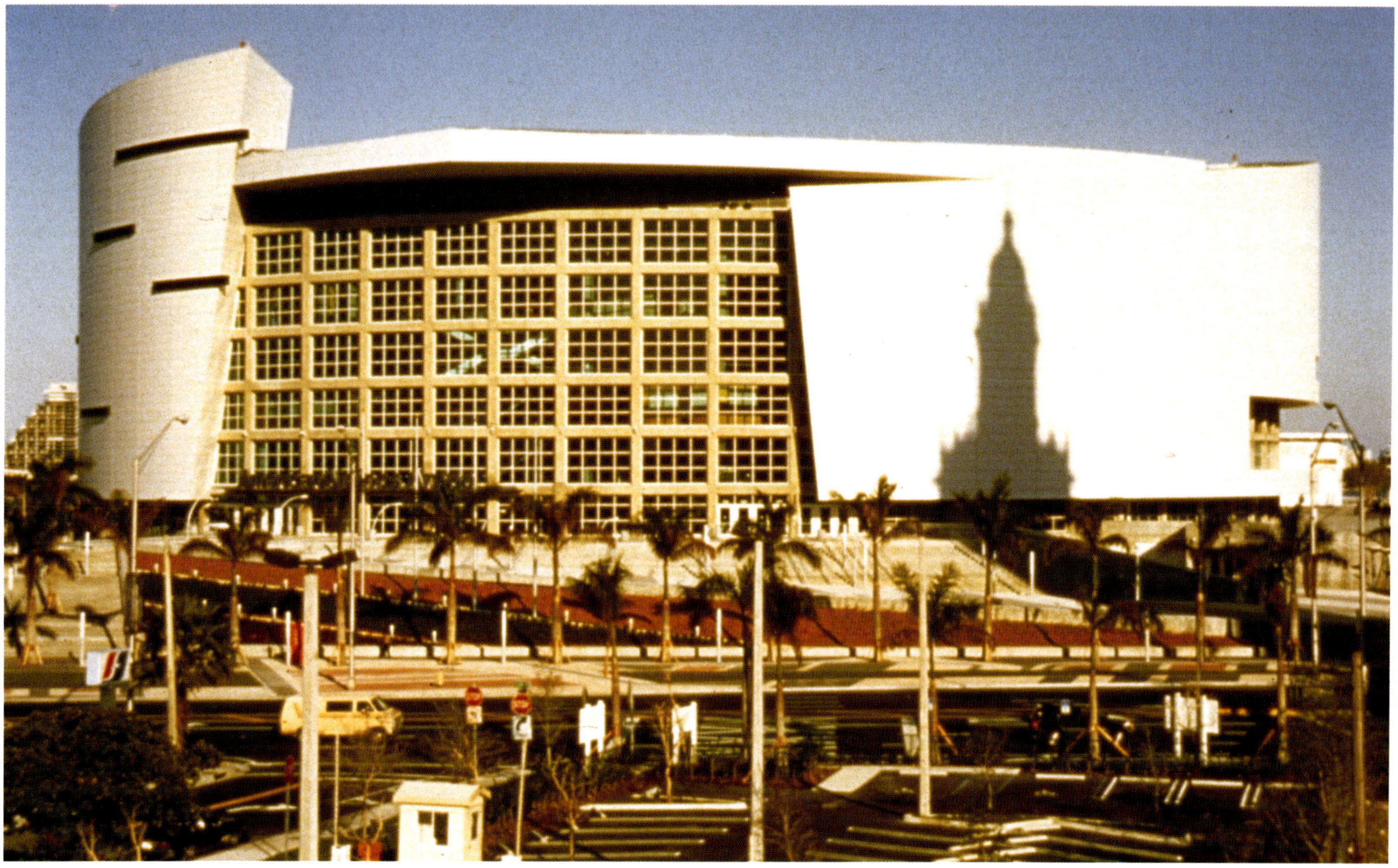

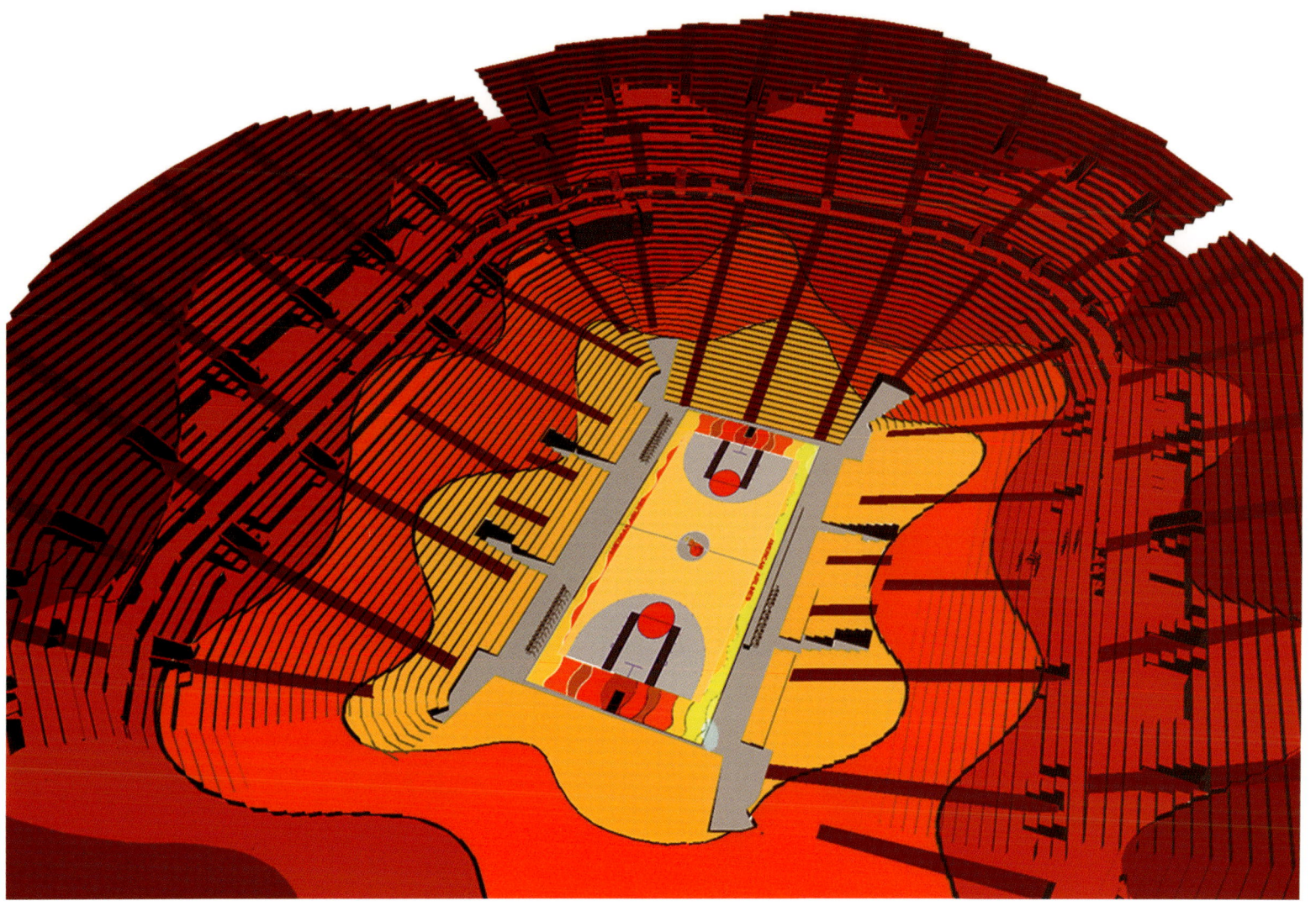

Perspective

Casa Club de Golf Fontanals

Architect: Josep Miàs i Gifre

Photographs © Eugeni Pons

Location: Puigcerdá, Spain
Year completed: 2004

THROUGH A GREAT DEAL OF AMBIGUITY BETWEEN INTERIOR AND EXTERIOR, AND THE USE OF MATERIALS FOUND IN THE AREA, THIS BUILDING MADE A STRONG ATTEMPT AT HARMONIZING WITH ITS SITE, AS WELL AS ORGANICALLY MOLDING ITSELF TO THE EXISTING TOPOGRAPHY IN SUCH A WAY THAT THE LANDSCAPE AND GROUND WOULD SEEM TO CREEP INTO IT.

CASA CLUB DE GOLF FONTANALS

As it is a member of a species that typically yields imposing and heavy buildings, this clubhouse is unique in its humble approach at blending into the existing topography so as to seem as though it naturally belonged there.

With a program of over 37,500 built sq. feet, this building's close profile to the ground is achieved through the design of an underground level—lit by skylights—that contains the sport service areas: dressing rooms, massage area and sauna, gymnasium, and covered pool. Concrete retaining walls divide the program on this lower level, and also serve as screens that hold up the main metal structure of the building. Atop this skeleton arises the most visible part of the structure of the building: a laminated wood structure that divides the social spaces on the upper level, all of which are open to the landscape thanks to a glass-and-aluminum enclosure. This upper level is covered by a large, dark sheet-like roof that delicately rests atop the wood structure and presents a series of sloping planes that engage in dialogue with the topography of the site. The entire building is clad in materials typically of the Pyrenees—panels finished in wood, rectangular slate tiles and matt-colored black zinc in difficult-to-span corners. To bolster the dialogue with the site and in order for the building to merge into its surroundings, the green slate floors extend outdoors, the roof reaches out over outdoor spaces and the area around the pool extends outward to form a terrace.

As it does not resist the flowing existing topography of the site, this clubhouse is a successful design filled with subtle details: to an extent in is the antithesis of what one usually expects of such an institutional building.

Sections

Sections

Floor plan

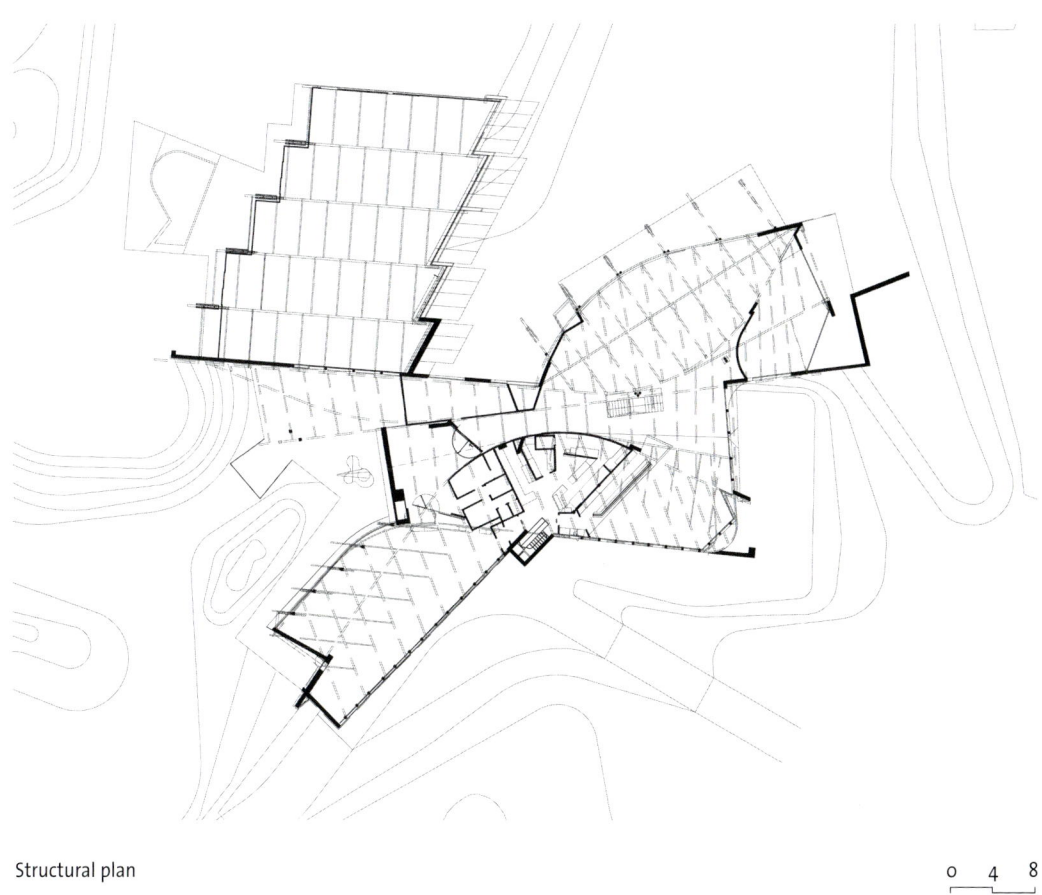

Structural plan

o   4   8

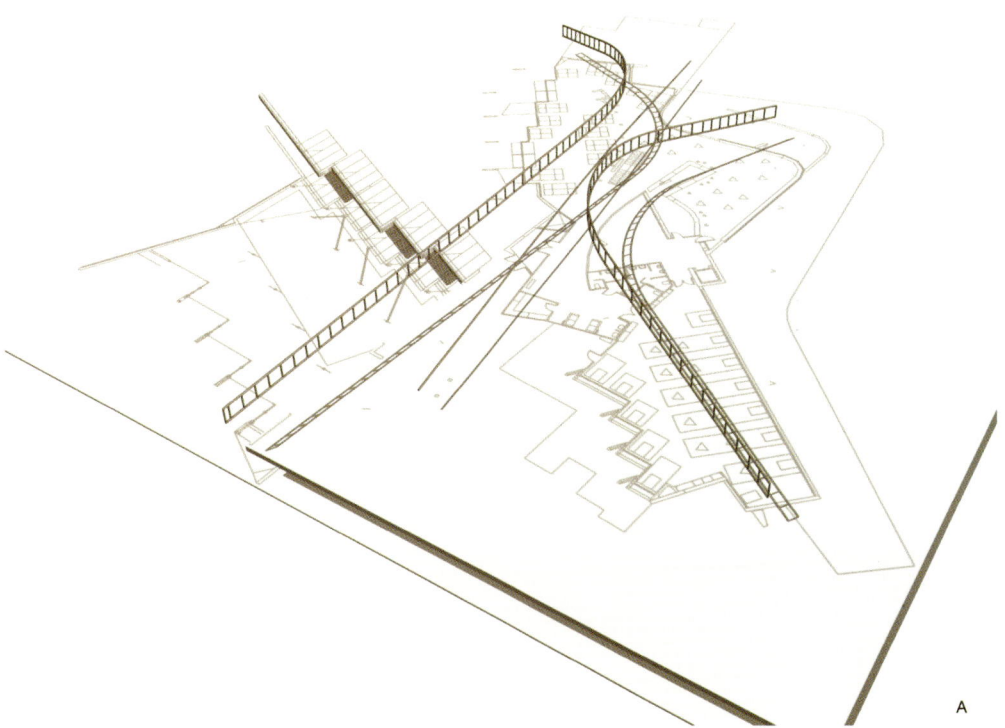

Structural plan

F

Structural plan

Structural studies

Structural studies

BERGISEL SKI JUMP

ARCHITECTS: ZAHA HADID ARCHITECTS
COLLABORATORS: CHRISTIAN ASTE (STRUCTURAL ENGINEER)

PHOTOGRAPHS © HÉLÈNE BINET

LOCATION: INNSBRUCK, AUSTRIA
YEAR COMPLETED: 2002

This ski jump appears to be a sculpture in the landscape—it is a work of spatial engineering that seems to have been placed atop Bergisel Mountain to watch over the city of Innsbruck.

Bergisel ski jump

It was the team led by Iraq-born Zaha Hadid that won the contest announced by the city government of Innsbruck to built a new ski jump on Bergisel Mountain, which was to enjoy prime views out over the city. The intervention forms part of a project to renovate the older, existing facilities, which were no longer up to international regulations.

The facility built, which betrays a complex and attractive formalism, combines highly specialized sporting equipment and facilities with public spaces, such as a café and a terrace/overlook. These two programs are fused in a single volume that extends and projects the topography of the slope towards the heavens.

Almost 270 feet long and 150 feet tall, this project is a conceptual combination of a tower and a bridge, and makes use of parameters that are unique to this type of architecture. Furthermore, it makes references to industry, which is typical of such buildings. Structurally speaking, it consists of a vertical, concrete tower and a metal enclosure that integrates the ramp to the café.

Two elevators lead the visitors to the café, which is located 120 feet atop the peak of Bergisel, from which visitors can enjoy the surrounding Alpine landscape in addition to watching how the athletes launch into the air with the city of Innsbruck in the background.

Sketch

Floor plans

0   3   6

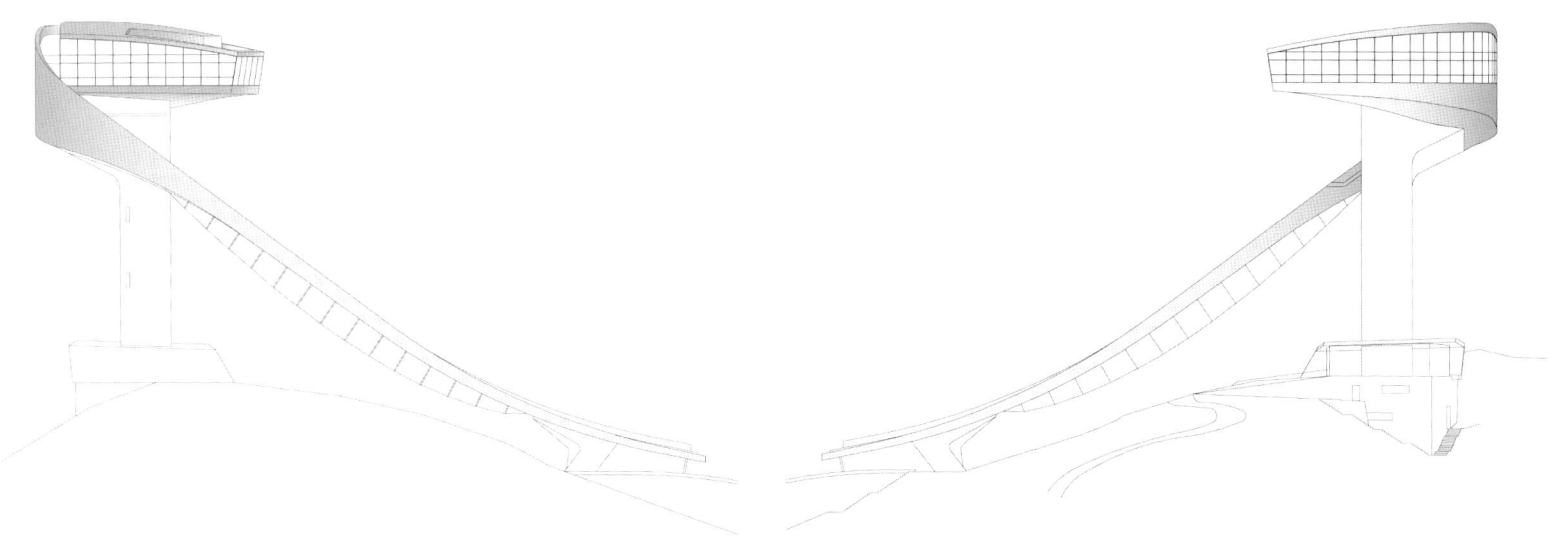

Elevations

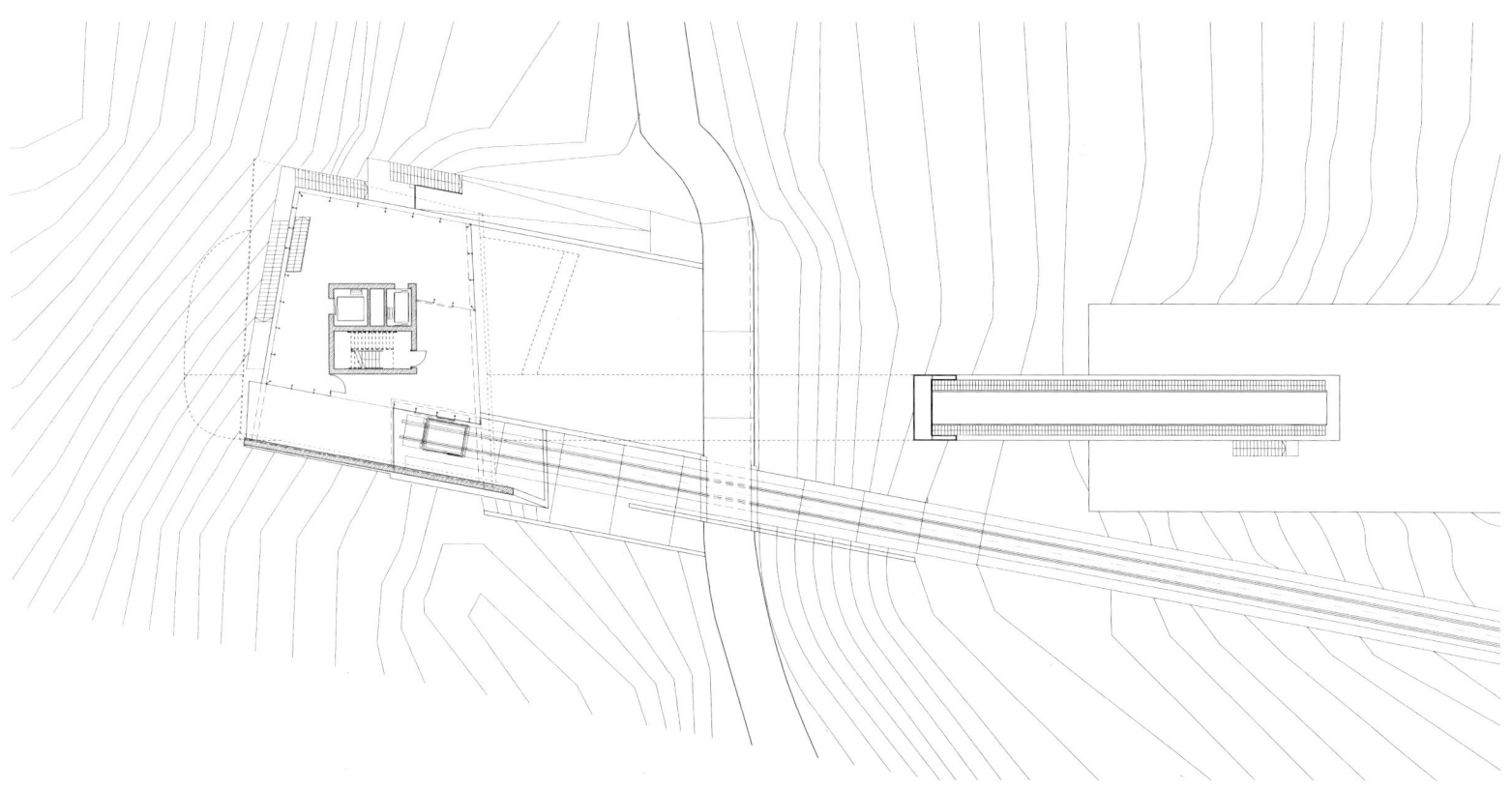

Ground level plan

GUIERA SPORTS PARK

ARCHITECTS: HERNANDO & SAUQUÉ ARQUITECTOS
COLLABORATORS: ÁNGEL OBIOL (STRUCTURAL ENGINEERS), JG ASOCIADOS (SERVICES)

PHOTOGRAPHS © JORDI MIRALLES

LOCATION: CERDANYOLA DEL VALLÈS, SPAIN
YEAR COMPLETED: 2003

THIS SPORTS COMPLEX, DESIGNED BY ARCHITECTS HERNANDO & SAUQUÉ, IS AN EXCELLENT EXAMPLE OF FUNCTIONALITY AND SUSTAINABILITY, AS IT MASTERFULLY ORGANIZES THE VARIOUS ACTIVITIES OF THE PROGRAM THROUGH AN ECOLOGICAL DESIGN THAT SAVES A SUBSTANTIAL AMOUNT OF ENERGY.

GUIERA SPORTS PARK

The Guiera Sports Park is a large sporting and recreational facility located in a small town 13 miles outside the city of Barcelona, at the foot of the Collserola Natural Park. The project is the result of a collaborative effort between the town hall, the owner of the land involved, and the Catalan Handball Federation, which will act as administrator of the facility.

The building will be built in two phases, to be finished between 2003 and 2008, and will house a range of indoor sporting activities in facilities including a pavilion for team sports and several gymnasiums. It will also be home to a number of outdoor sports, including tennis courts, paddle courts, a athletic track, a children's play area, and several swimming pools. Furthermore, the complex will also include facilities that are not directly related to sporting activities, so as to diversify and integrate the social life of the local community—these include a bar, hotel, and the offices of the Federation.

Despite the complexity of the program, the designers came up with a system of connections between the different areas that would allow for access between them without interfering with the everyday functioning of the park, and would also allow for controlled access to given areas.

From the beginning, the development of this project kept in close step with the tenets of sustainability: the construction design allows for the building to be easily dismantled, thanks to the number of prefabricated components it uses—steel elements, its metal and wood structure, and its lightweight façade, which is crafted from metal plates. In addition, energy savings are achieved by naturally ventilating all the spaces and through the use of solar panels. Furthermore, those spaces that require a greater number of technical services have been gathered into the center, so as to rationalize the connections between them. Finally, a separate waste water treatment network was planned to be able to take advantage of part of the waste water generated.

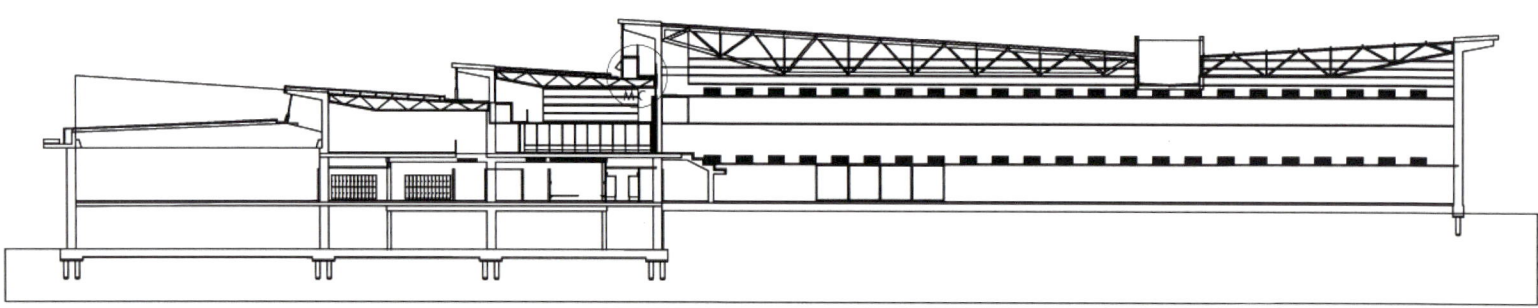

Section

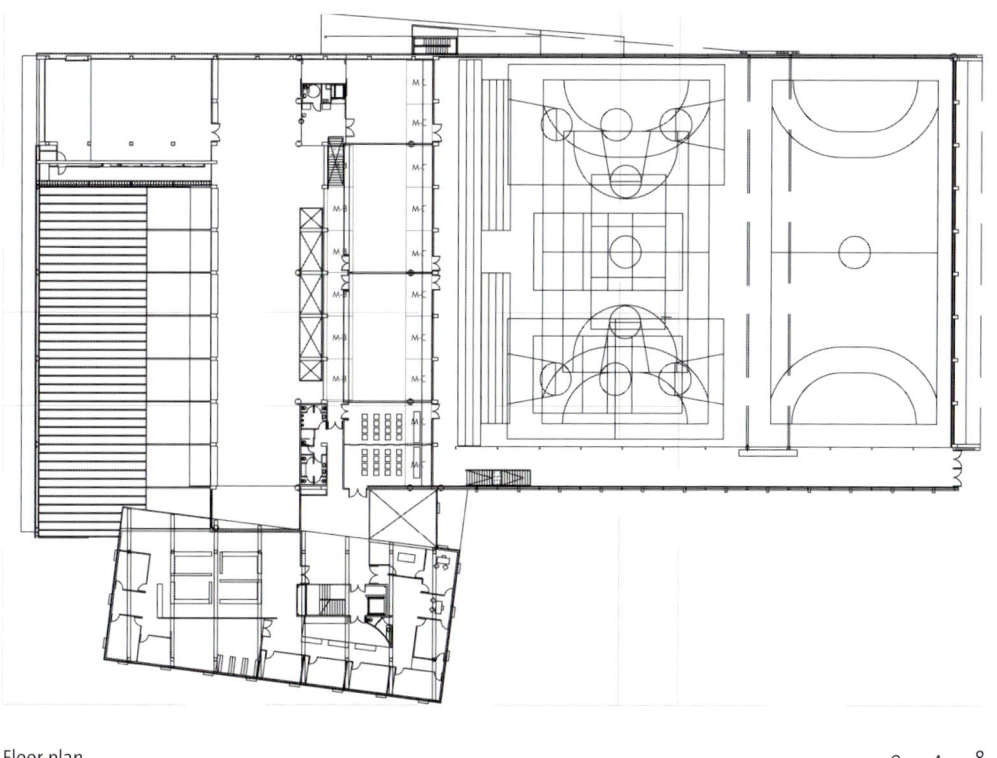

Floor plan

0 4 8

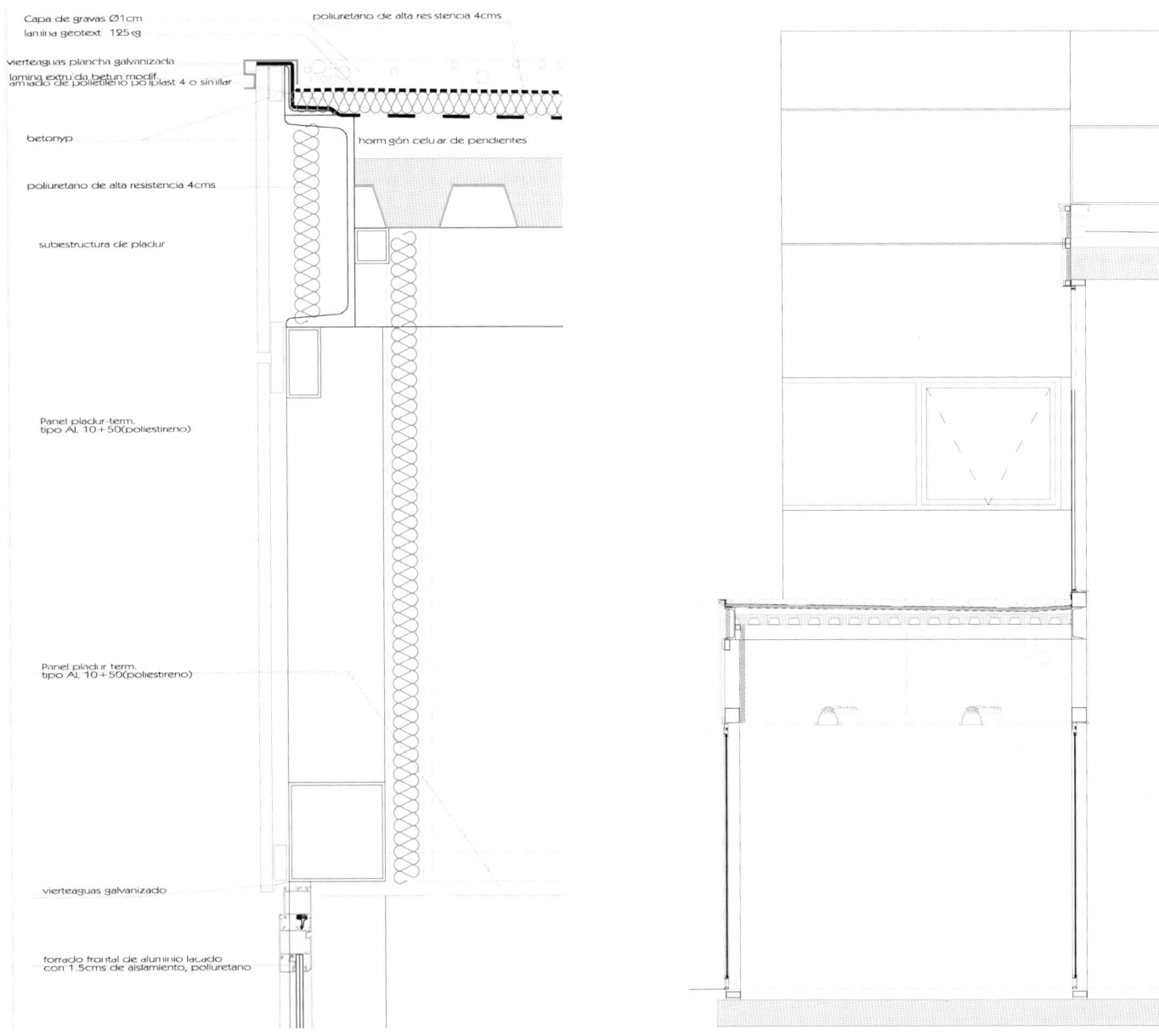

Capa de gravas Ø1cm
lamina geotext 125 kg

poliuretano de alta resistencia 4cms

vierteaguas plancha galvanizada

lamina extruida betun modif
armado de polietileno poliplast 4 o similar

betonyp

horm gón celular de pendientes

poliuretano de alta resistencia 4cms

subestructura de pladur

Panel pladur-term.
tipo AL 10+50(poliestireno)

Panel pladur term.
tipo AL 10+50(poliestireno)

vierteaguas galvanizado

forrado frontal de aluminio lacado
con 1.5cms de aislamiento, poliuretano

Construction detail

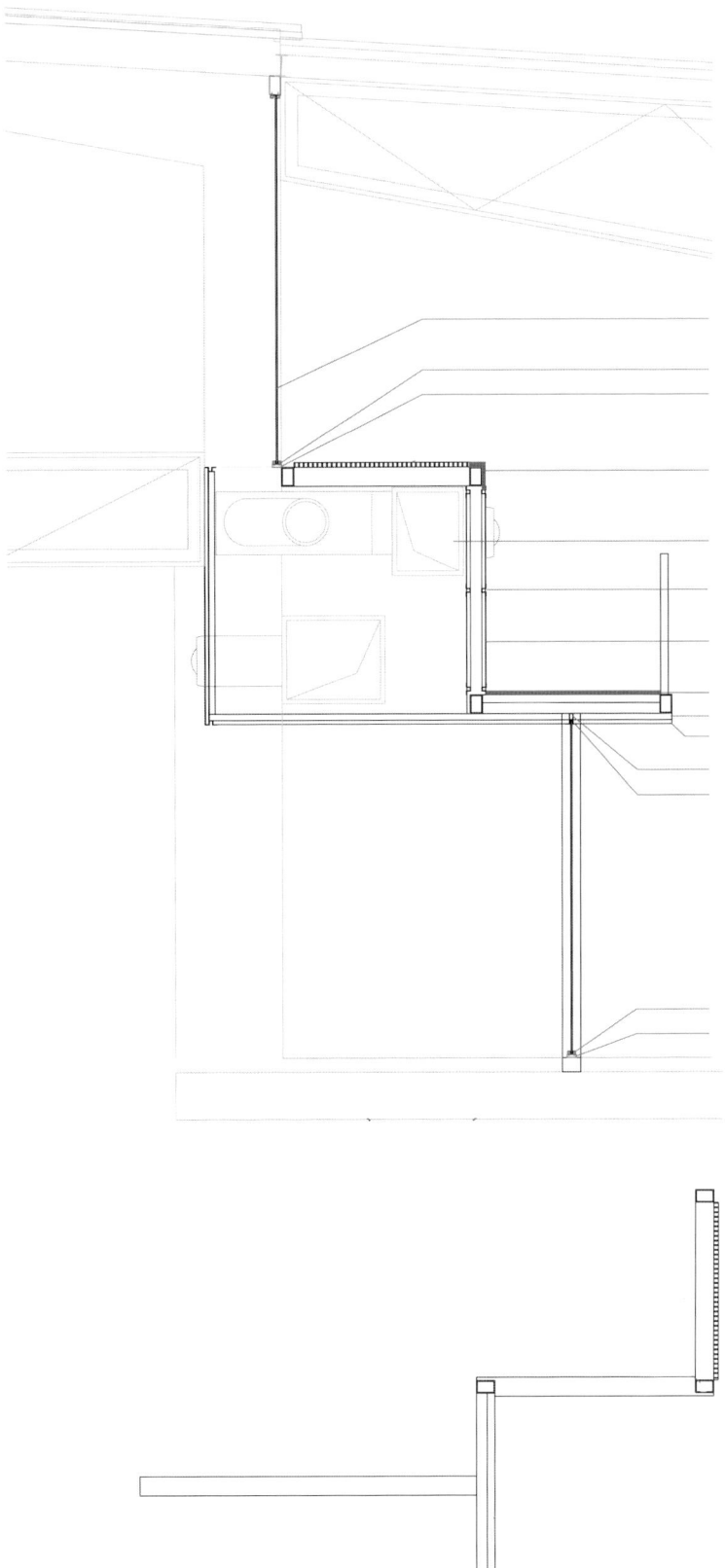

Construction details

OITA STADIUM

ARCHITECTS: KISHO KUROKAWA ARCHITECT & ASSOCIATES

PHOTOGRAPHS © KOJI KOBAYASHI

LOCATION: OITA, JAPAN
YEAR COMPLETED: 2001

OITA STADIUM

Oita Stadium was chosen to serve as one of the host stadiums for the 2002 World Cup, and an expansion is being planned in order for it to be able to house a series of athletic championships in 2008—it will then be one of the largest sporting complexes in the country.

Thanks to the curves of its spherical design, the stadium harmonizes with its natural surroundings. The choice of a sphere was obviously the expression of an abstract symbolism, although this geometry allowed for part of the roof of the stadium to be retractable, and thus opened or closed based on the weather or the functional necessities of any given competition. The use of innovative Teflon panels eliminated the need for artificial lighting during the day, even when the roof is closed. Furthermore, to achieve an ideal solar lighting, the stadium was located on a north-south axis. An opening was also left between the stands and the ceiling so that spectators could enjoy views out over the adjacent forest.

The stadium's structure combines reinforced concrete for the footings and the base, while large, arcing stainless steel beams were chosen to hold up the roof.

Despite having been designed as a football stadium, it has also come to house a wide range of athletic activities, such as track and field competitions, and concerts. The stands are also retractable, which allows for a range of possibilities based on whatever activity is being carried out—in this way, the spectators can always sit right up next to whatever is going on, and feel like they are really part of the game.

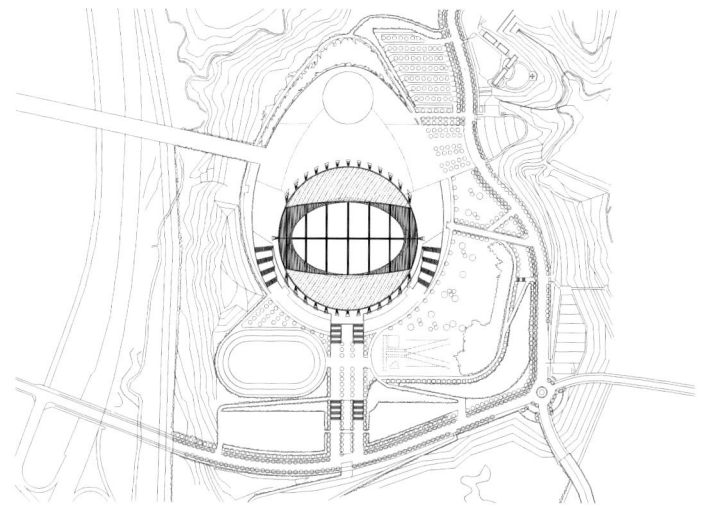

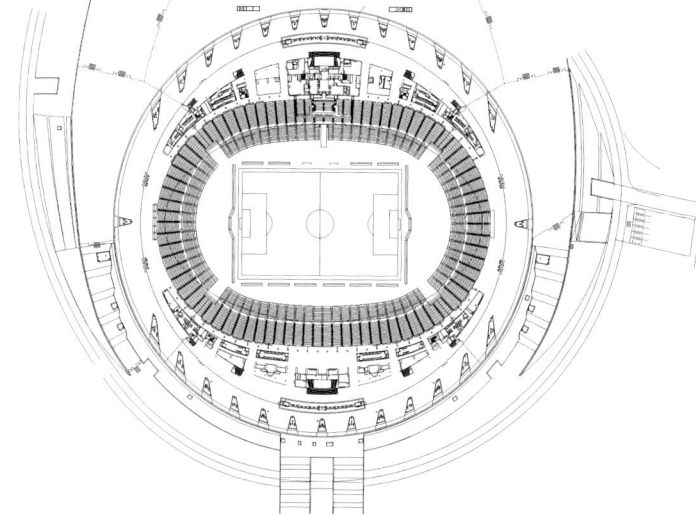

Location plan

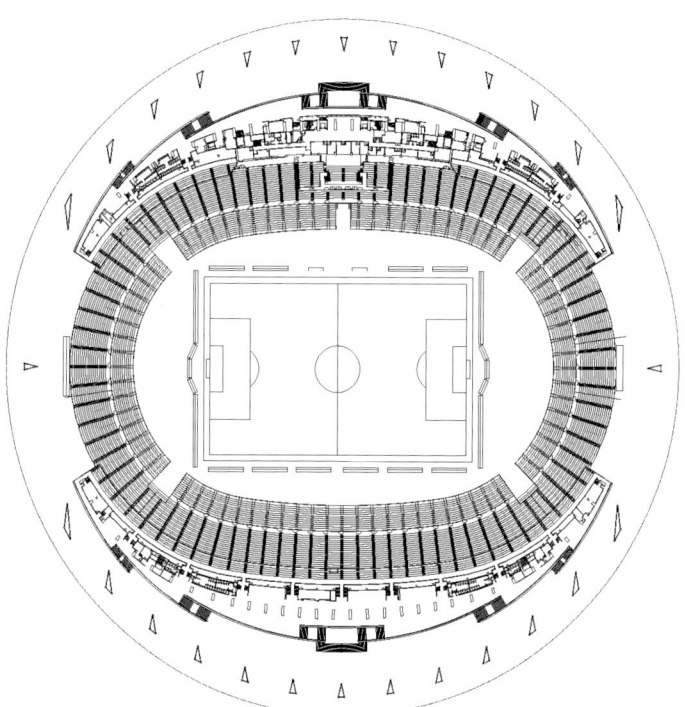

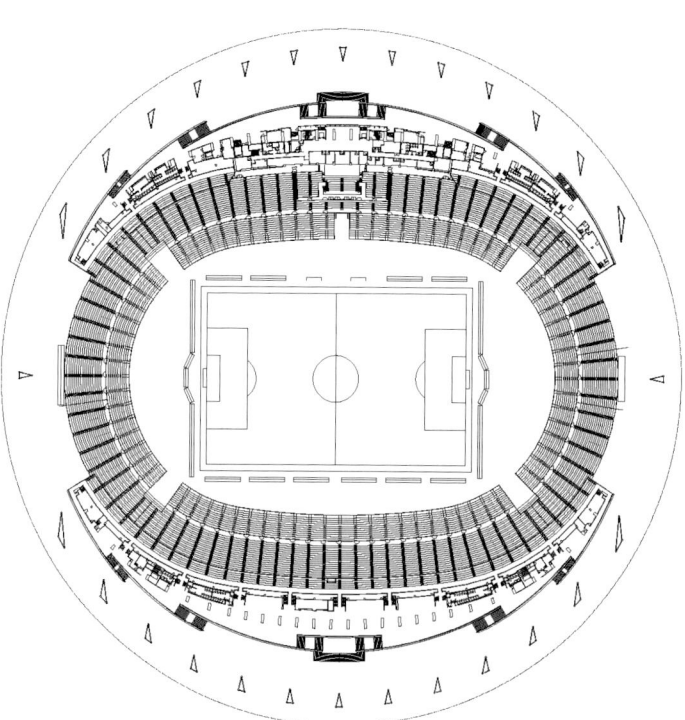

Plans

0   20   40

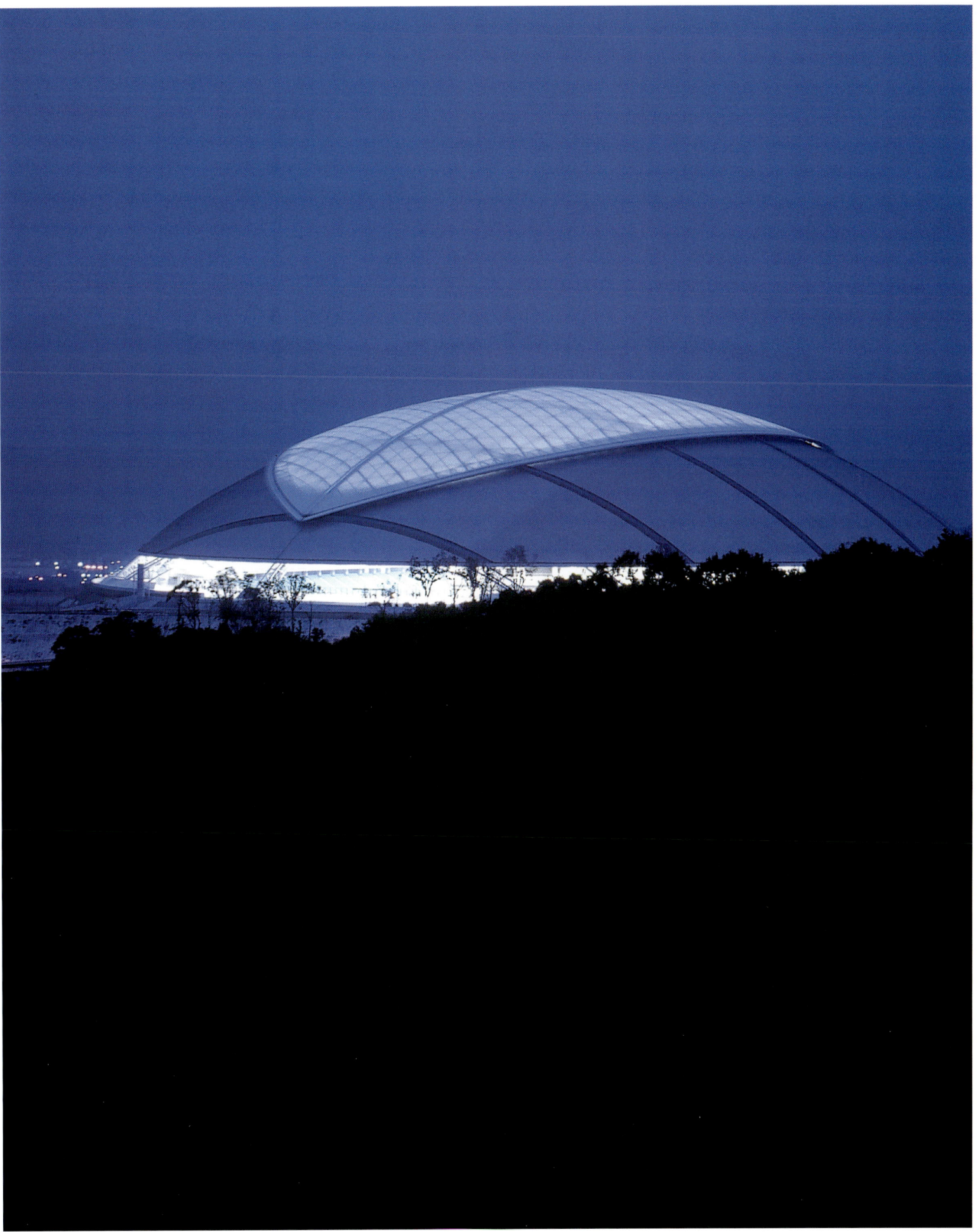

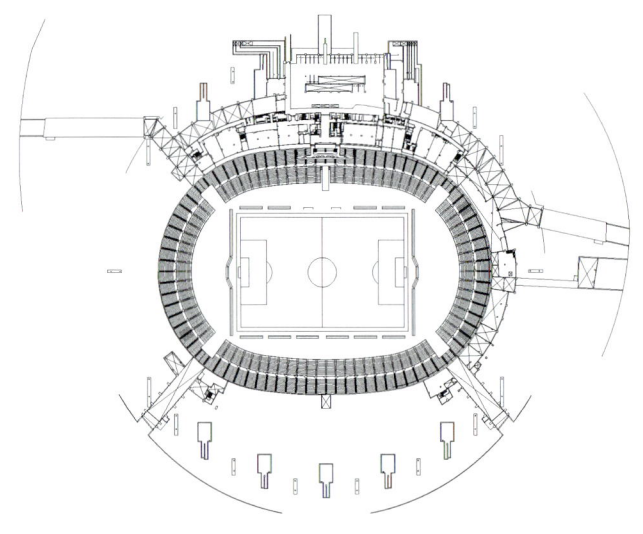

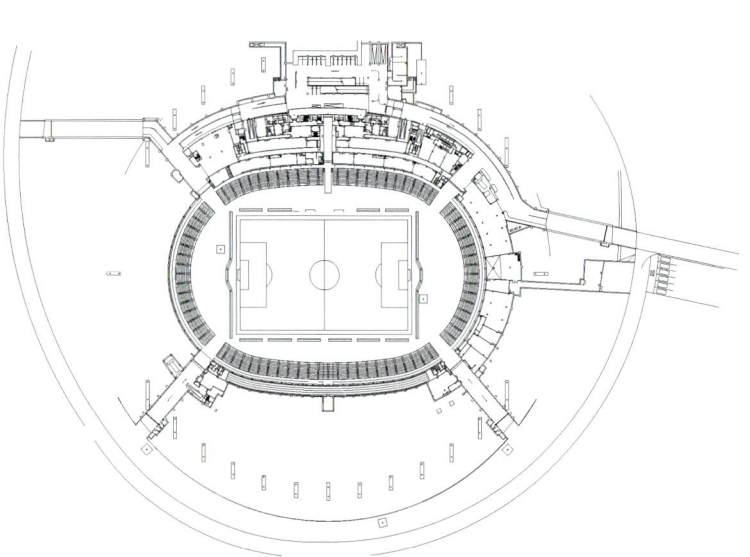

Plans

0   20   40

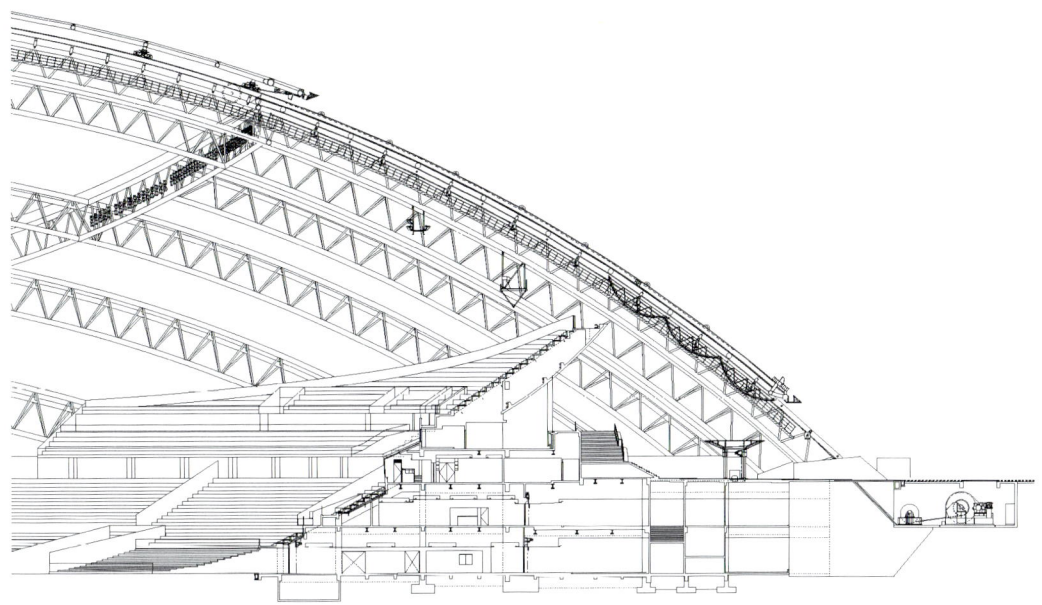

Section

Ca N'Arimon Sports Center

Architect: Moisés Gallego Olmos
**Collaborators: Manuel Raventós, Pere Castelltort (structures), P. Vicente Ibáñez
(services), Alex Gallego and Martí Sanz (collaborating architects)**

Photographs © Jordi Miralles

Location: Mollet del Vallès, Spain
Year completed: 2000

For the town of Mollet del Vallès, Can Arimón has traditionally served as a recreational center focused especially on swimming. Over the years, however, the original facilities had grown out of date, which had come to required that it be renovated.

Ca N'Arimon Sports Center

The project here entailed a continuous set of buildings along an east-west axis that would extend along the rear part of the site and that would also highlight the basic organization of the town and the roads leading to it. The continuity of the cornice across the set of buildings creates a certain unity between them, in a simple yet emphatic way. The building's impact on its surroundings it mitigate by its placement at a minimum distance from the school grounds behind it and a terraced area of landscaping.

Achieving a unified exterior—as the indoor ceiling heights in the pool area and the sports center differ—required designing a structural system of ribs atop the roof plane, which in the area of the pool appears as a parapet that conceals the solar panels. Part of the existing outdoor pool was maintained, as was the children's pool, and two sporting fields were laid out. The new facilities were laid out on two floors in parallel to the main façade: the lower level was dedicated to the users and the upper floor was designed for spectators and the common areas. Perpendicularly, a transversal volume runs through the space and extends out to the street, and comprises the entrance to the building. This is a prism that divides the open space into two parts; that of the bathrooms is located on one side, and the sports center on the other. Additionally, it acts as a physical and visual barrier. This project paid special attention to achieving energy savings through the use of solar panels to heat running water as well as the water in the swimming pools.

Site plan

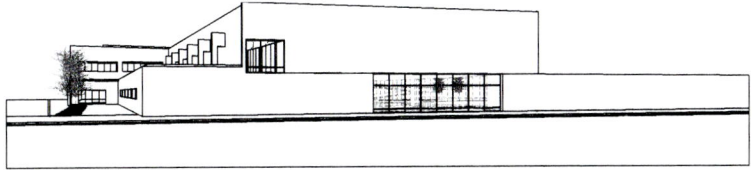
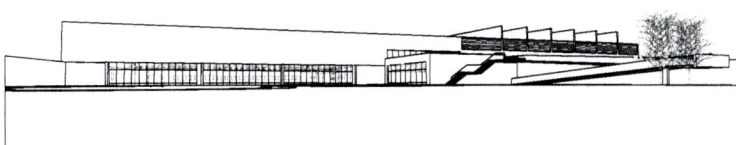

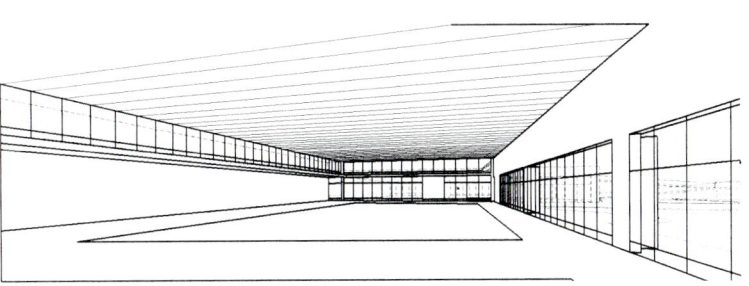
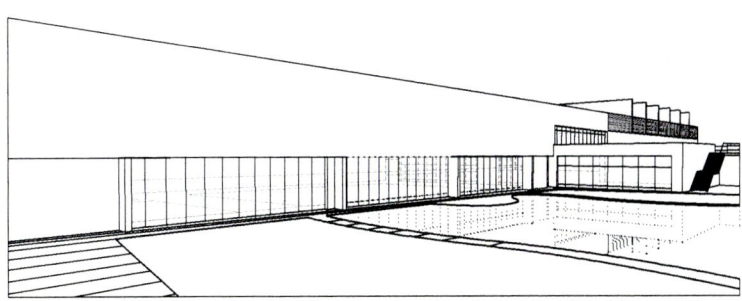

Perspectives

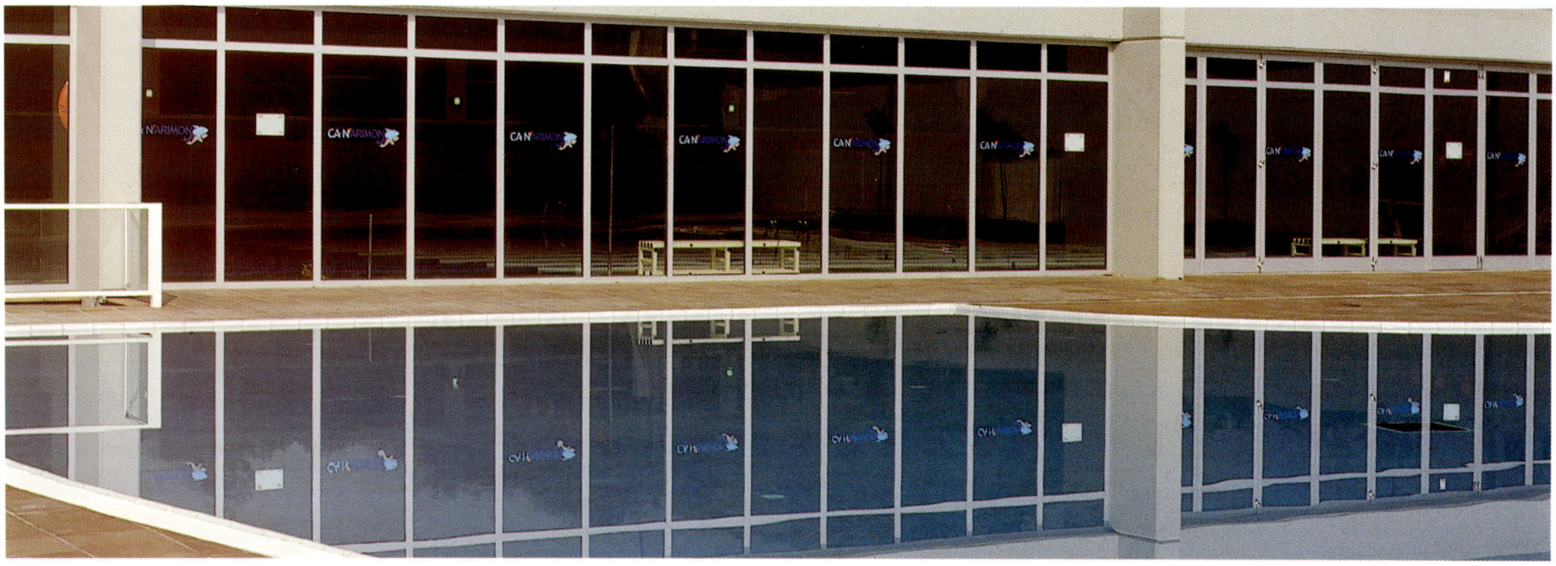

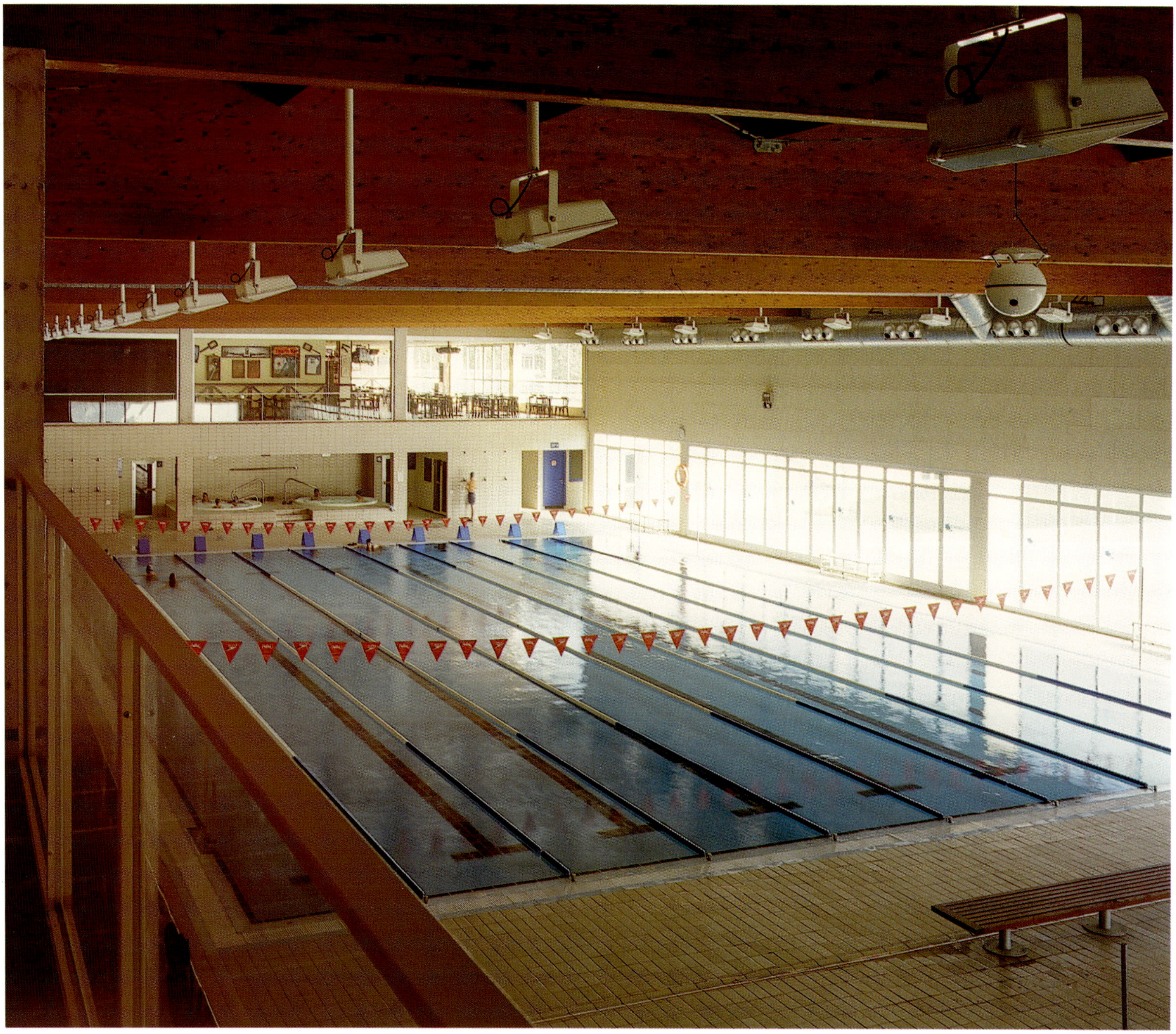

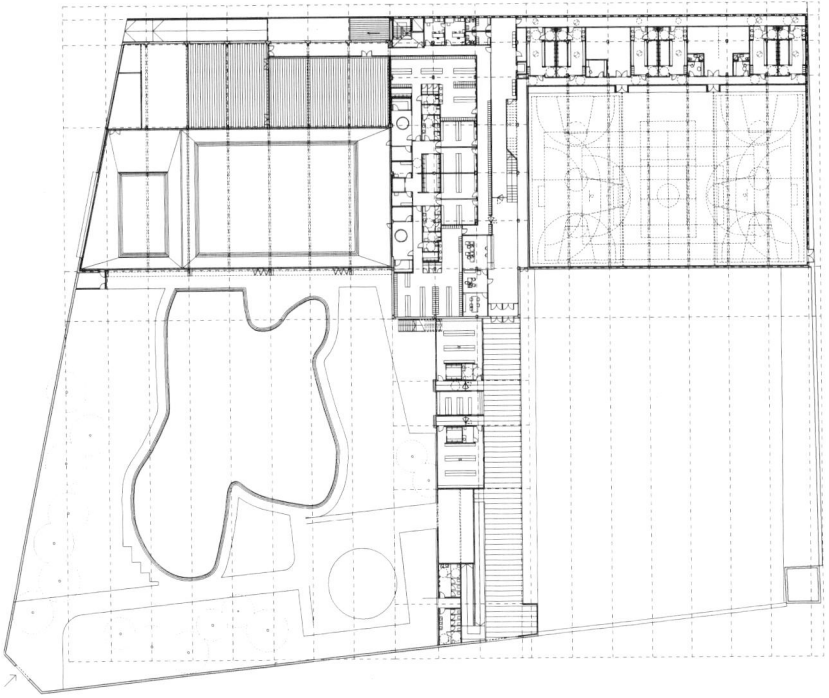

Ground floor

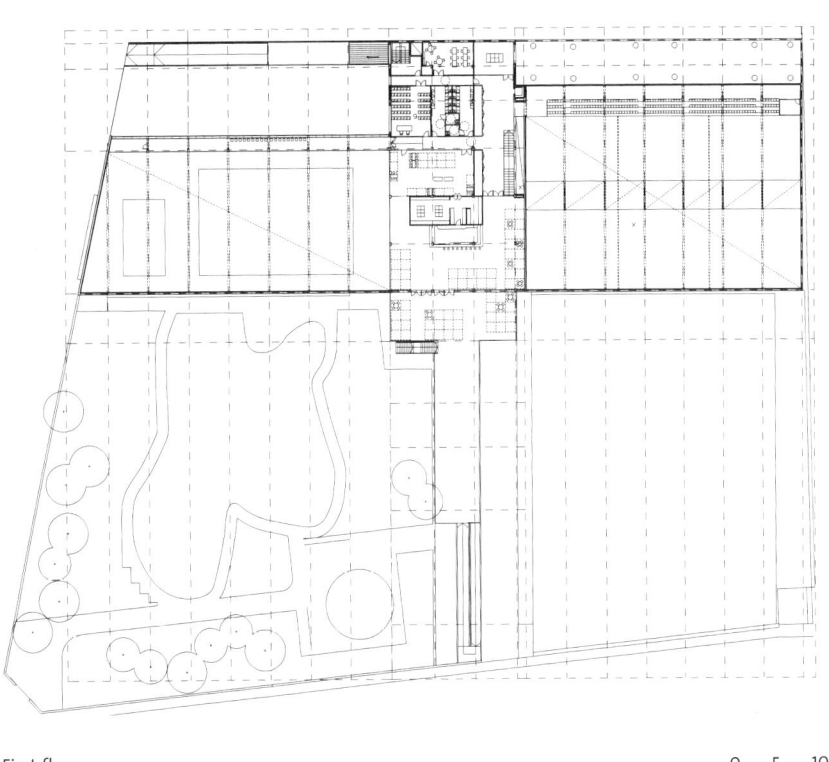

First floor

0   5   10

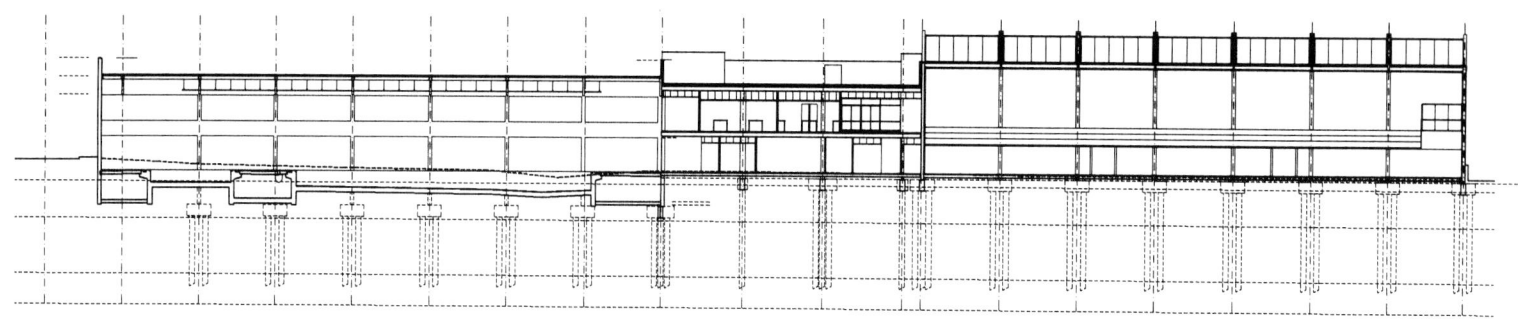

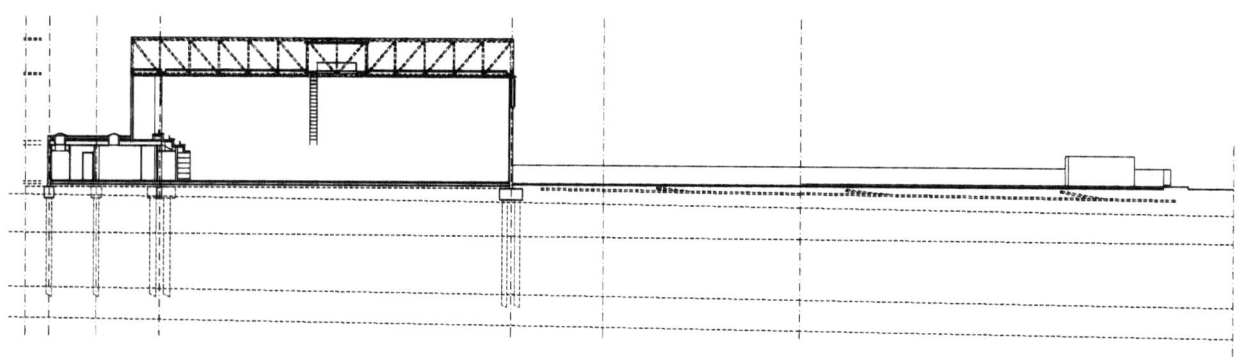

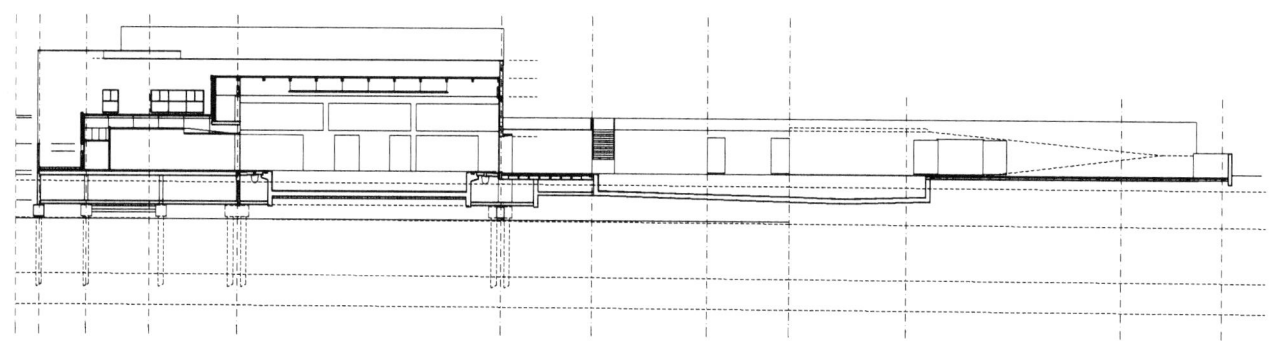

Sections

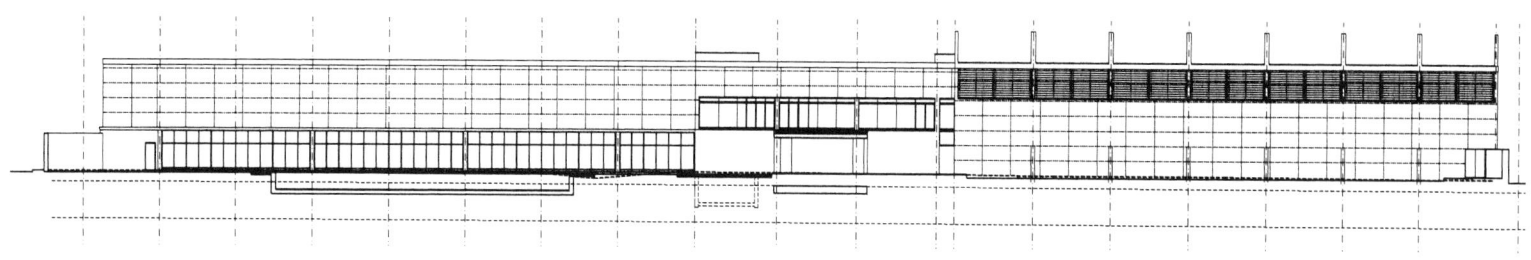

Elevation

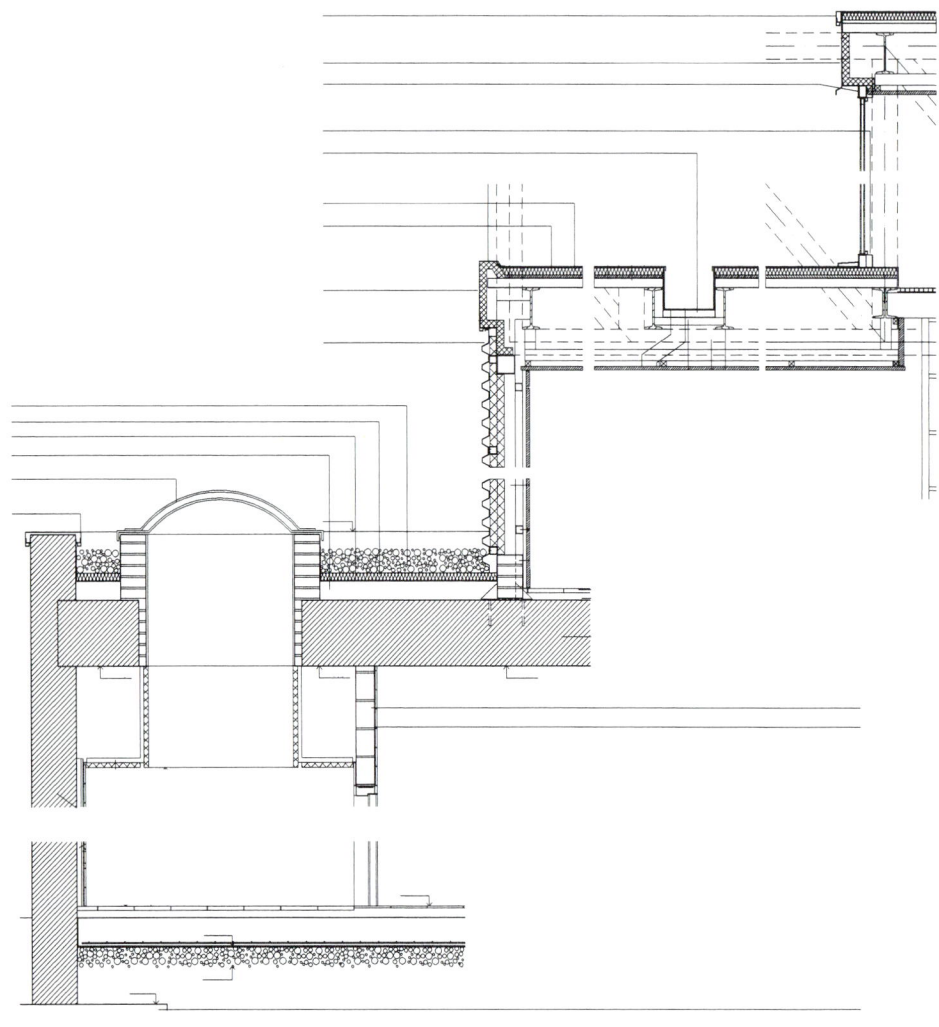

Construction details

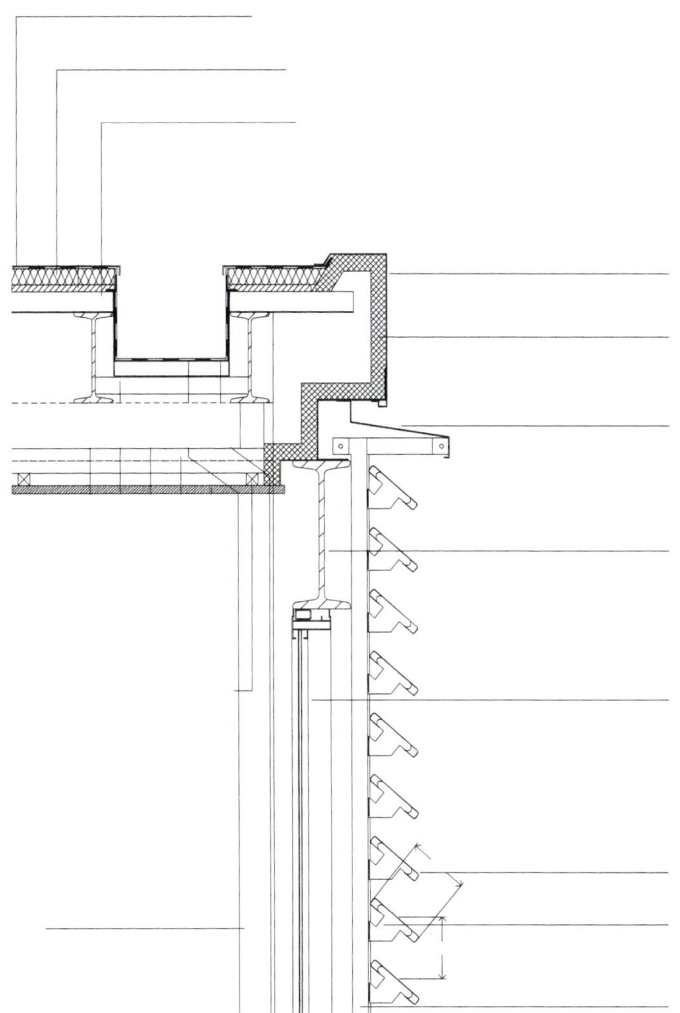

Façade detail

RHEIN ENERGIE FOOTBALL STADIUM

ARCHITECTS: VOLKWIN MARG/ARCHITEKTEN VON GERKAN, MARG UND PARTNER

PHOTOGRAPHS © JÜRGEN SCHMIDT, HEINER LEISKA

LOCATION: COLOGNE, GERMANY
YEAR COMPLETED: 2004

THE RHEIN ENERGIE STADIUM REPRESENTS A RESTRAINED DESIGN THAT PREDICATED RECTANGULAR SYMMETRY, AND ADDITIONALLY SOUGHT TO MAKE A RATIONAL USE OF MATERIALS AND STRUCTURAL SOLUTIONS—THE LATTER INCLUDE SUCH ELEMENTS AS SUSPENDED CEILINGS AND PREFABRICATED STANDS.

RHEIN ENERGIE FOOTBALL STADIUM

The Rhein Energie Stadium is located in the city's largest sporting facility, which is a large complex that includes tennis courts, pools, and an expansive green area. It is an entirely new construction, which was built to replace the erstwhile Müngersdorfer stadium so as to offer visitors modern amenities and to increase seating capacity.

The building appears from the access to the complex as the finishing touch at the end of a large avenue of trees and columns—these represent the only elements that were retained from the original design. A glass ceiling covers the main entrance to the ring of distribution that divides the stand into two areas. From this access point, one enjoys a full view of the interior through an enormous window located underneath the main grandstand, which includes fifty-two VIP booths as well as others for the press. On the opposite end of the stadium, another grandstand encompasses a conference center and a VIP restaurant, both of which have independent entrances.

The rectangular nature of the stadium is maintained both in plan and in section, and is highlighted by the concrete structure that holds up the prefabricated stands. The corners are crowned by four 180-foot-tall steel towers that sustain the roof structure, and include a sophisticated lighting system designed by Philips. So as to be able to remove columns from the structure, the architects designed a system of hanging ceilings, which include tensile elements suspended between the towers that direct the weight of the roof towards the ground along their external vertices. The four independent roofs are clad in metal on the outside and in glass in the interior, to ensure an optimal growing environment for the grass in the field.

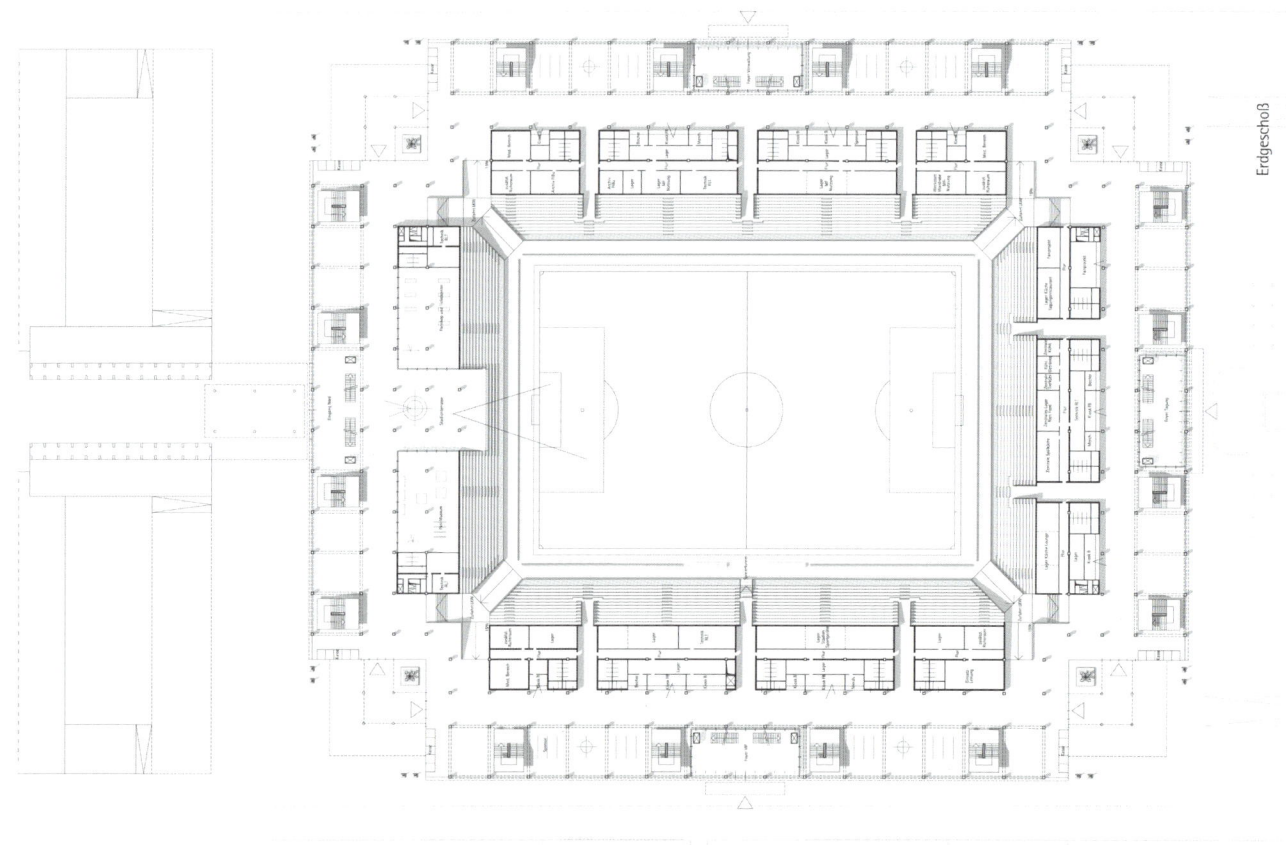

Floor plan

0　5　10

Section

Sports Center in Zoug

Architects: Bétrix & Consolascio Architekten
Collaborators: Eric Maier, Harald Echsle, Nathalie Rossetti

Photographs © Guido Baselgia

Location: Zoug, Switzerland
Year completed: 2001

THE SUBTLETY OF THE COLORED GLASS FAÇADES OF THIS SPORTS CENTER ALLOW FOR A DIFFUSE INTERIOR LIGHTING THAT CREATES A SOPHISTICATED AMBIENCE AND CONFERS A DIMENSION THAT SUPPLEMENTS ONE'S AESTHETIC EXPERIENCE OF IT.

SPORTS CENTER IN ZOUG

Located at the west entrance to the Swiss city of Zoug, this sports center is inserted into the context of the urban periphery. To the south of the site, a leisure complex is coming into being, and furthermore indicates that the neighborhood is undergoing a process of change. What had once been pastureland was taken over by industry, only to later be dedicated by the city hall to public use, by first slowly transforming it into training fields and subsequently into an area encompassing a wide range of sporting facilities.

From the beginning, the architects aimed to provide the building with a unique and precise architectural motif, so as to mark a different feel from the industrial air of the facilities that preceded it. In this changing context, this sports center emerges as a free-standing box, without being in alignment with any of the other buildings nearby. A perfect square in floor plan, this sports center avoids making references to the spatiality of the city, whose presence is not at all felt in the area.

To solve the issue of pouring the foundation on an unstable site, the volume of the building was sunk three feet below ground level, and pilotis were designed to affix it to the bedrock. In this way, the courts are located below ground level, while one enters the building four and half feet above ground level, via a ramp that leads visitors to the lockers rooms or the stands.

This building—which is clad in painted glass along its rear façade—avoids transparency and explicit symbols, and furthermore refuses to reveal the nature of its functions: all in all it cultivates an air of mystery. In addition, its colors change over the course of the day and over the course of the year, by appearing to be a different hue every morning, and occasionally reflecting the colors of the earth around it.

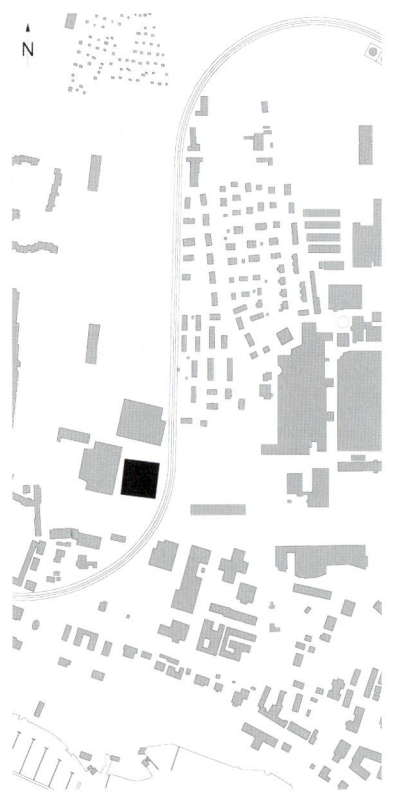

Site plan

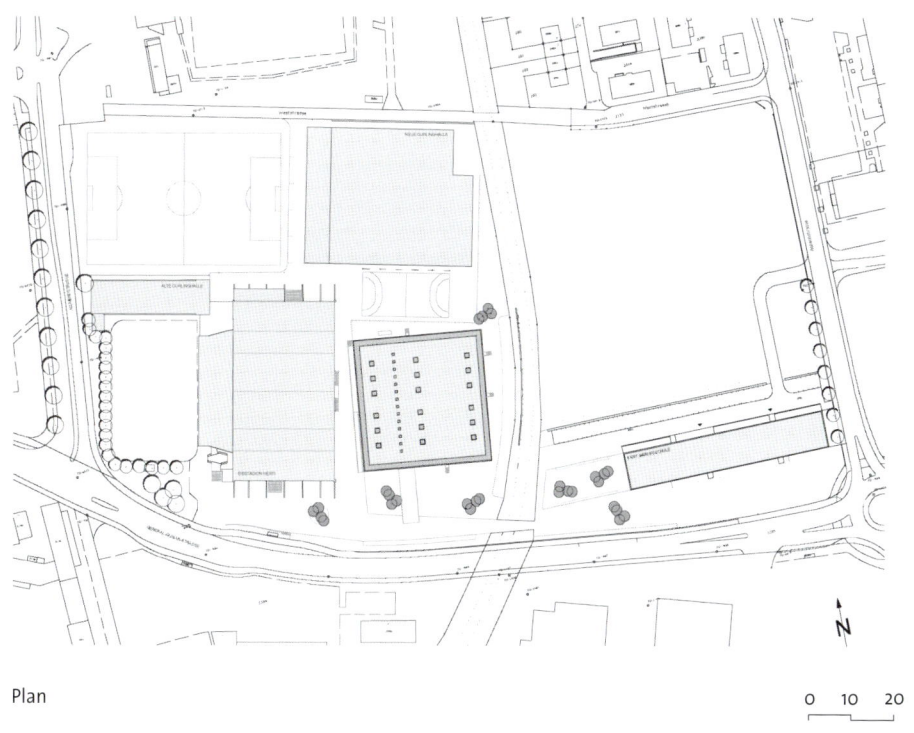

Plan

0   10   20

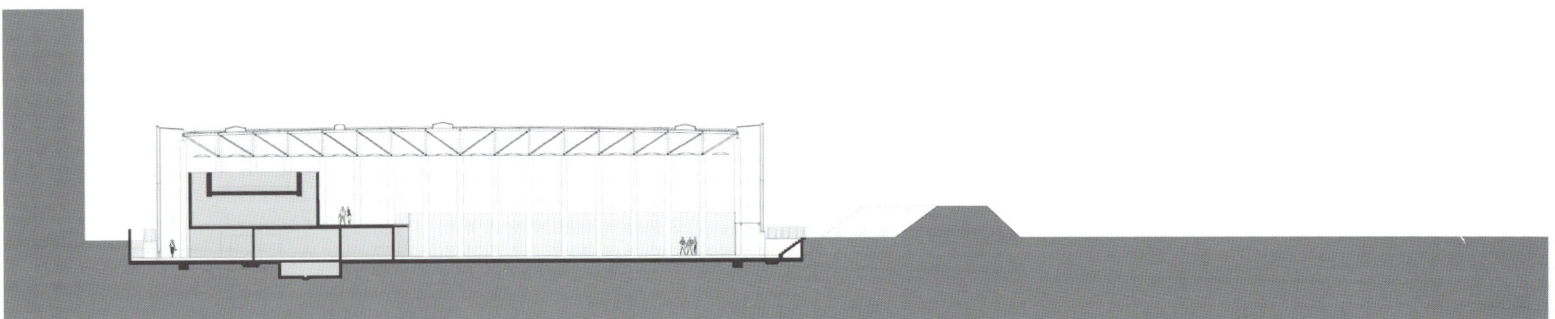

Sections

0   1   2

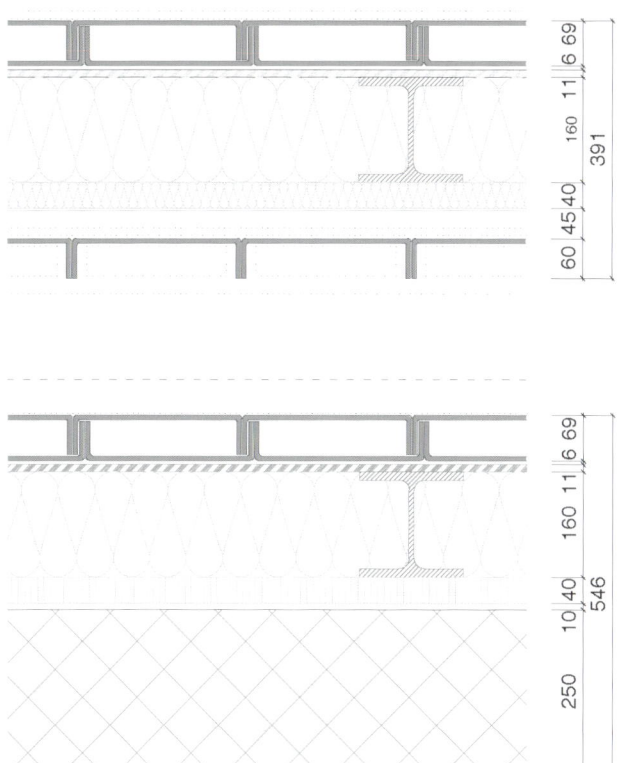

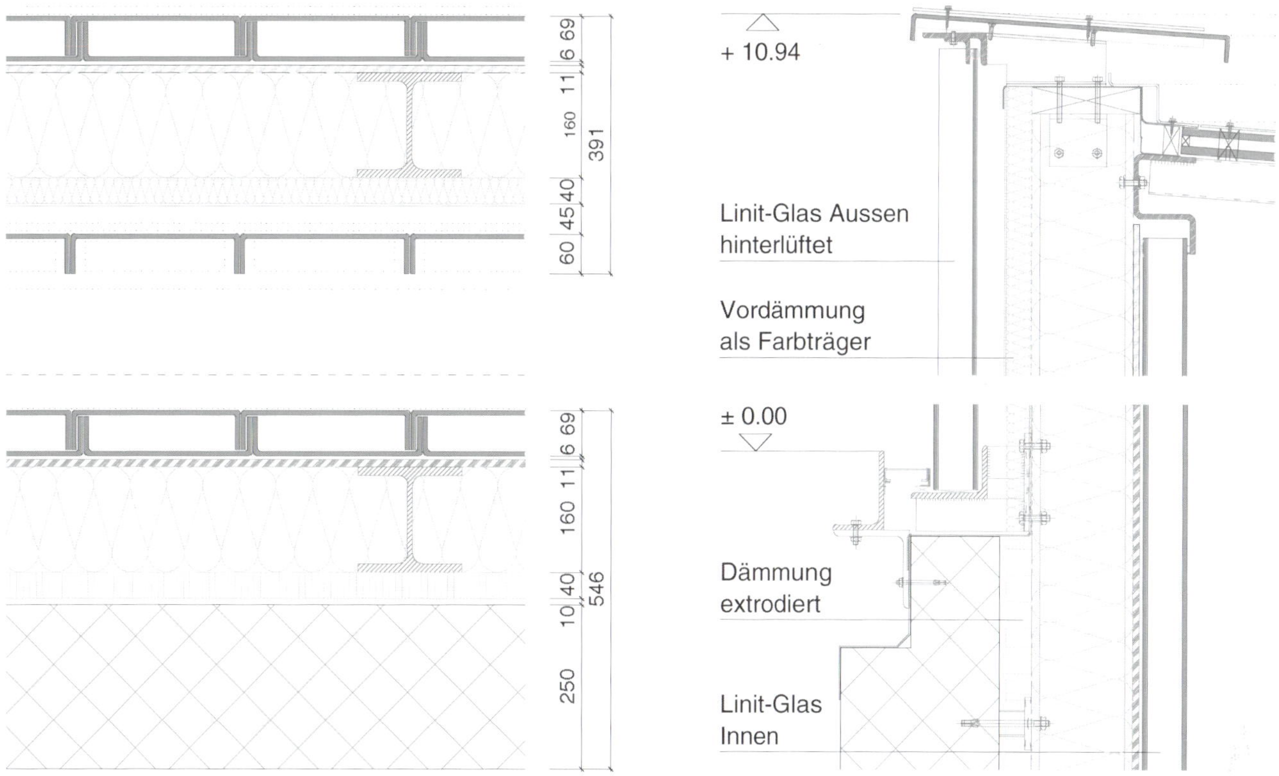

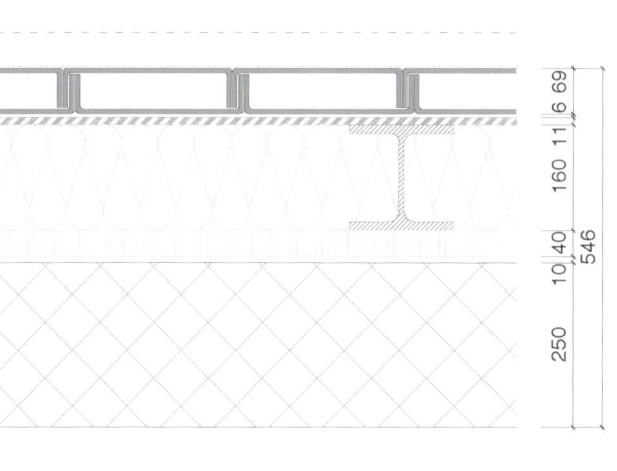

6 69
11
160
391
40
45
60
+ 10.94
Linit-Glas Aussen
hinterlüftet
Vordämmung
als Farbträger
6 69
11
160
40
10
546
250
± 0.00
Dämmung
extrodiert
Linit-Glas
Innen

Construction details

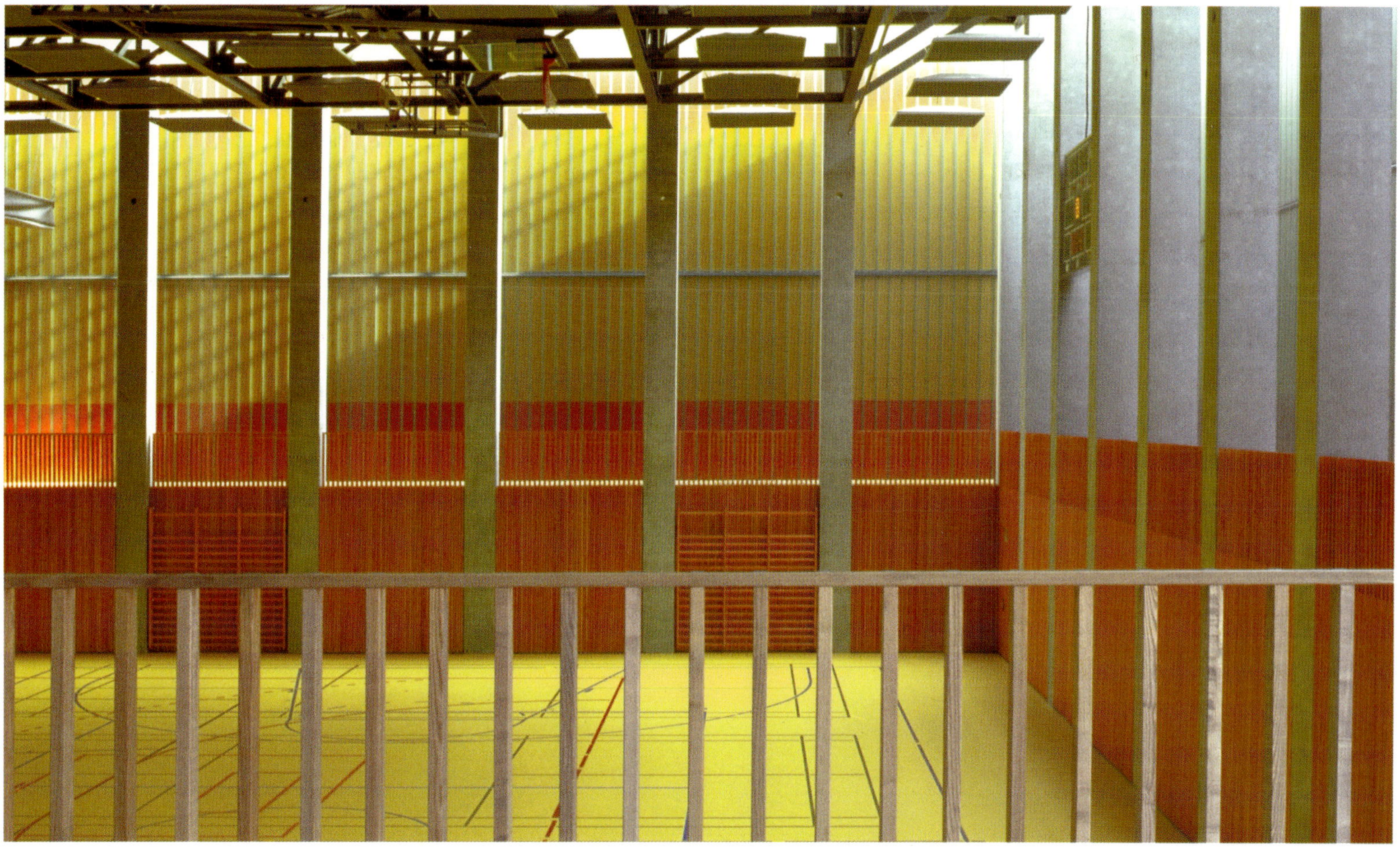

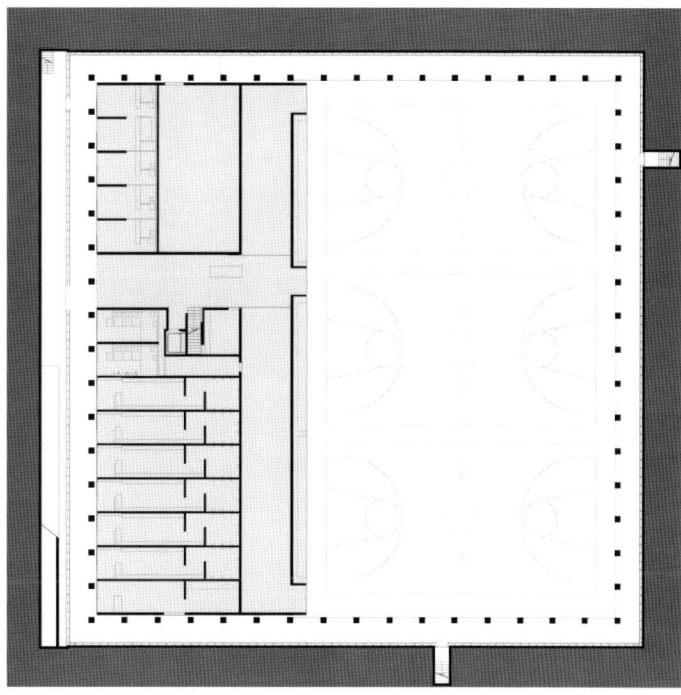

Basement

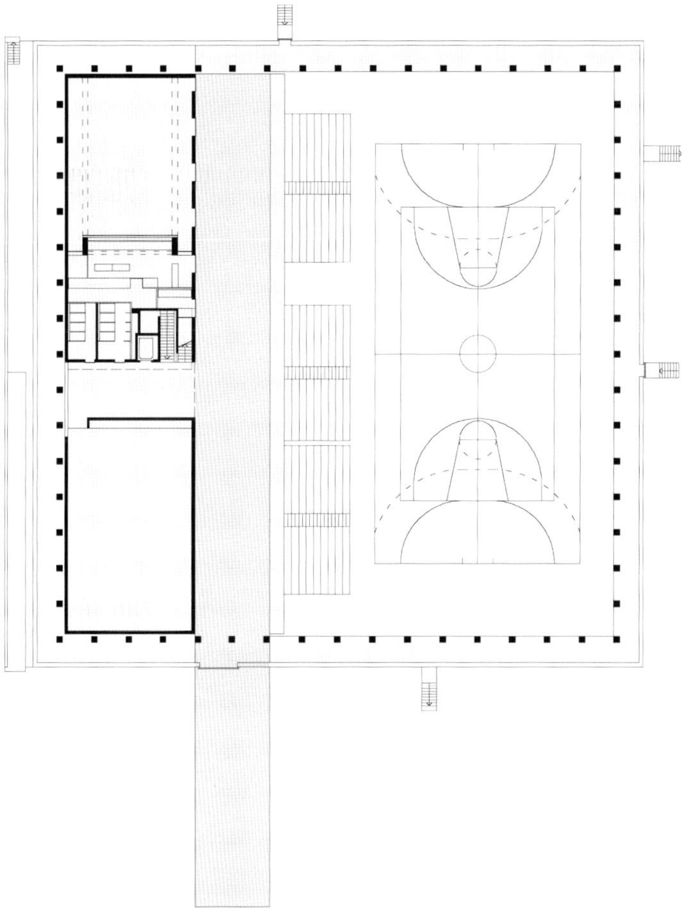

Ground floor

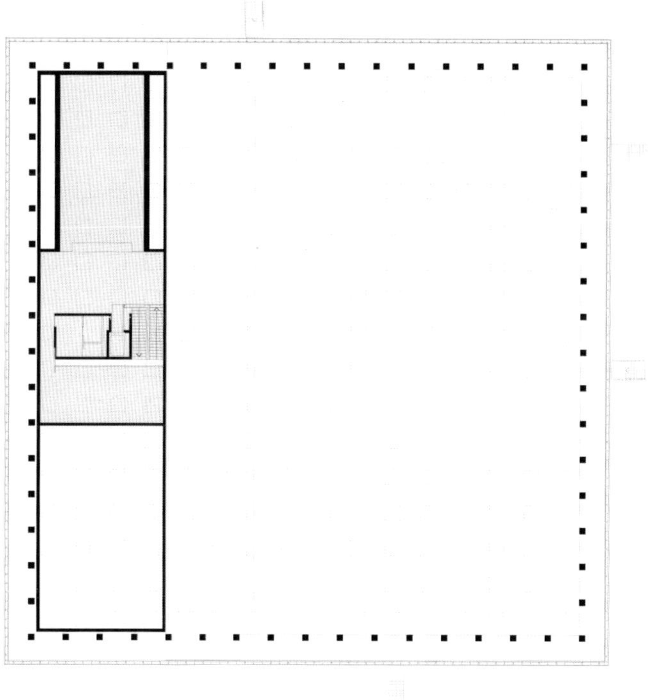

First floor

0   10   20

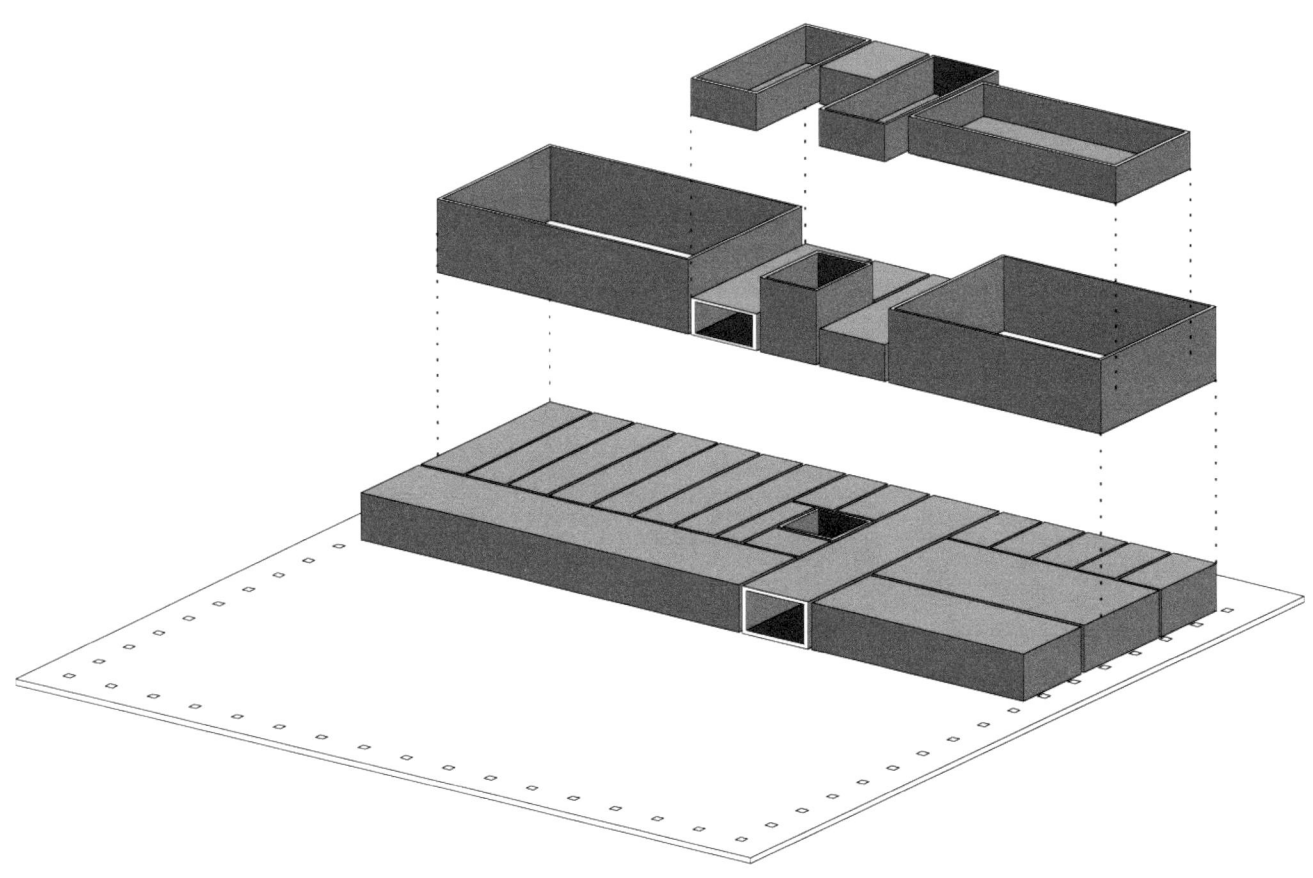

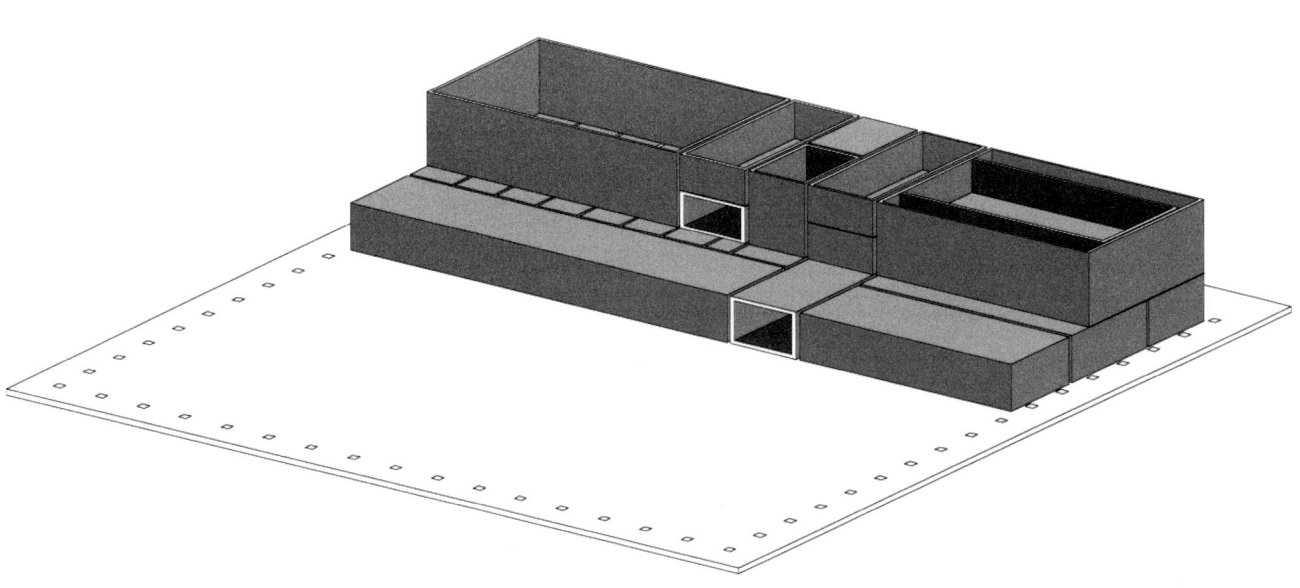

Perspectives

TUSSOLS-BASIL ATHLETIC TRACK AND FIELD

ARCHITECTS: RCR ARANDA PIGEM VILALTA ARQUITECTES,
COLLABORATORS: BRUFAU, OBIOL Y MOYA (STRUCTURES)

PHOTOGRAPHS © EUGENI PONS

LOCATION: OLOT, SPAIN
YEAR COMPLETED: 2002

THIS ATHLETIC TRACK AND FIELD BENEFITS FROM AN INTIMATE
RELATIONSHIP WITH THE WHITE OAKS IN THE FOREST THAT
SURROUND IT—THIS WAS BROUGHT OUT THROUGH THE USE
OF STANDS MADE UP OF TERRACES OR GENTLY SLOPING RAMPS
IN THE OPEN SPACES.

TUSSOLS-BASIL ATHLETIC TRACK AND FIELD

At the boundary between the city of Olot and the Natural Park of the Garrotxa, the Tussols-Basil recreation area stretches along the banks of a river. The architects in charge of this project— Aranda, Pigem, and Vilalta—designed a number of facilities and infrastructures, such as a bathing pavilion, a natural path and an athletic track and field, all of which have served to enhance the natural beauty of the place as well as to bring people engaged in sporting activities into closer contact with nature. The location and construction of the stadium in two clearings in the white oak forest represented the most conflict-ridden element of the plan: ecologists demanded that not a single tree be felled to built the space, while athletes required a playing field free of vegetation that would obstruct overall visibility. An equilibrium between these two points of view led to the stadium's being carefully located in a landscape in which trees act to filler light, and the use of lighting posts disguised as tree trunks that rise above the forest to illuminate the stadium. As another desire was to minimize the impact of the stands, the spectators were given wooden benches or grassy knolls to sit on—these seem as though they have always been there.

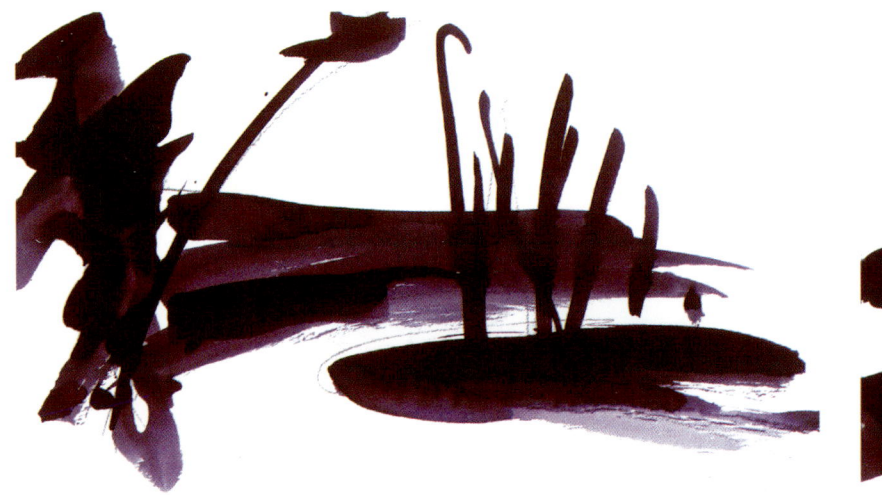
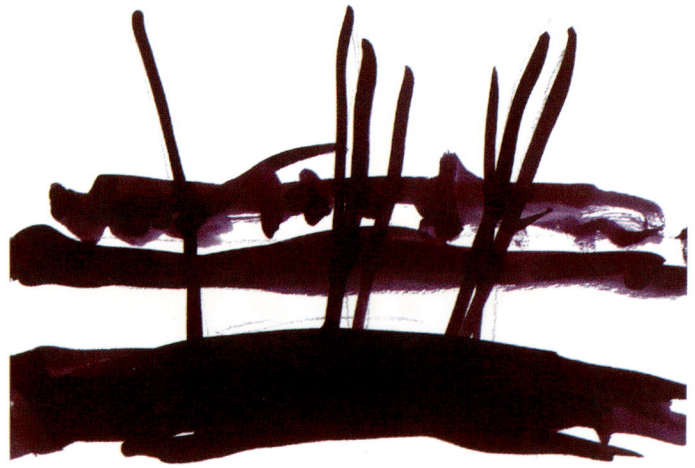

Sketches

Sketches

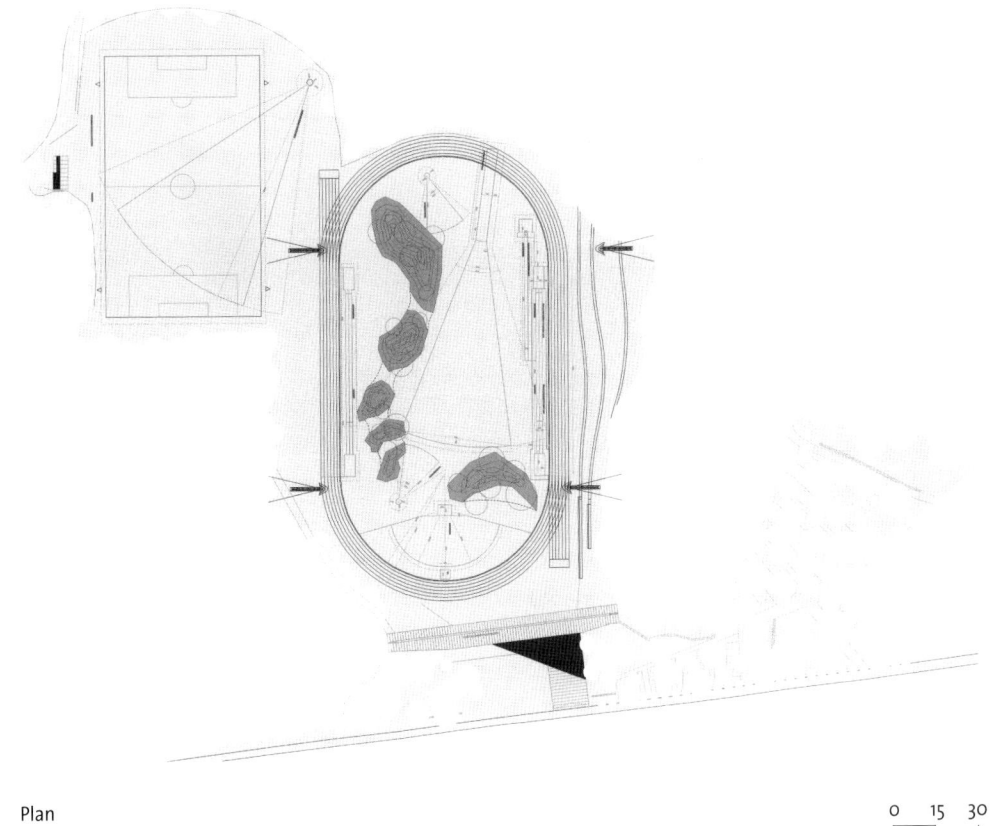

Plan

0   15   30

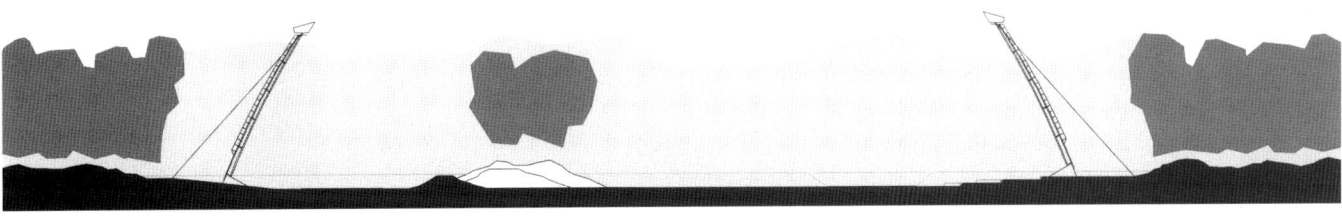

Elevations

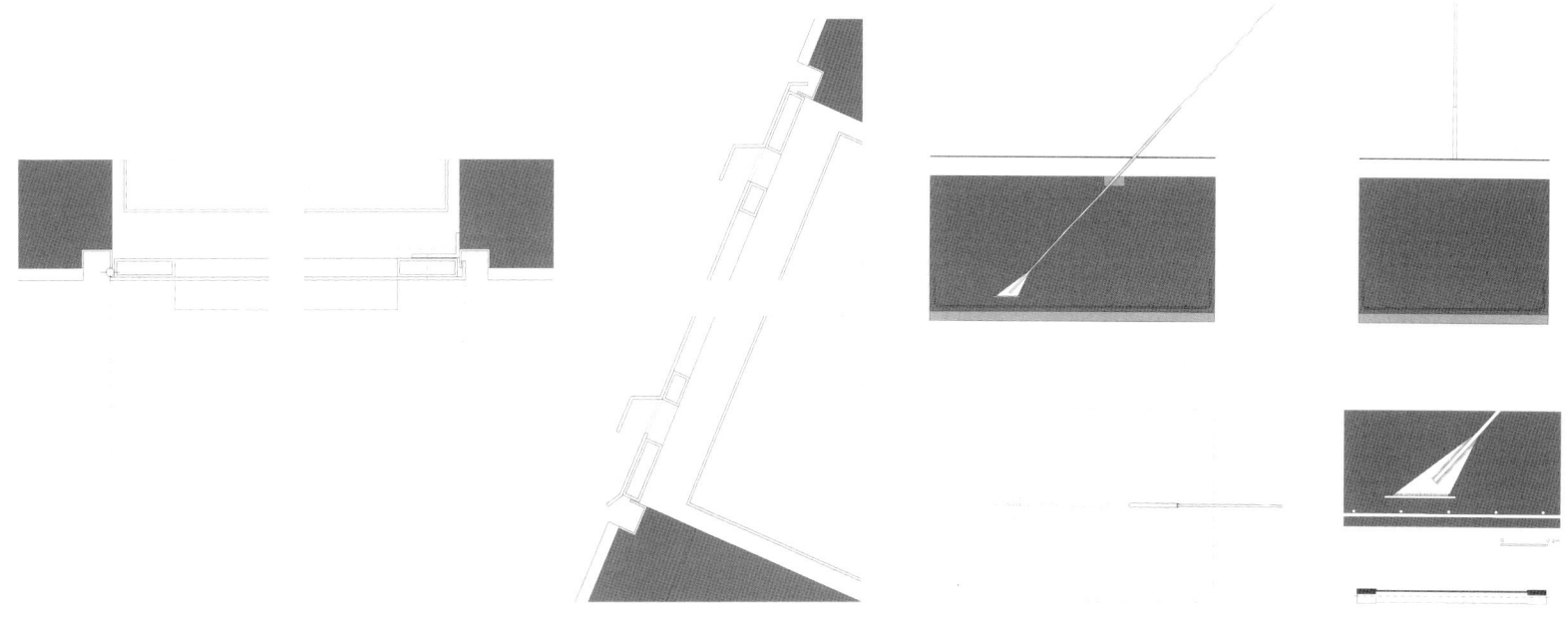

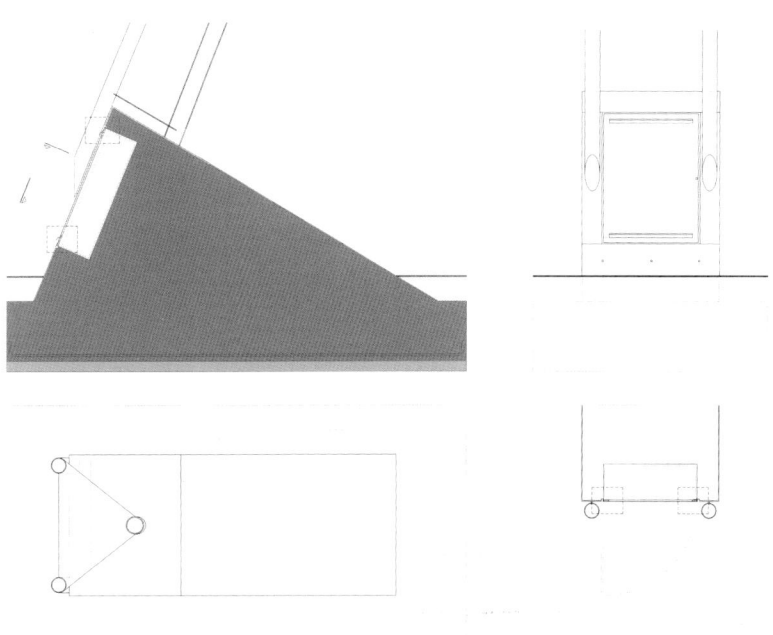

Construction details

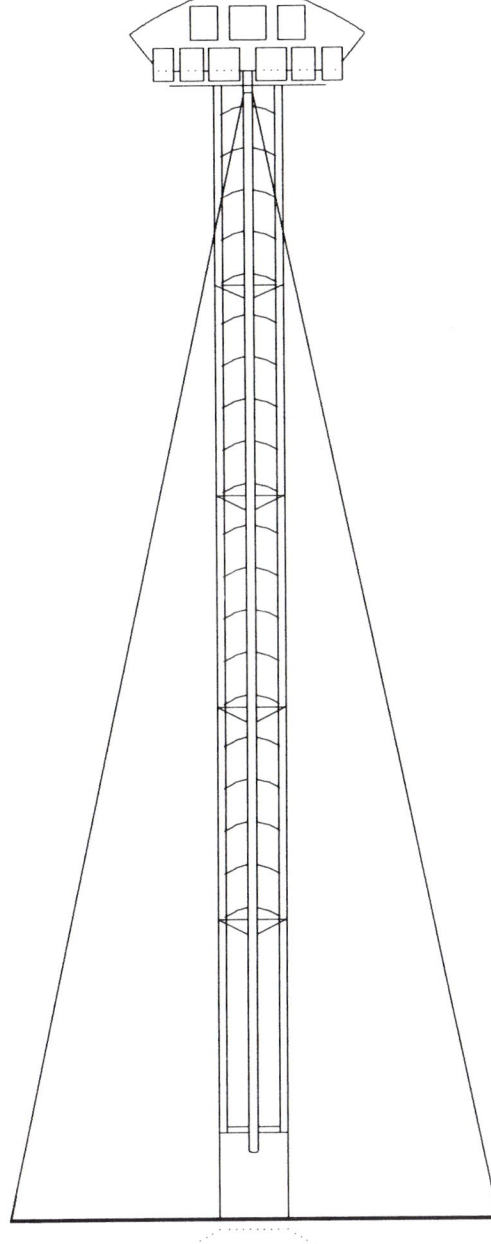

Elevation

JADE STADIUM

ARCHITECT: ATHFIELD ARCHITECTUS
COLLABORATOR: ELLERBE BECKETT

PHOTOGRAPHS © STEPHEN GOODENOUGH

LOCATION: CHRISTCHURCH, NEW ZEALAND
YEAR COMPLETED: 2003

THE STAIRS AND RAMPS THAT LEAD THE PUBLIC TO THE LOWER LEVEL OF THIS COMPLEX, WHICH IS THE LOCATION OF THE ACCESS AREAS AND VESTIBULES OF THE STADIUM, GENERATE NEW URBAN ENVIRONMENTS, WHICH ARE MORE QUIET AND INTIMATE, AND BLEND INTO THE SURROUNDING URBAN FABRIC.

JADE STADIUM

This new stadium entails the final phase of a master plan designed by the architects in charge of the stadium, in which a series of discreet, juxtaposed quadrants were used to create a progressive composition that would culminate in this building of great formal complexity. The fact that the site is located adjacent to Lancaster Park—a green space traditionally open to the residents of the city—determined both the final location of the building, in addition to its function and how it would be accessed. The final design respects the character of the park as an urban overlook, and makes the most of the distant views that one can enjoy from this location.

One of the main strategies behind the design was to clearly divide the circulation of athletes from that of the general public. In order to achieve this, a lower level was designed 15 feet underground to house the entrances and vestibules for the general public. The entrances, services and hallways for the athletes were then able to be placed at street level.

The structure of the building is based on a system of load-bearing walls, which support three sloping platforms that serve as stands and simultaneously as roofs for the levels beneath them. By means of this structural scheme, the architects achieved a maximum number of seats protected from the elements, as well as and an unique formal language for the building—this is further enriched by the additional boxes that separate vertical circulation and the general services. This stadium had served as an architectural reference point for the city and has sparked the development of a new residential and commercial area in its immediate vicinity.

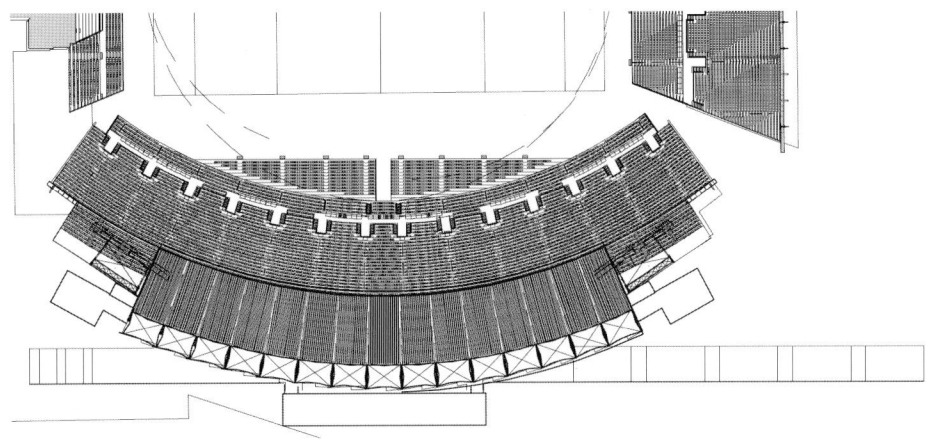

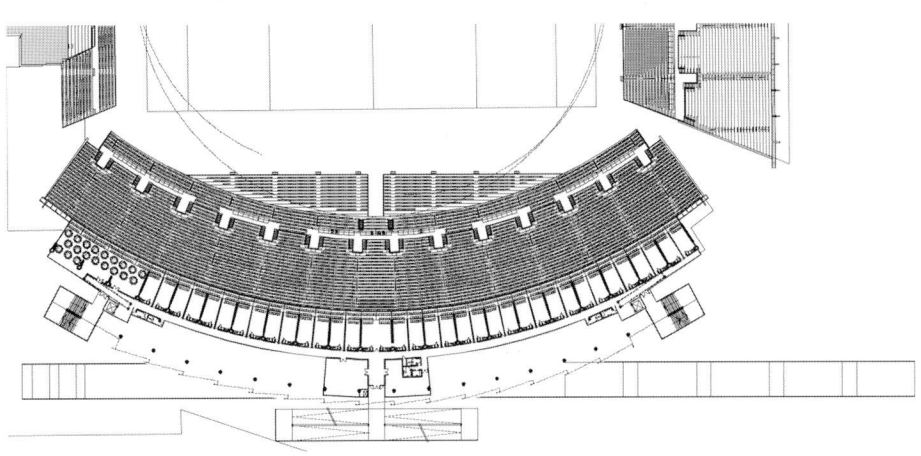

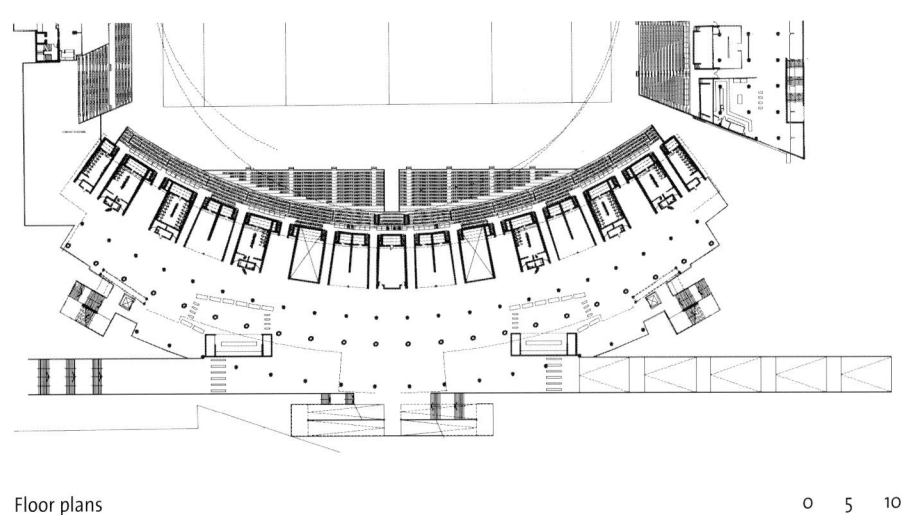

Floor plans

0   5   10

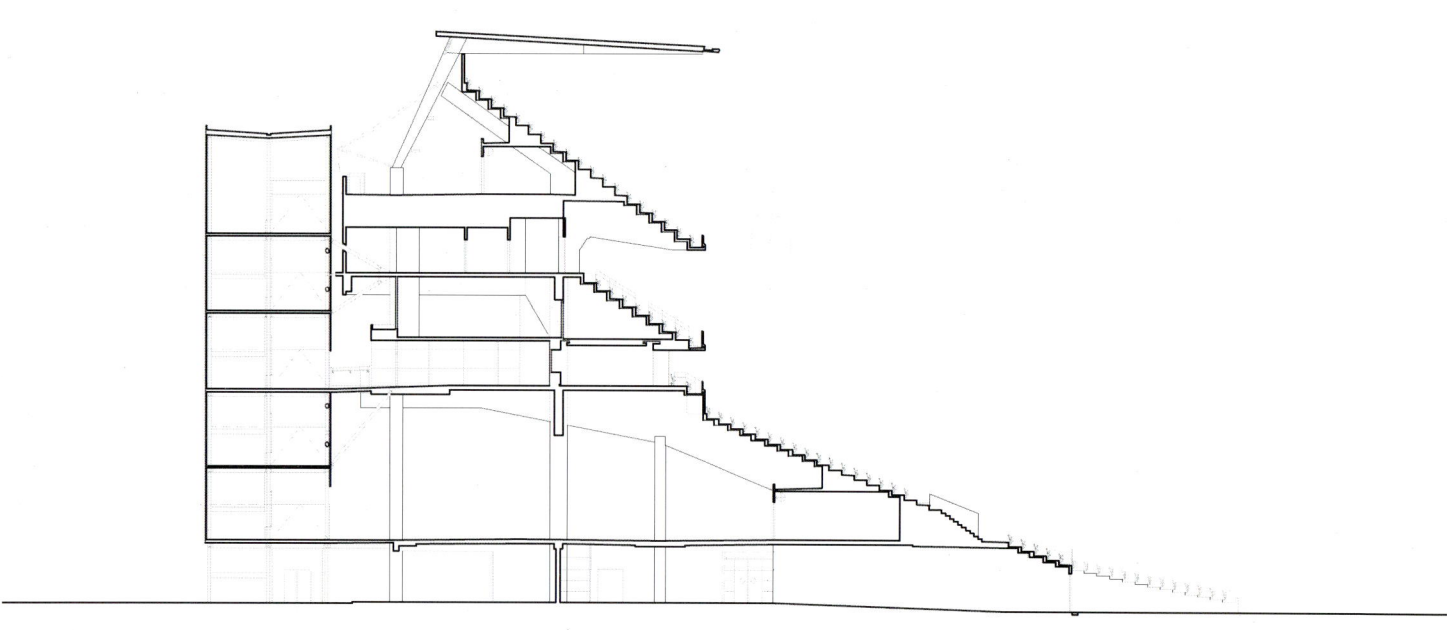

Section

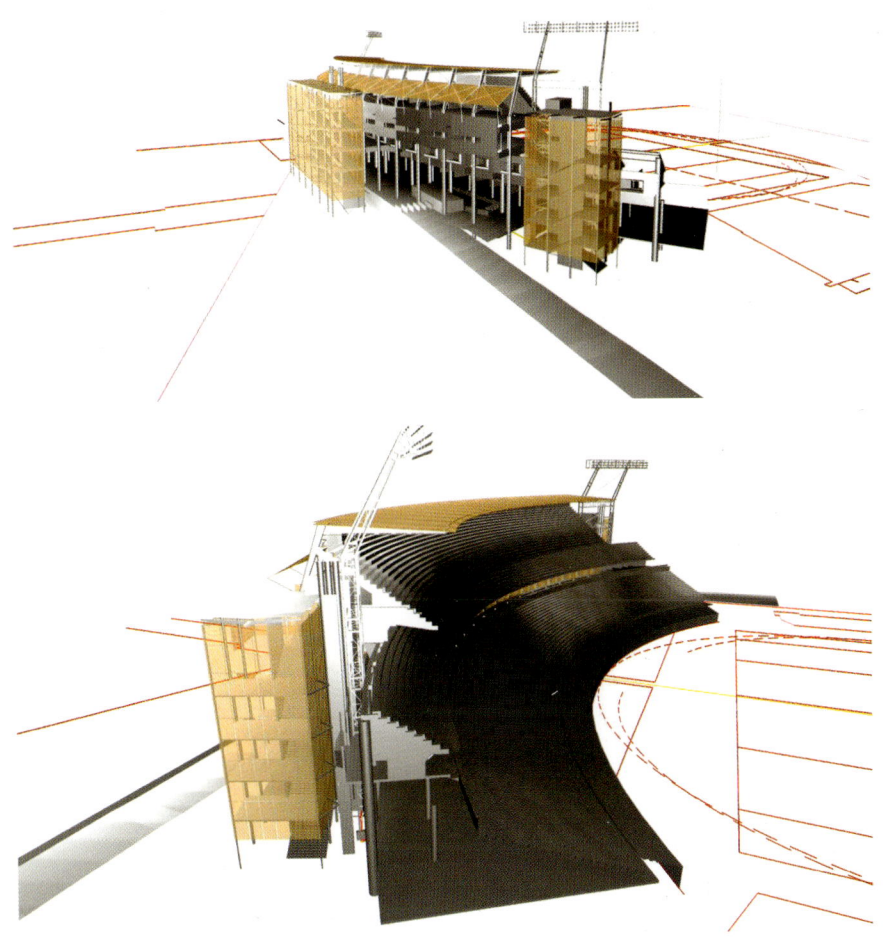

Perspectives

Olot Public Swimming Pool

Architects: Rob Dubois, Shuichi Kobari, Jordi Hidalgo, Daniela Hartmann/DKHH
Collaborators: Andreu Pico (draftsman), Josep Viñas (engineer)

Photographs © Eugeni Pons

Location: Olot, Spain
Year completed: 2002

GLASS, STONE, AND STEEL WERE COMBINED HERE TO CREATE A DIVERSE RANGES OF OPAQUE AND TRANSPARENT SPACES THAT ENVELOP AND CONTAIN THE INDOOR SPACES OF THIS COMPLEX.

OLOT PUBLIC SWIMMING POOL

The development of this pool in the Catalan city of Olot stemming from adapting to a complicated location that required an intervention capable of establishing a new identity in the region. The site was flanked by two, two-story townhouses, as well as by one of the city's bypasses. The mountains of the volcanic region of the Garrotxa, located to the south of the site, also played an important role in determining the position of the pools themselves— so that the shadows these mountains cast over the course of the day could be avoided.

The definition of the building in an L-shape and its positioning atop a large rectangular platform approximately three feet above street level are the designers' main proposals in response to such a complex site. The fact that the ensemble is elevated off the ground allows for it to be insulated from its surroundings, both in terms of noise from traffic and the views of passers-by. The different levels of the topography were manipulated to adapt to the new zero level and to achieve a maximum horizontal extension for the grassy lawns around the pools. Given that the outdoor pool did not require a large amount of construction, it was conceived of as a large, empty volume, and was built solely out of a stretched mesh that would envelop the solid pieces and simultaneously create adjacent spaces such as porches or open-air passageways. The proposal divided the program of the building into two volumes that would be clearly distinguished from one another as either full or empty parts: the full parts would be occupied by opaque volumes clad in dark natural stone, which would fuse with the colors of the nearby landscape; while the empty parts would be fully glassed-in interiors and the corresponding empty parts would be enclosed by the mesh. The mass and opacity of the stone volumes contrast with the lightness and transparency of the galvanized metal mesh.

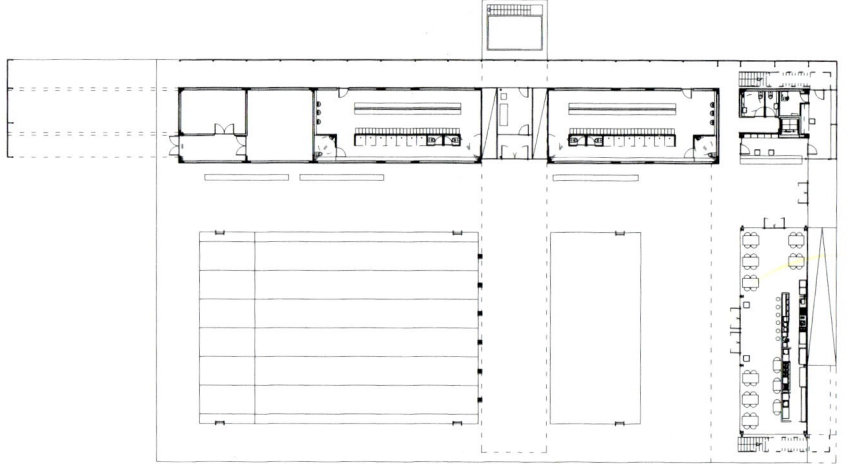

Ground floor

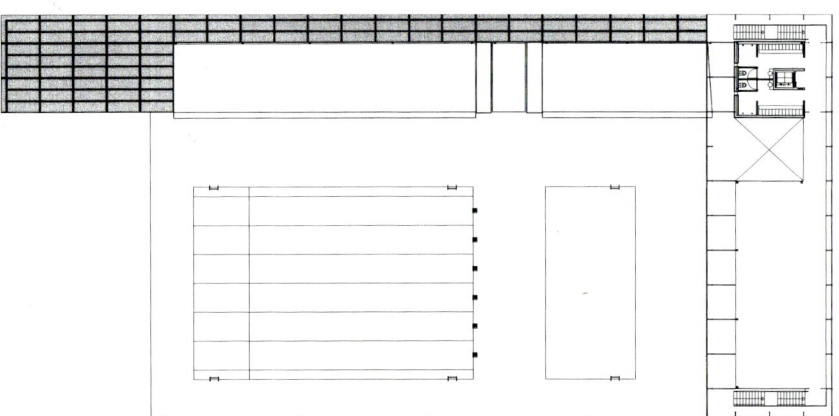

First floor

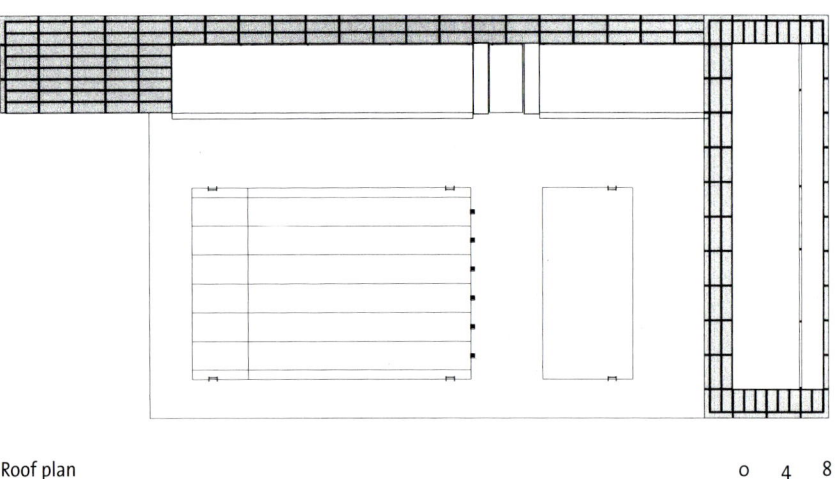

Roof plan

0 4 8

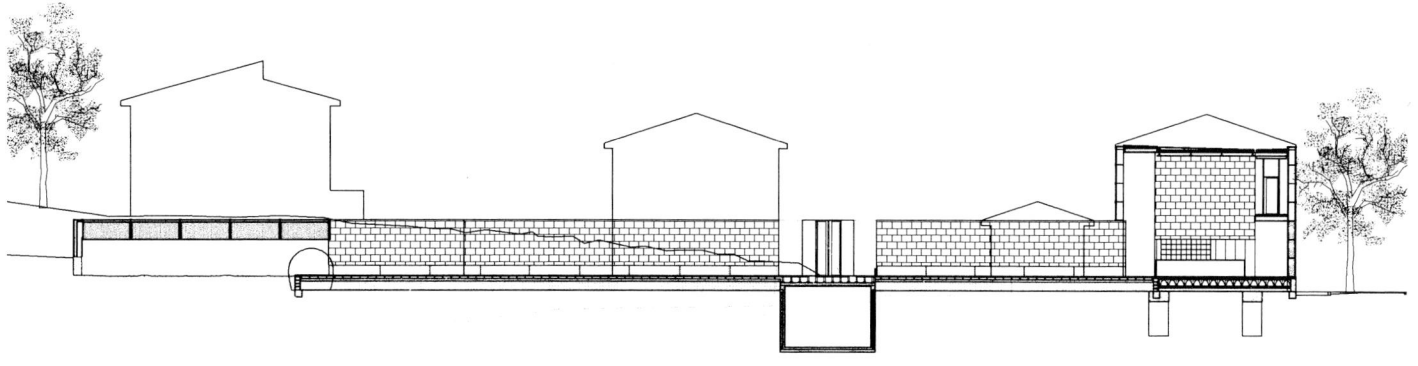

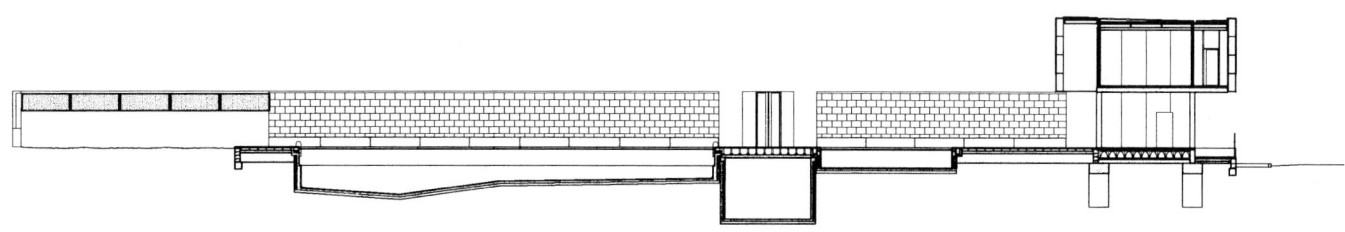

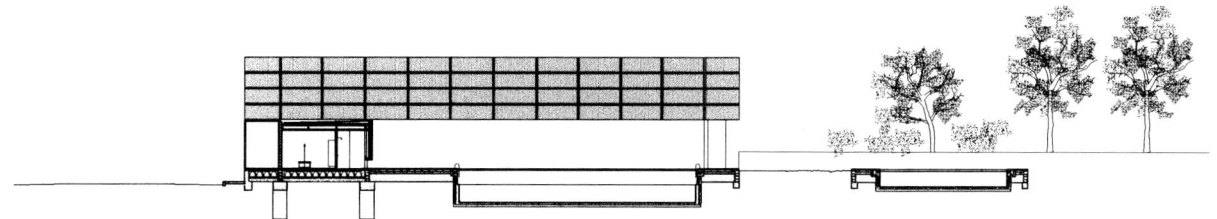

Sections

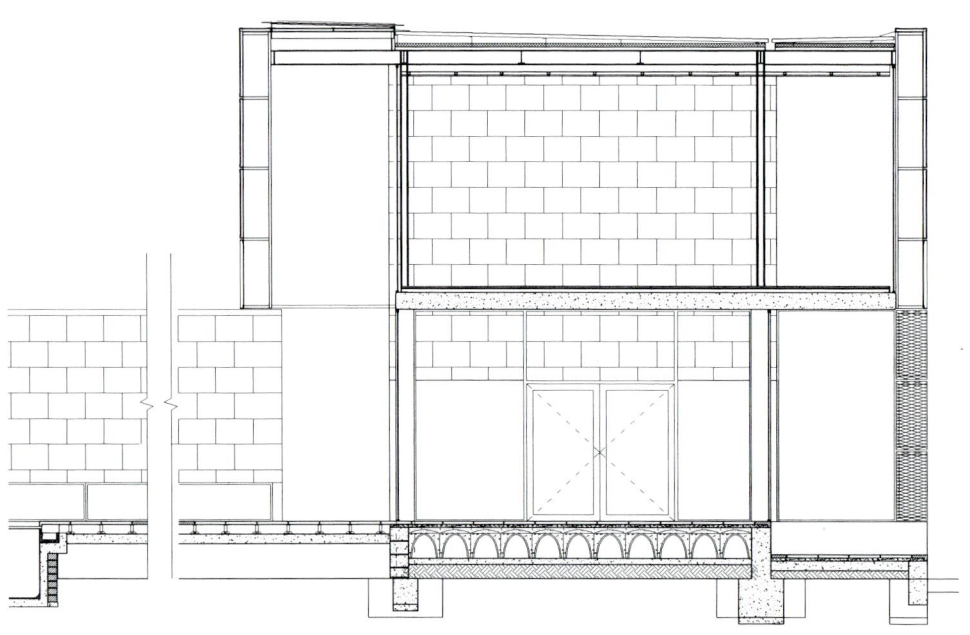

Construction detail

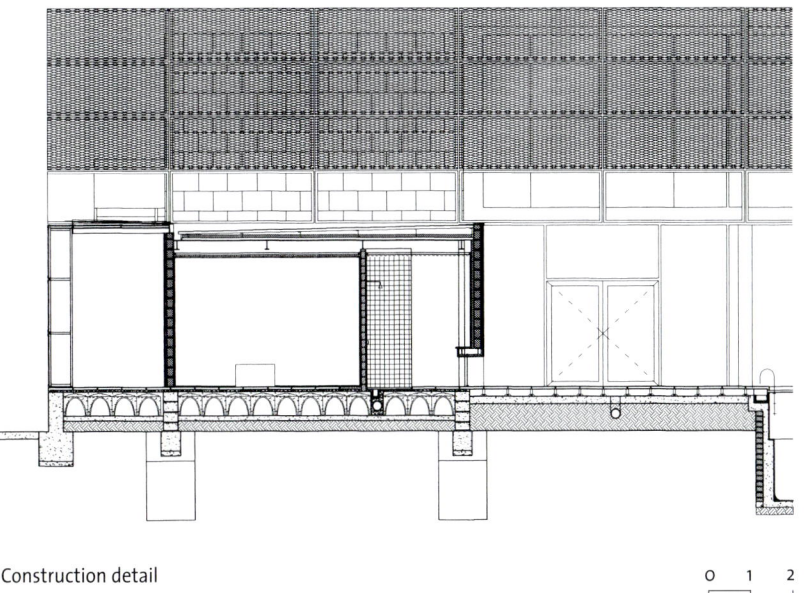

Construction detail

0   1   2

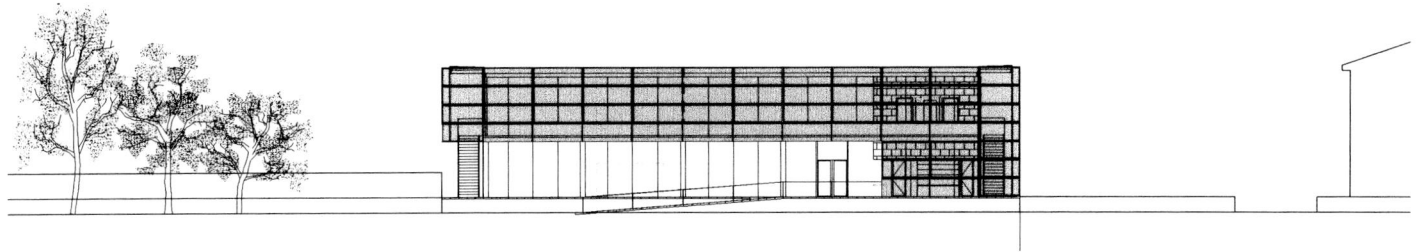

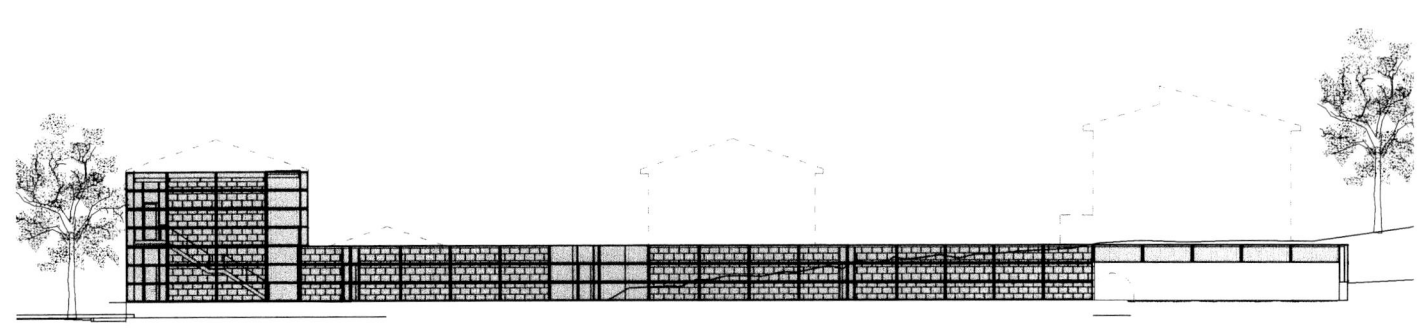

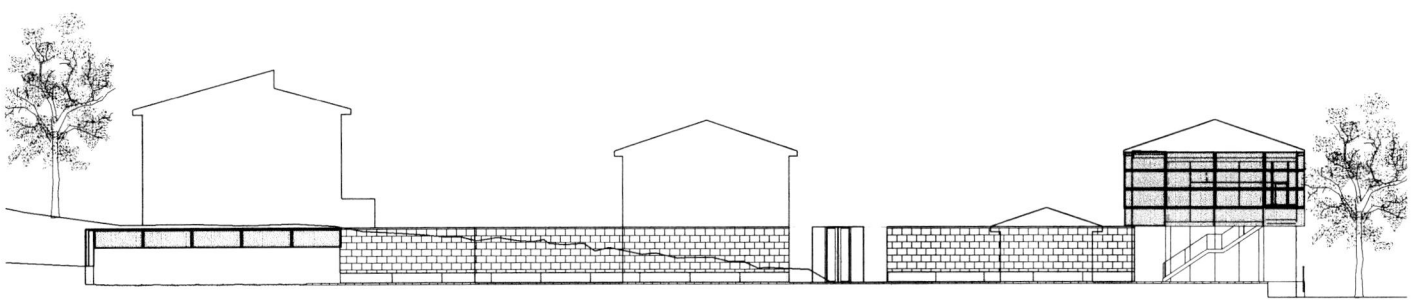

Elevations

Sports Center in Herrenkrug Park

Architects: Andreas Veauthier, Tanja Klein/AV-A Veauthier Architekten
Collaborators: IPK Magdeburg (electronics), IB Thorwarth (services), Hortec (landscaping)

Photographs © Werner Huthmacher

Location: Magdeburg, Germany
Year completed: 2004

TO DESIGN THIS SPORTS CENTER, WHICH CAME ABOUT DUE TO THE RENOVATION OF AN EXISTING TENNIS CLUB, THE BERLIN-BASED STUDIO VEAUTHIER ARCHITEKTEN UNDERTOOK STUDIES INTO ITS FUNCTIONALITY, LIGHTING, COLOR, AND PROFITABILITY.

SPORTS CENTER IN HERRENKRUG PARK

This project is located near the River Elbe, in a park that was designed by landscape architect Peter Joseph Lenné in the 19th century. It had initially been opened as a tennis club, but after several months was closed due to financial reasons. Furthermore, the flooding that occurred in the area in the summer of 2002 caused serious damage to the club. As such, it was eventually decided that the club should be transformed into a larger sports center—this commission was entrusted to the team of Veauthier Architekten for the entirety of the following year. The architectural concept behind the project is based on expanding or modifying the existing facilities without removing the original structure of the club; the new additions were designed to be read as additive elements to the original complex. Additionally, new materials were introduced so as to transform the monotonous atmosphere of the club into an intense and vivid environment.

What had served as a bowling alley was converted into a spa, which includes saunas, an area for massages, places to relax and engage in aromatherapy, and cosmetic facilities—all of these lead to a higher level that includes terraces for sunbathing and enjoying the views out onto the park. The restaurant—a place for the users of the spa to relax and enjoy each others' company—was divided onto two floors, the first floor representing a more informal environment and the second a more sophisticated setting, replete with wood floors and leather furniture.

The lighting was another of the elements from which the renovation drew energy; of note are the large, twelve-by-six-foot lamps that were hung from the ceiling in one of the exercise rooms. In addition, as the application of color was a determining factor, the designers decided on red and green and shades thereof for the colors of many of the components— everything from furniture to the showers, and even closets and tiles.

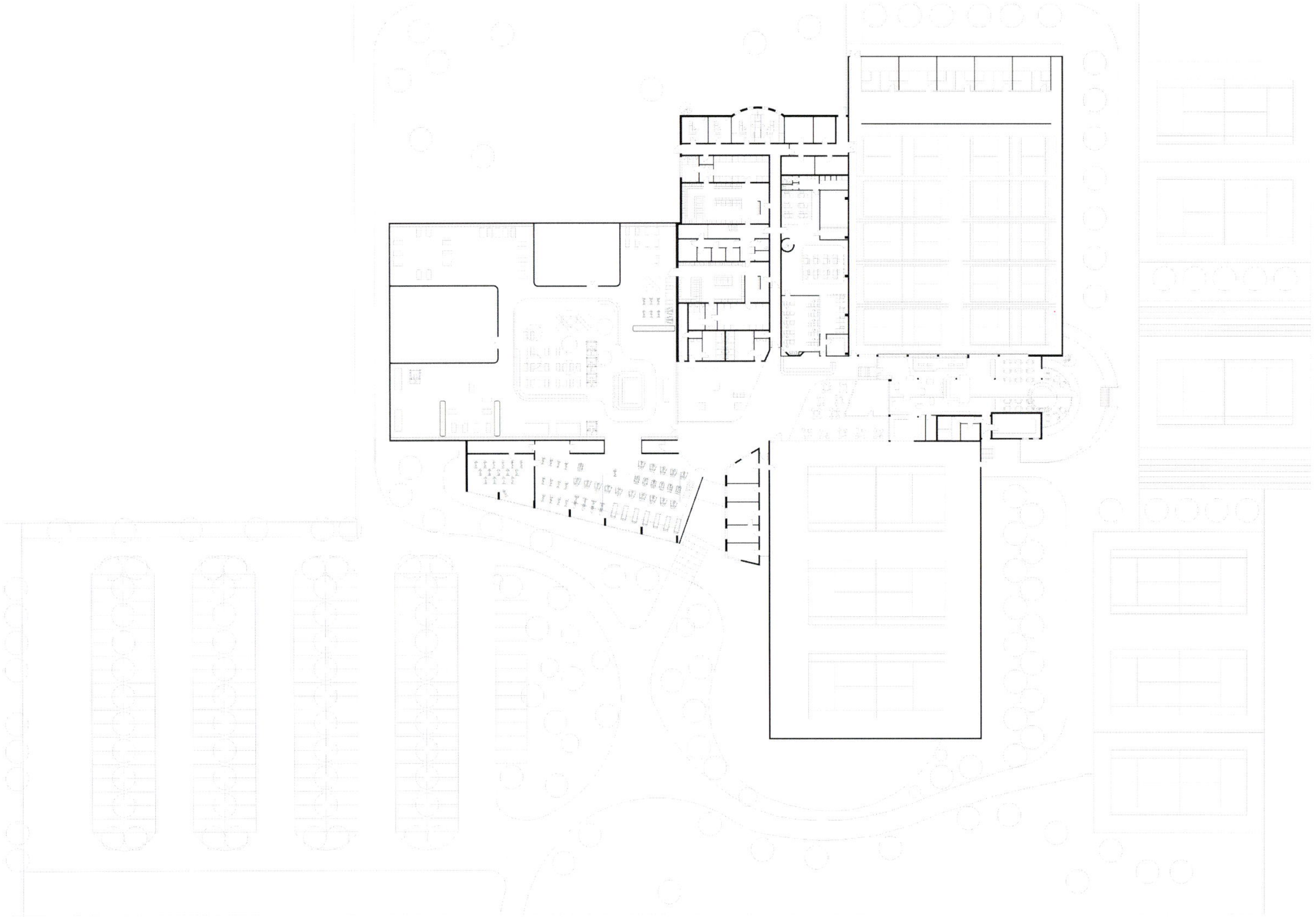

Floor plan

0   5   10

TOYOTA STADIUM

ARCHITECTS: KISHO KUROKAWA ARCHITECT & ASSOCIATES

PHOTOGRAPHS © KOJI KOBAYASHI

LOCATION: TOYOTA, JAPAN
YEAR COMPLETED: 2001

THE RATHER SMALL SITE UPON WHICH THE TOYOTA STADIUM WAS TO BE BUILT REQUIRED AN EXHAUSTIVE STUDY INTO HOW THE PROGRAM OF THE STADIUM WOULD BE ORGANIZED, AND A PRECISE STRUCTURAL AND CONSTRUCTION SYSTEM TO TAKE FULL ADVANTAGE OF WHAT SURFACE AREA WAS AVAILABLE.

TOYOTA STADIUM

This stadium represents part of an urban development project undertaken to commemorate the 50th anniversary of the city's receiving its charter. It is located adjacent to the Toyota bridge, a significant element in the city's infrastructure, which also serves as the main way for pedestrians to access the stadium. The complex was initially in the running to house events for the 2002 World Cup, but was eventually eliminated from the running—as a result, the planned capacity was reduced from 60,000 spectators to 45,000. This change in program required the designers to work on concepts such as flexibility and multifunctional spaces, which led to a sliding roof that would allow different spaces to be set up to meet the needs of any given activity. The site chosen was limited on one side by a river, and protected irrigation fields on another; this seriously restricted what surface area could be used. Hence, each square inch of project space had to be maximized. One of the measures to this end taken was to erect sloping walls to hold up the stands, and four giant, free-standing columns to support the roof. Despite FIFA's strict regulations requiring football fields to be illuminated by natural light, it was also decided that the stands should be covered by a projecting roof to protect them from the direct rays of the sun. Thus, the roof was built out of two parallel elements that can be retracted using a pneumatic system, in an echo of the workings of a traditional Japanese fan.

The structure, which was engineered by Ove Arup & Partners Engineers, kept to the sophisticated concept designed by Kisho Kurokawa, and was designed in a thought-provoking way so as to withstand typhoons or the frequent earthquakes that plague the area. It is built from steel elements covered with pre-tensioned concrete.

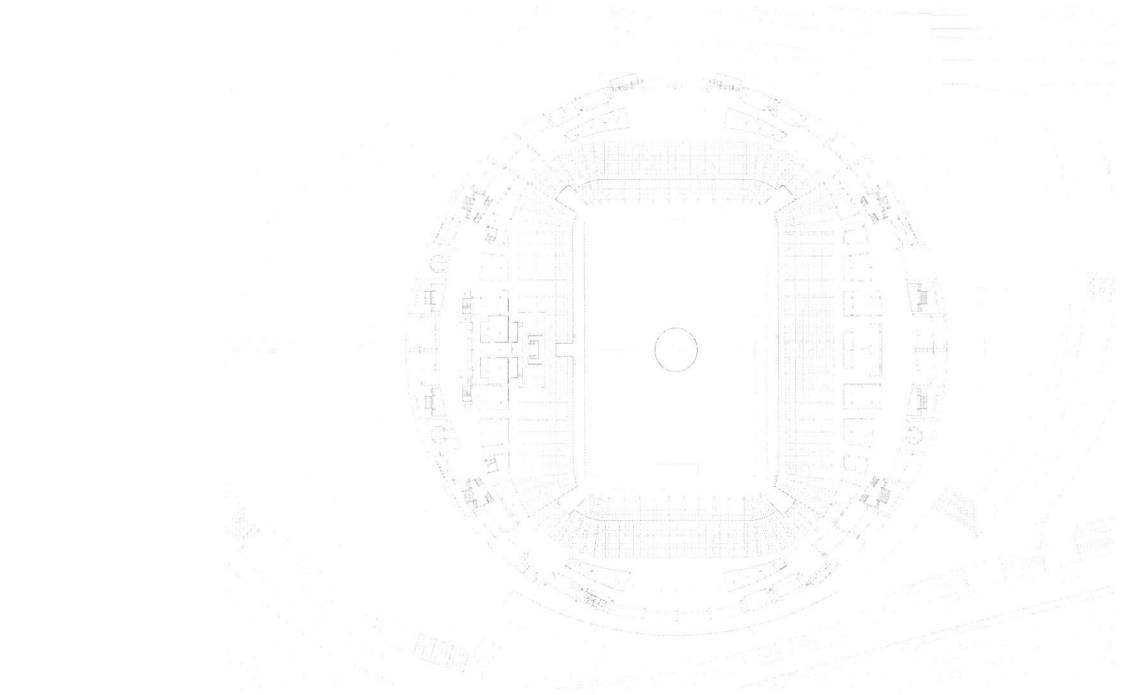

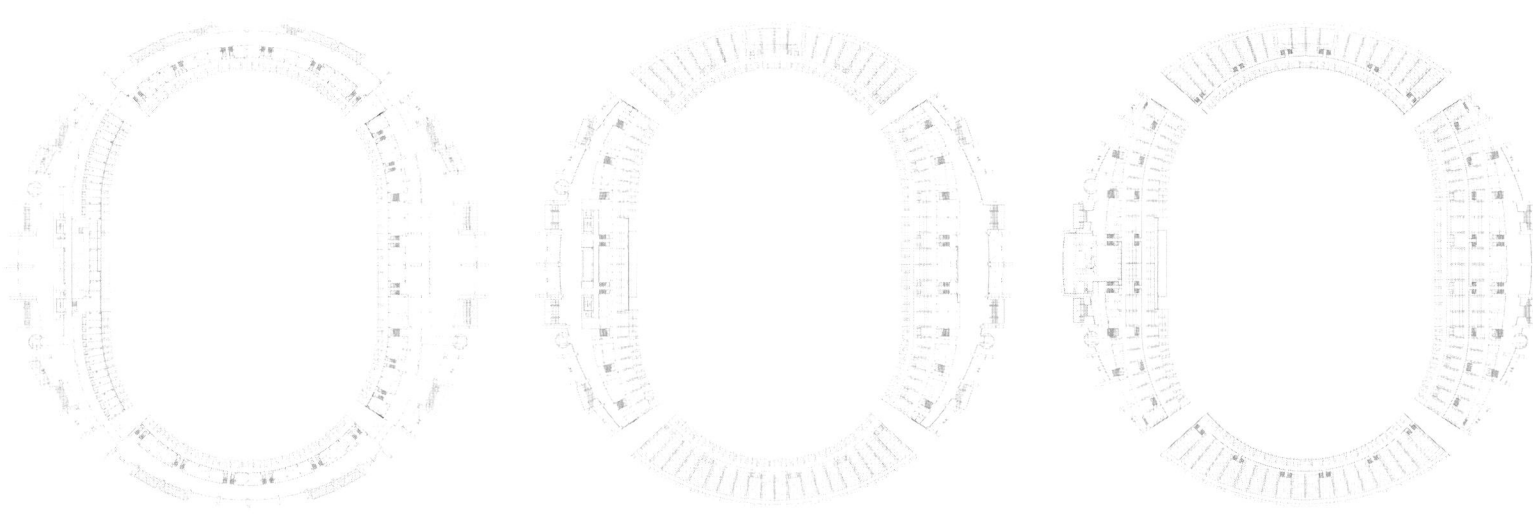

Floor plans

0   20   40

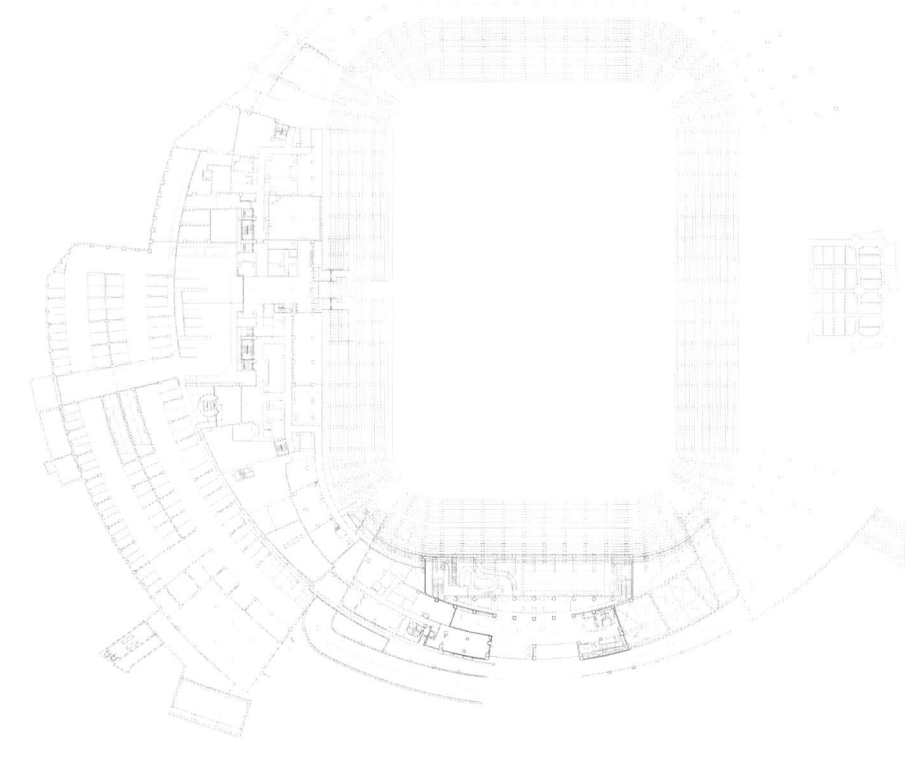

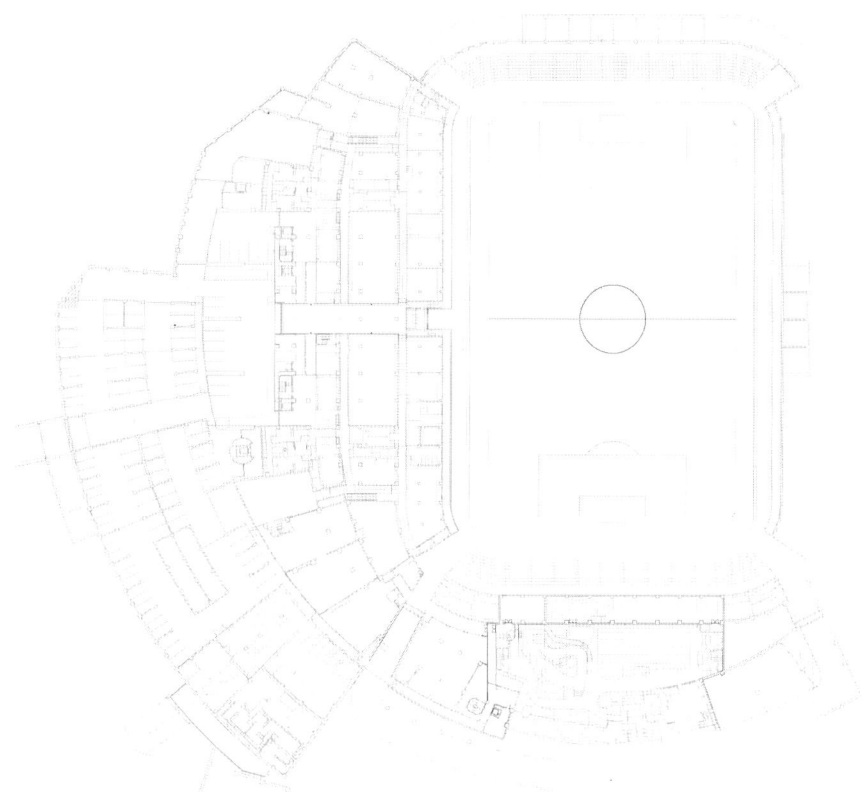

Floor plans

0   20   40

Structural details

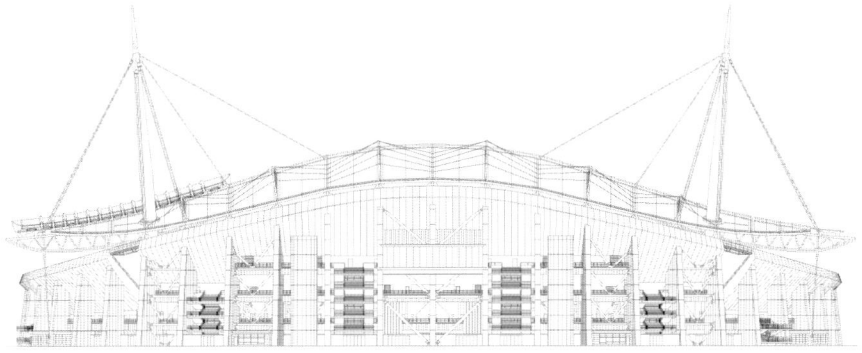

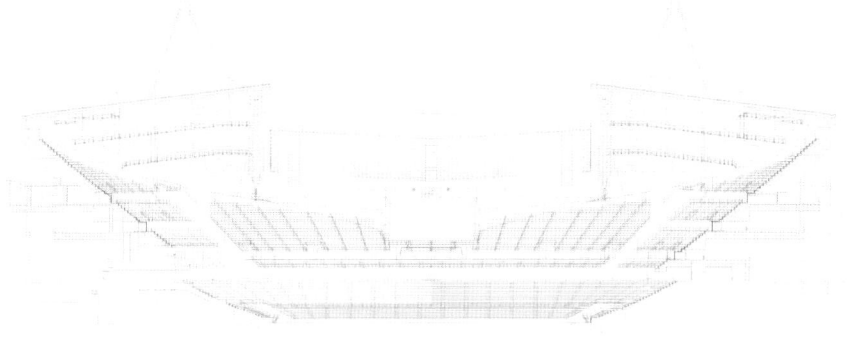

Sections

Alpicat Sports Complex

ARCHITECT: Salvador Giné Macià

COLLABORATORS: Cabezas y Góngora Consultores (structures),
Mafo Enginyeria (installations), Emili Fornells (draftsman)

PHOTOGRAPHS © Jordi Miralles

LOCATION: Alpicat, Spain
YEAR COMPLETED: 2004

THIS SITE, CHOSEN BY THE SPANISH VILLAGE OF ALPICAT UPON WHICH TO BUILD A NEW SPORTS COMPLEX, HAD ALREADY BEEN EARMARKED IN A DEVELOPMENT PLAN FOR THE FURTHER CONSTRUCTION OF PUBLIC SWIMMING POOLS AND A FOOTBALL FIELD.

ALPICAT SPORTS COMPLEX

Topographically speaking, the site consists of a flat terrain elevated above street level, and one must climb up a gentle slope to reach it.

This project entailed a three-volume building that would take advantage of the uneven existing terrain by plunging itself nearly six feet into the ground—in this way its impact on its surroundings is far less than what is typical of these kinds of buildings. This also came in response to program requirements and the various formal aspects of the building—which from the beginning had been designed in such as way so as to avoid creating a massive volume. The interior was also made more dynamic and filled with more light thanks to its having been planned on a north-south axis—this is especially well-suited to sporting activities.

The main mass of the building contains the sports court, while the auxiliary volume—which has higher ceilings—contains the services, dressing room and gymnasiums, and emerges from the ground plane. The roof of the latter is a terrace that offers breathtaking views of the gardens surrounding the complex. Furthermore, this platform also comprises a balcony that opens onto the indoor court. The third volume, which faces the street, contains the entrance to the facilities as well as to the balcony-overlook.

In urban design terms, this building was made to fit into the adjacent garden through the creation of a network of pedestrian paths that divide the park into different areas and facilitate access to all of the facilities.

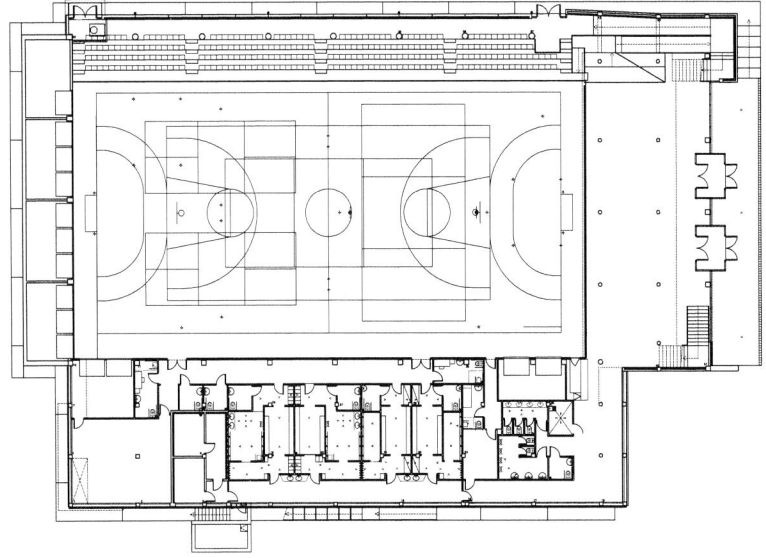

Ground floor

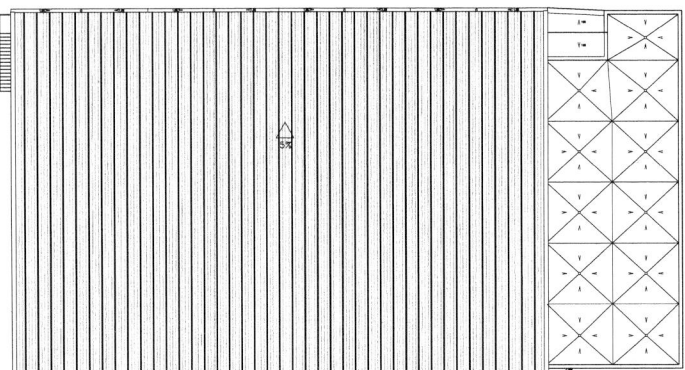

First floor

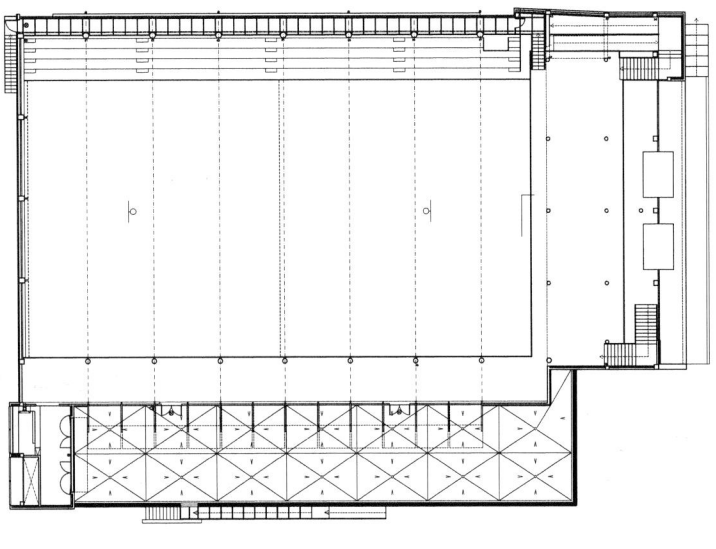

Roof plan

0   2   4

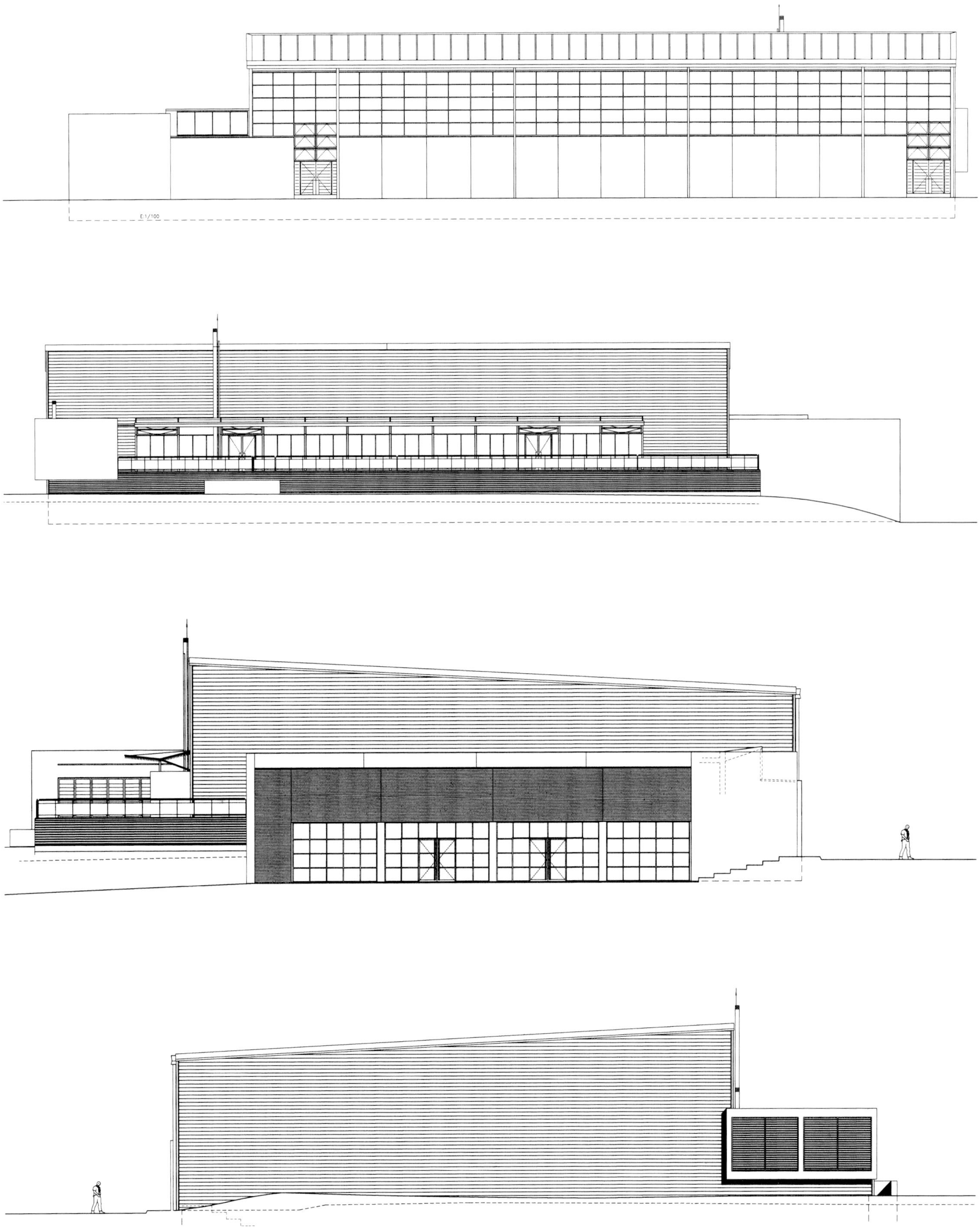

E:1/100

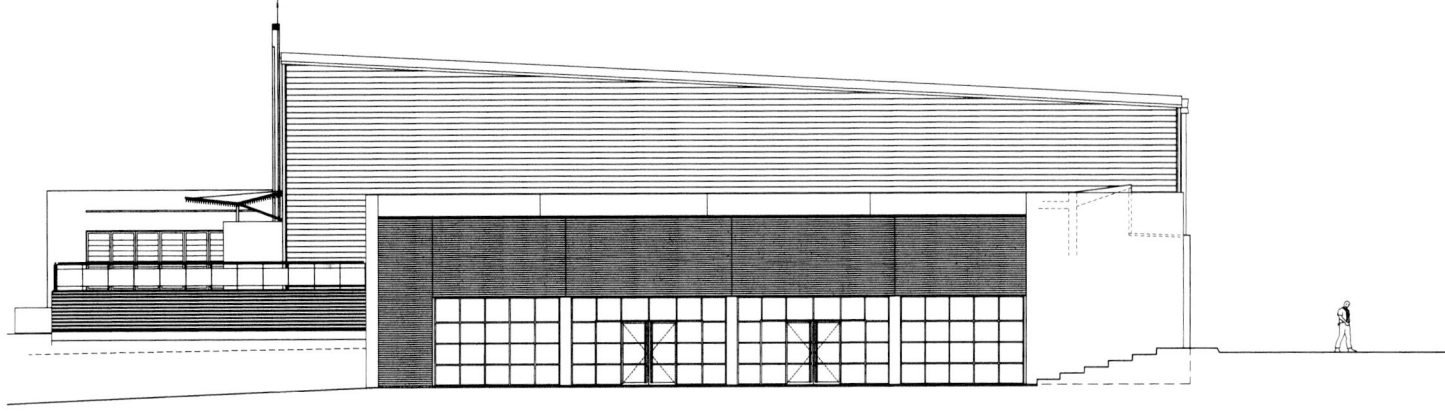

Elevations

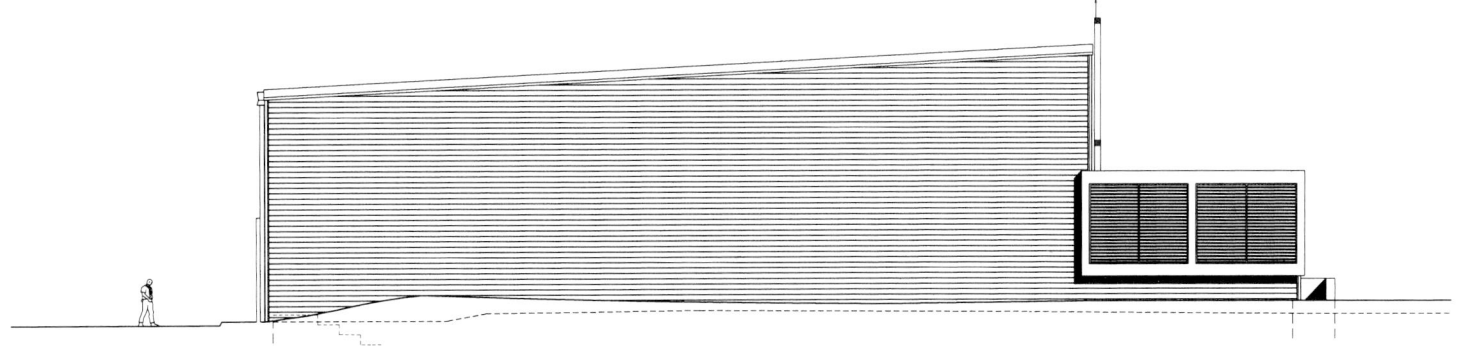

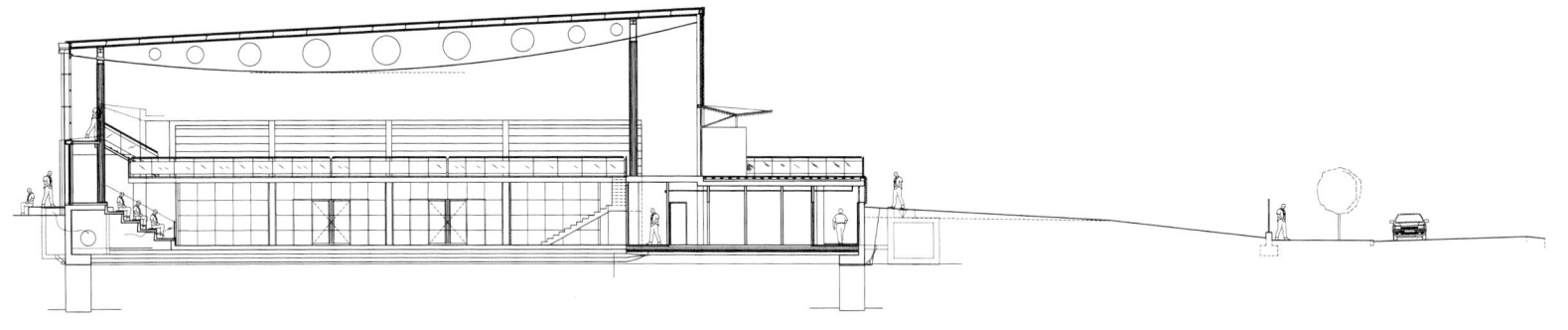

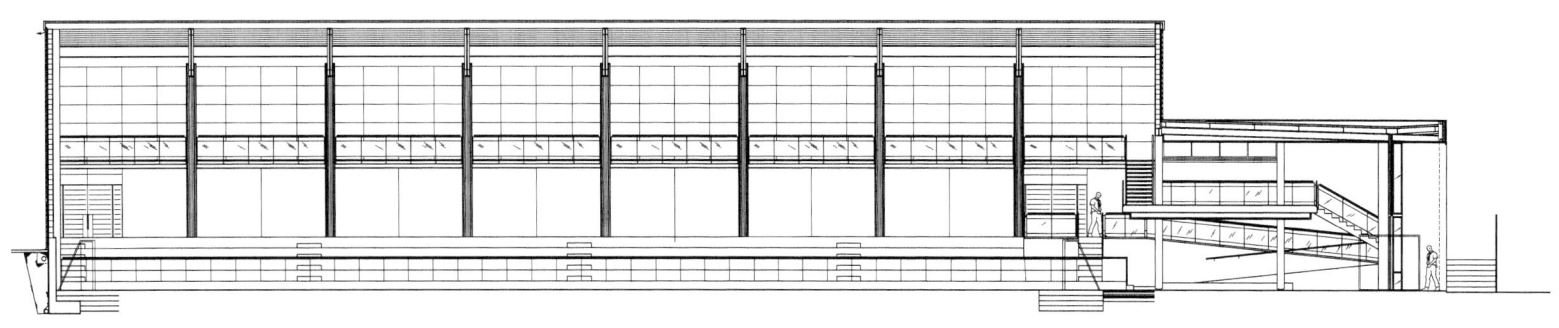

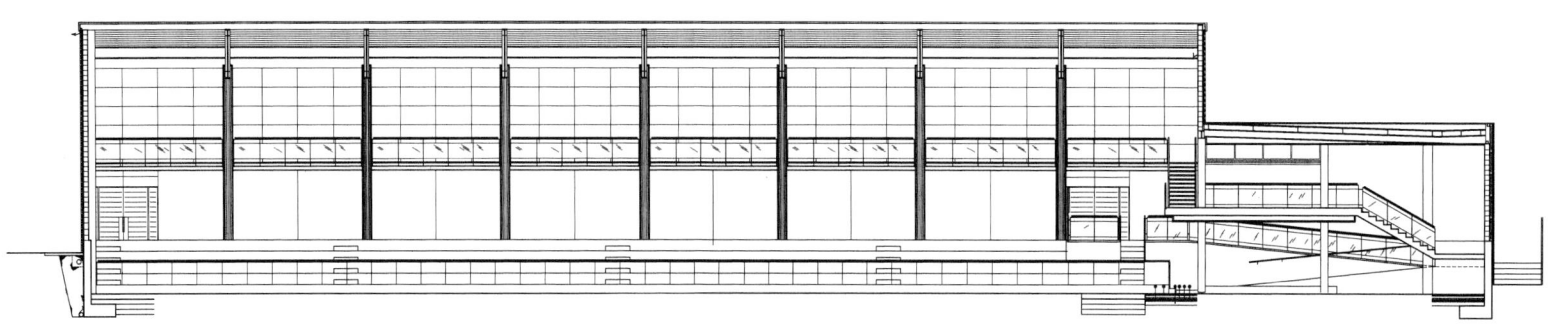

Sections

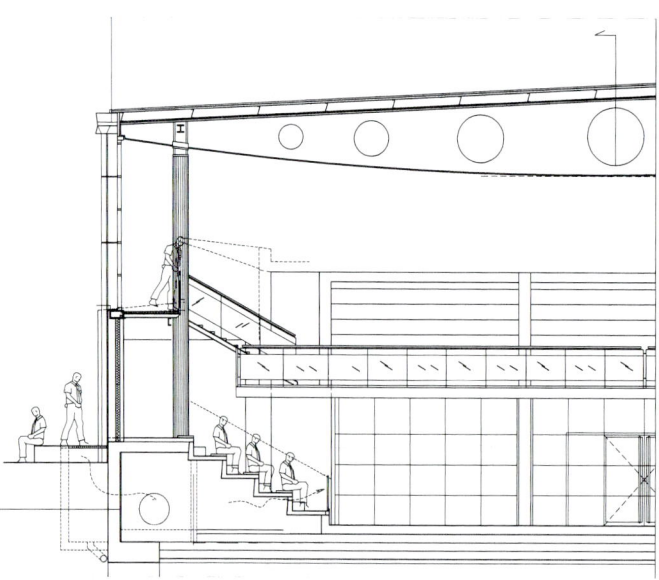

Construction detail

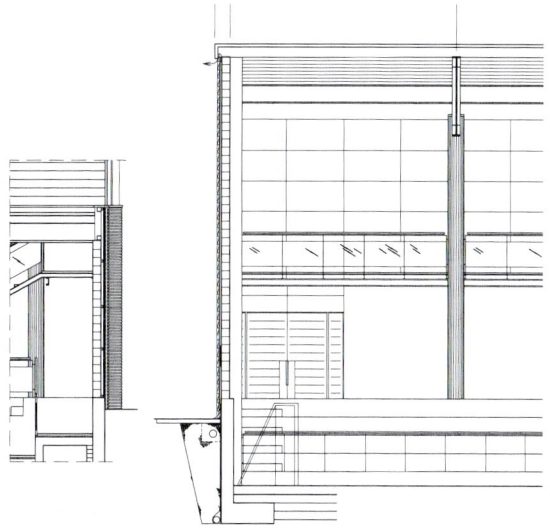

Construction detail